CONTEMPORARY ENGLISH LITERATURE

CONTEMPORARY ENGLISH LITERATURE

By

Dr. Lopa Sanyal, *Ph.D.*

Associate Professor

Dyananda College of Science & Arts

Bangalore

DISCOVERY PUBLISHING HOUSE

NEW DELHI-110002

Published by:
Namit Wasan

DISCOVERY PUBLISHING HOUSE PVT. LTD.
4383/4B, Ansari Road, Darya Ganj
New Delhi-110 002 (India)
Phone : +91-11-23279245; 23253475; 43596065
E-mail : discoverybooksindia@gmail.com
discoverypublishinghouse@gmail.com
namitwasan9@gmail.com
web : www.discoverypublishinggroup.com

Edition: **2020**

ISBN: 978-81-8356-137-2

Contemporary English Literature

Printed at:
Infinity Imaging Systems
Delhi

Preface

In the study of the rich expanse of English contemporary literature a great deal has been accomplished in recent years, and the literature of the subject multiplies. During recent years much important work has been done on various aspects of Contemporary literature, and the time seems to have come when some attempt should be made to present the general results of this research. It was obviously impossible to deal in detail with all the theories which have been brought forward at one time or another. Only those which have received a support so general that they may be considered established, together with the more plausible or more interesting of the remainder, could be dealt with at all fully; a brief reference is all that has been possible for the majority. Nor did this seem to be the occasion on which to bring forward any individual views of the author for the first time. In a synthesis such as this it is essential that the theories and opinions included should have been subjected elsewhere to the approval or criticism of other workers in the same field.

The organization of material in this book conforms with that of the other books in this series. After a brief consideration of the historical background and time-spirit of the different phases of the contemporary period, the method of procedure is topical. Within the topical divisions of poetry, novel, drama, and miscellaneous prose, the arrangement is generally chronological. In the treatment of particular movements and groups, however, it has seemed more practicable at times to proceed from a discussion of major figures to those of lesser importance. In the many instances in which an author's works extend to several literary forms, the works, regardless of type, are considered in the principal entry of the particular author. Thus Hardy's novels and poetry, Galsworthy's novels and dramas are considered under the entries of Hardy and Galsworthy respectively.

The general bibliographies are arranged according to literary type, with subdivisions indicated in so far as they prove helpful. The reference works on poetry, for example, are subdivided into anthologies, biographical and critical studies, and discussions of poetic theory and principle. In the bibliographies of individual authors, the order of arrangement is generally from comprehensive treatment to the treatment of particular facets of the author's life and works. And in end, an alert consciousness of current scholarship must go along with a direct and independent reading of the literature itself. To promote and guide such a reading program is the primary purpose of this book.

Contents

1
Chapter
Preamble

MODERNISM

The Twentieth century has ended. The literature world is in what might be called a *fin de siècle* mood. What sense can we make of this long era? What legacy has it left? Every day we hear more talk about how the century began, with the simultaneous invention of movies, automobiles, skyscrapers, and abstract art. The high culture we have called Modernism has now been with us for most of the last century, longer than any other cultural *-ism* since the French began naming them back in the eighteenth century. This book is an attempt to describe literature in these contemporary times.

The result we have before us is a narrative history of ideas, a thing that has become rare. Narrative, some now say, is obsolete, to which accusation the many have replied by building our time's demand for meaningful story—indeed, for any kind of story—to something like a fever pitch. History too is now accused of obsolescence, and "theory" contends it is impossible to adopt a point of view and interpret the past from it. But it is extraordinarily hard to avoid doing that, and there are many reasons why one ought not to try. Some accuse ideas themselves of being obsolete, since all ideas are artifacts of subjectivity and cannot be passed on without intersubjectivity.

They are all of them individuals, and all of them are, in their way, geniuses. A genius we take to be a person who does something no one else can do until enough time has passed for a lot of other people to learn how to do it too. One can be a genius without being a hero.All are presented here, in a nod to a form of history as old as Plutarch, as profiles in genius, notables of their intellectual specialties, from mathematics to painting. On the other hand, they ought not to be thought of as acting alone, like the mythic American frontiersman. Some, indeed, are women. They learned from each other, something that is harder to do in the more advanced state of intellectual specialization typical of our own times. The intellectual and cultural environment in which the first Moderns found themselves as the twentieth century began was rich and complicated, composed of every sort of social relationship in Western culture, including academic disciplines, family, nation, class, and language, habitual cafés and cabarets in particular cities, and of course circles of correspondents, blessed by the historian because they leave such good evidence behind. Ideas may well occur to people who have no relationships, but they are not ideas history can find out about.

Writing about Niels Bohr, the genius who came up with Modernism's epistemology of science:

> *The creative individual is, in a sense, complementary to the society in which he lives, rather as a soloist in a concerto. Both the basic ideas of science and the key inventions of mankind have generally been conceived in the minds of individuals, while the effort to gain the data on which the ideas and inventions have been based, and the subsequent effort to turn them to good account, have required the contributions of many besides the inventor and originator of ideas. So the individual and the community are necessary to one another. . . .*

> *For these individuals the necessary community, in many cases, was the entire Western world, at least insofar as it communicated with itself in the major Western languages. The great cities of* 1900 *where the first Modernists found themselves were already very populous, and usually multicultural. The nineteenth century had accomplished that. Communication was extremely swift, whether by postal correspondence (five deliveries a day in Munich), by publication (one month plus one week from contract to presentation copy for Kafka's first book of fiction), or by telephone and telegraph. It was possible for the poet Jules Laforgue to be born in Uruguay, educated at one of the best provincial secondary schools in France, employed as a reader by the Dowager Empress of Germany, and commissioned to translate the American works of Walt Whitman. James Joyce could write a novel meticulously set in the Dublin of* 1904 *while he was teaching English to Italians in the main seaport of the Austro-Hungarian Empire. In this sort of world an aristocratic Russian like Igor Stravinsky could change the course of Western music with a ballet score written in Switzerland and performed in Paris. Niels Bohr could write his classic paper on the atom in English while teaching in his native Denmark, publishing it in the journal of the British Royal Society under the guidance of a New Zealander who had made his scientific reputation in Ontario, Canada, by extending the work of a Polish woman living in Paris. This kind of "hopscotching the world," as early film newsreels called it, suggests an absence of system, certainly to those who prized nineteenth-century distinctions based on ethnicity and language. But the system was there, and it was itself transnational. In fact, the insistence on a supra-ethnic community of thought and of art is one of the positions now often defined as Modernism.*

Historian of literature Charles Newman and historian of science Stephen Toulmin dubbed literature and science "postmodern." Dance, critics archly assumed, was also postmodern, though not so often.

According to Andrew Ross, who taught "Postmodernism: Theory and Practice" in the Princeton English department, postmodernism was an "emerging concept . . . a contemporary response to the modernist division of high culture from mass culture." Not so, countered Claude Rawson, whose field is eighteenth-century studies:

> *The massive works of what are called postmodern novelists are . . . in their difficulty, allusive density, and simpering air of in-group donnishness . . . in their bulky appearance and learned showmanship, reminiscent of dissertations. . . . The trend was already potential in an earlier modernism, with its delight in esoteric allusion and its self-conscious (part satirical, part participatory) obsession with pedantry.*

Ada Louise Huxtable didn't like postmodernism either, but hers was different. It was "the renunciation and devaluation of everything the modernists believed in and built," and embodied "something somewhat nastier—a parvenu, old-tie, anti-liberal snobbism of the new, and young, far Right." (Huxtable had probably been reading *The New Criterion*, which had become, under Hilton Kramer's editorship, the U. S. voice of those whose only quarrel with Modernism was that it had been too utopian or too austere, not to mention anticapitalist, and never too democratic.)

The educated reader uses the term "Modernism" all the time, possessed of certain spreadeagled definitions learned, perhaps, in courses in art history or twentieth-century fiction and reinforced by daily trips through the glass canyons of downtown; but in fact we know less about it than we do about any other -ism—very little indeed. Communism or liberalism, even classicism or romanticism, would be less of a problem for us, if only because they are not so general. Unlike Modernism, none of these others requires us to understand a bit of everything and to indulge in the wholesale crossing of what we have come, in the twentieth century, to call "disciplinary barriers."

If Modernism may be too broad a term to be meaningful, it may also be too long. What is the duration of an -ism? The first to name itself was romanticism (classicism is retroactively applied), and it lasted little more than a generation, though much later and even now, thinkers will be called "romantic" if the old ingredients are there. Realism in the later nineteenth century has the same sort of history, though it seemed to last longer. By the 1880s -isms had begun to succeed each other at roughly five-year intervals. Five years, in the age before international telephoning, was barely enough time for bright members of a generation to find each other. Now, with postmodernism we have -isms that cover more than a generation and have little coherence. Perhaps because the bright young people in a generation don't cohere, or because there are too many of them, or because we are now in the habit of -ism-ing and can't find an alternative, critics and commentators have taken over, and instead of making terms that refer to new ideas and those who come up with them, they make terms that refer to themselves.

So what is Modernism? One premise of this book is that we had better define Modernism soon or we will lose the use of the term as soon as the last generation of Modernists follows the first to its centenary, putting an end to what may be the longest-lived cultural movement our civilization has ever experienced. It has been a long time since the first Moderns. James Joyce was born in 1883 when Freud and Strindberg were twenty-four; Anton Webern and Niels Bohr were born in 1885 when Bertrand Russell was thirteen and Kandinsky going on twenty. Isadora Duncan, Ludwig Boltzmann, Georg Cantor, and Stéphane Mallarmé all died before their work could be fully understood. Stravinsky and Picasso lived long, but not forever. Oskar Kokoschka was still alive when this book was planned, but he did not reach one hundred. The last of the quantum physicists, Paul Dirac, died in 1985 at eighty.

Symbolism is also a more useful term than most for the cultural historian, since it was adopted not only by playwrights and novelists but also by poets and painters; but it is fundamentally an aesthetic, too narrow to provide a core for Modernism. Unless it is stretched to include some Freudian psychologists, it describes no scientists at all. Such deepening divisions between the "disciplines" have made it difficult for academics in one of them to feel competent to write about others; as a result, a full history of Modernism, including all the arts and sciences, has never before been written. Successors of Louis Untermeyer's old biographical dictionary exist, but they all use the order we call alphabetical. What seems to be needed is a set of centrally located ideas, informing more than one discipline, that can together be termed Modernist retroactively if necessary but without serious anachronism.

Smoothness, in fact, was one of the ruling metaphors of the age. Nineteenth-century minds disagreed about almost everything except how much they disliked hard edges. Between one thing and another, whether on the canvas of an academic painter or in the natural and social worlds, there was always a *sfumato,* a transition. Marx, Hegel, and Darwin agreed that change was, if not regular, at least smooth. The tidal wave of dialectic, the *Aufhebung* (elevation) of Being, the evolutionary origin of a species, was a spectacular show, but it was neither catastrophic nor unpredictable. It was more like the forbiddingly complex but entirely harmonic development of a Brahms symphony. And its tempo, like that of a classical ballet, was *legato*. The reader of novels, mimicking the omniscient narrator, could assess something called "development of character" over hundreds of pages that mimicked real time.

One might expect an academic to do things of that sort on a high level of abstraction, but my academy is a secondary school. The reader will recognize no sense of obligation here to narrow the field of research or to restrict what is written about Modernists to things that have never been published before. The usual academic taboos against supplying a lay reader with a general history are not in effect, and this book uses biographical and chronicle forms, rather than those ritually adopted for launching a new salvo in one or another specialists' debate. These biographical profiles of the great first Modernists are focused on their most ground-breaking works, linked and arranged so that those works appear in chronological order. In this way there can always be one or more stories to tell: the story of how a particular poem or theorem was made, the story of one individual life or another, and the story of early Modernism as a whole.

Telling stories is not only, we hope, the more appealing way of arguing a case, but also by far the most Modern. Philosophers of the most contemporary dash now argue that there is no theory by which to judge truth—only more or less plausible stories. Given a collage of remarkable events, chronologically arranged, the reader will hopefully not mind the narrator's occasional insistence on consequence and coincidence among them, his assumption of near-omniscience, or his observance of the tradition that there be always one damned thing after another. The French critic Remy de Gourmont already understood this attitude a year before the twentieth century began, when he wrote that "ideas, like the atoms of Epicurus, hook up to each other as best they can, whatever the risk of confrontations, shocks and accidents." The story of Modernism begins with German mathematicians and moves on to physicists in Vienna, Berlin, Bern, and Copenhagen; a French painter; French and American poets; a histologist and a politician from Spain; a Viennese psychologist; a Dutch biologist; English, German, and Italian logicians; a New York filmmaker; a Parisian painter from Spain; a Swedish playwright; musicians from Vienna, New Orleans, and St. Petersburg (Russia); a novelist from Dublin; and a Muscovite painter in Munich. In addition to these central characters there were architects from Glasgow and Vienna, dancers from California and New Jersey, African nationalists from Georgia and the Caribbean, and writers of fiction from a dozen countries, including New Zealand and Norway. Finding each other was not hard for them, in the age of the telephone and the railroad and the heyday of the World's Fair. This book tries to bring them together by pausing occasionally for a sudden confluence of minds in

Vienna, Paris, or St. Louis, Missouri. Sometimes, as at the Upton Inn in *Tom Jones*, everyone was in the same place without ever meeting each other at all, while the emerging professions and disciplines ignored their cross-talk and fervently organized and subdivided themselves. More often, however, these geniuses did meet, conveniently or incongruously, deliberately or by the remotest chance, in person or in the educated minds of our own late twentieth-century culture. As the French say, "les grands esprits se rencontrent"; but if great minds have met in this century, it is because they have had no choice.

THE BEGINNING

The death of Queen Victoria in the first year of the twentieth century marks with a convenient definiteness the beginning of a new age. In international politics England's position of "splendid isolation" was abandoned in favor of an *entente cordiale* with France, which the new sovereign, Edward VII, had a considerable share in arranging. Great Britain had emerged from the Boer War victorious, but with diminished prestige; the German Emperor's congratulatory cablegram to President Kruger had aroused British animosity, and the British Government's counter stroke of sending the White Squadron out into the North Sea had excited German fears. Germany set about the increase of her own fleet to a strength that caused further irritation of British susceptibilities, and Europe seemed to be divided into two armed camps. All that the diplomatists could do was to defer the outbreak of the inevitable conflict to 1914.

The Great War suspended every peaceful human activity, and reduced the arts, including literature, almost to silence. Indeed the period for all World might be divided into pre-war and post-war, for the whole world suffered from the results of the disaster for a very long time. The delicately balanced economic and financial relations by which the world's business was carried on were upset. The War transformed Lloyd George from "the orator of the new social order" into "the organizer of victory," and when peace came, his power crumbled along with that of every other statesman who had endeavoured to patch up the miseries of a disordered world by the Treaty of Versailles (1919). His Coalition Government gave place to a Conservative administration, which was speedily defeated at the General Election of 1923. The Labour Government, which succeeded, stayed in for less than a year, and the difficulties either party – Conservative or Labour – experienced in attempting to govern the country, without a sufficient majority in the House of Commons, culminated in 1931 in the appointment of a second Coalition Government, headed by a Labour Premier, Mr. Ramsay Macdonald, but depending for its existence upon Conservative support. The financial and economic problems of peace proved even more incapable of solution than the problems of war. The European Governments found themselves alike unable to pay the debts they had incurred to the United States and the debts they had incurred to each other, including the reparations to which the Germans had unwillingly submitted as the price of peace. The result was a world-wide dislocation of financial and commercial relations which involved every nation except Russia in acute distress through the universal fall in prices, destruction of values, and consequent unemployment.

It is evident that the state of political and social unrest, which preceded and followed the War was unfavourable to the production of imaginative literature, and the effect of these unfavourable conditions was enhanced by a decay of religious faith. Sidney Low and Lloyd C. Sanders, summing up the achievements of the Victorian era at the beginning of the twentieth century, record the impression: "To some pessimists the orthodoxy of economics, the orthodoxy of science, and the orthodoxy of faith seemed alike 'bankrupt.' " Even so acute a thinker and so detached an observer as Professor Henry Sidgwick, writing at the end of the nineteenth century and looking back over the victory for liberalism he had helped to win, said: "Well, the years pass, the struggle with what Carlyle used to call 'Hebrew old clothes' is over, Freedom is won, and what does Freedom bring us to? It brings us face to face with atheistic science: the faith in God and Immortality, which we had been struggling to clear from superstition, suddenly seems to be in the air." This attitude, though characteristic of the twentieth century intellectuals, was not confined to them. Writing of England after the War, Charles E. G. Masterman says: "Shortly after the War, a report was issued, signed by members of all the religious bodies, of the experience of chaplains in dealing with the ordinary adult male soldier during the War. The report, if pessimistic, had at least the merits of candour. The general testimony was that, with occasional distinguished exception, this great mass of British male young adult life was facing death and being killed without any of the conviction of a spiritualexistence, a dominating Providence, or a future life, which have been entertained unchallenged for nearly two thousand years. It was not the War which had made this change. England, according to these testimonies, was no longer Christian, and had become pagan; and the great majority of the male population of England had completely ceased to believe in the faith of their forefathers."

This statement of the spiritual condition of English youth in 1914-18 may seem to some exaggerated. But similar testimony is given by leading representatives of English orthodoxy. To E. F. Benson, son of the Victorian Archbishop, writing in 1932, it appeared too mild a phrase to say that "a wave of irreligion" swept over the young generation in the years 1914 to 1918. "For some years already a growing indifference to religious matters had been sweeping over them: it might be called a wave, or it might be called a tide. . . . Already, before the War, the national indifference to matters of religion had been on the increase, and the Church had been losing hold, and these four years had vastly accelerated the process. Some, those chiefly who had seen service, rejected it with scorn and bitterness, but apart from them, the attitude of the mass of the nation was to turn from it as from some topic that lacked interest and reality. There was no slogan or crusade against it; it was merely a bundle of discarded and obsolete pieties, rubbish that lay littered in the house of life, and had perhaps better be cleared away, lest the microbes that bred in those medieval rags should again infect the spirit of man with fevers of childish superstition. The house must be cleaned and set in order, made habitable for a race that now looked on the world with a more enlightened eye." "All around," said the Bishop of Birmingham in his charge to the clergy at his episcopal visitation of 1932, "they saw decay of faith.

Of the great institutional systems, Anglican, Free Church, Roman Catholic, Unitarian, not one escaped. Ingenious advertisement, confident assertion, violent misrepresentation, conservative tenacity, earnest social enthusiasmall failed to avert loss, both of adherents and of prestige. Profound doubts had developed, not merely as to particular details of Christian dogma, but as to the most fundamental of Christian belief's – the existence of God. A widespread feeling existed that Christianity was antagonistic to that free and splendid progress, the glory of the thought and life of the present era, a feeling that in the churches intellectual incompetence was associated with spiritual insincerity." The fact of paramount importance in the spiritual life of England, he asserted, was the "loss of religious certainty."

This sense of spiritual uncertainty was also of paramount importance from a literary point of view. There was no longer a common body of religious belief to which writers of imaginative literature could appeal in confidence that they would find a general response in the hearts and minds of their readers. When Hamlet says "there's a special providence in the fall of a sparrow," and

There's a divinity that shapes our ends,
Roughhew them how we will,

Shakespeare knew that this expression of faith in divine Providence would find an echo in the hearts of all. So, too, Wordsworth, two centuries later could set forth his assured belief

That the procession of our fate, howe'er Sad or disturbed, is ordered by a Being Of infinite benevolence and power; Whose everlasting purposes embrace All accidents, converting them to good.

Midway in the nineteenth century ('In Memoriam,' 1850), Tennyson could only

Stretch faint hands of faith, and grope, And gather dust and chaff, and call To what I feel is Lord of all, And faintly trust the larger hope.

By the end of the nineteenth century even this "faint trust" in a beneficent Providence had largely disappeared from the minds of thinking men, and there was no longer any general expectation of a future life in which the woes of suffering humanity would be relieved, and its wrongs redressed.

From a merely literary point of view the lack of Christian faith might have been less serious if some other form of belief had commanded general acceptance. But, as was ironically remarked by the Bishop of Southwark, "Our ethical teachers – the novelists – are agreed only on the absurdity of the Christian faith. They completely disagree, however, upon what should replace it." If the mechanistic determinism which had been the favourite philosophy of evolutionary science in the nineteenth century had continued to gain ground in the twentieth century, the poets and novelists might have accommodated their minds to it; but it went almost completely out of fashion. The dogmatic faith in science as the guide of life, characteristic of so much of nineteenth century thinking, faded away under the light of twentieth century research, especially in astronomy and physics. Two Oxford professors, Sir James Jeans and Sir Arthur Eddington, are the leading exponents of the new science which, according to the distinguished Cambridge mathematician, Bertrand Russell, is "undermining the whole structure of applied reason and presenting us with a world of unreal and fantastic dreams in place of the Newtonian solidity." "Science now presents nothing but the most disorderly, random, and preposterous universe of events, connected by little except a structure composed of human concepts." Sir James Jeans, at the conclusion of 'Eos, or the Wider Aspects of Cosmogony" (1929), writes that the picture the scientist sees may be merely a creation of his own mind, in which nothing really exists except the mind itself; "the universe which we study with such care may be a dream, and we brain-cells in the mind of the dreamer." Professor John Scott Haldane, another Oxford scientist, while avowing himself a free-thinker because he cannot accept the creed of any existing church, sees no hope in science as a revelation of the significance of human life. "Science by itself cannot guide us, since from its very nature it does not deal with the values which are supreme. Science is not enough. Reason in its highest form as religion, and real religion extending into every part of our lives is what the world has most need of, and particularly just now, with old theological beliefs, which to a large extent embodied religion, disintegrating in every direction along with old scientific beliefs as well as old political beliefs."

Along with the general discontent and the decay of religious beliefs went the weakening of the standards of morality to which those beliefs gave the supports of an authoritative sanction and an impelling motive. In 'A Corner of England' (1932), an intensive study of a London slum by John Martin, the author states that the slum-dwellers have ceased to recognize the sanction of the rights of property. "A man loses little and may easily gain in local prestige if he is thought to be a burglar or a motor bandit." And outside of the slums, among selfrespecting and respectable working people throughout the length and breadth of England, there has been a noteworthy falling away from ancient standards.

Thus, though spiritual conditions seemed unpropitious to genius, the material conditions were by no means unfavourable to literary production. The extension of elementary education to the whole population, achieved before the end of the nineteenth century, was followed in the twentieth by the bringing of secondary education within the reach of the masses and by the provision of scholarships which opened the way for the poorest to the universities. There was no excuse for any "mute inglorious Milton" to perish unknown for lack of literary opportunity, and on the other hand, the reading public was so immensely enlarged as to increase the demand for literature and the profits of authorship to a degree undreamt of in previous centuries. The establishment of international copyright in the last decade of the nineteenth century added the American to the English market, and, especially in the novel and in the drama, gave the English author an opportunity such as had never before existed in the history of the world. The greatly improved facilities for international communication brought the ideas and methods of foreign authors speedily to the attention of the British public and British craftsmen, and writers in twentieth century England were no longer hampered by the national prejudices and Puritanical restrictions which had beset the frank description of and comment on life in novels and plays almost to the end of the Victorian era. The twentieth century novelist or playwright had all the liberty that he deserved or desired, and took full advantage of it. Henry James, as early as 1914, commended the younger English novelists of his time for their courage in hugging the shore of the real in matters of sex instead of flying to the open sea of sentiment at the least sign of difficulty. The popularity of psychoanalysis led to further frankness in this regard, and the twentieth century dramatist or novelist not only recovered the chartered liberty of eighteenth century literature but went beyond it.

Meanwhile, the bashful maiden whose blushes Mrs. Grundy wished to spare, had done something for her own emancipation with the aid of the bicycle, the tennis racket, the hockey stick, and the golf club. The greater opportunities offered by the War for women of all classes resulted not merely in the grant of the parliamentary suffrage, but in a greater feeling of independence. This was emphasized by the adoption of more sensible styles of dress, first for games and then for everyday wear. Fashions of hairdressing also became simpler, and the young women of the twentieth century were obviously taller, stronger, and more self-reliant than their predecessors in any age known to history. The opportunities for secondary and college education which were organized for women in the last thirty years of the nineteenth century were still further developed in the twentieth, and the professions of law and medicine, which had been wholly or partially closed to them, were thrown open. Changes in legislation or in the interpretation of the law gave married women a greater degree of personal liberty in addition to the control of their own property, and placed them on the same level as men in the divorce court. All these outward evidences of liberty and equality were accompanied by an inner conviction in the minds of women, which gave them a greater sense, not only of personal freedom, but of personal responsibility.

Literature (and still more, journalism) had a great deal to do with bringing about these changes and with conveying the knowledge of them to the unenlightened. Books, especially those which had a wide sale, dealt more and more with current issues; the novel and the play were made use of for all kinds of propaganda; and the circulation of serious discussions of political and economic questions, through cheap printing and free libraries, increased to an enormous extent. By the side of a great mass of printed matter of merely ephemeral interest, there were more books than ever dealing with serious questions in a serious way. Never before did problems of politics, economics, and sociology gain such widespread attention.

In such a period we may expect to find very wide divergence of opinion and the advocacy of measures which must seem to many people extravagant. The more daring, radical thinkers have something to suggest which may be worth consideration or may be utterly impracticable, but is at any rate more likely to be of interest than a mere plea for the maintenance of things as they are. The air is full of the consciousness of new conditions, such as the world has never faced before, and there is a general expectation of impending change, both in national and international affairs. In the conduct of its domestic policy and in its contributions for the solution of international problems, Great Britain has endeavoured to combine enterprise with moderation, and the English literature of the period, although much of it is transitional and journalistic, has features which are both of immediate and of permanent interest.

2
Chapter

The Evaluation of Modern Literature

What is so remarkable about the twentieth century, and what marks it off from previous centuries, is the intense awareness it has of its own processes, and its innumerable attempts to describe what is happening, while it is still happening. The Victorians were certainly aware of their problems and their predicament. As Matthew Arnold wrote to Clough, "these are damned times – everything is against one – the height to which knowledge is come, the spread of luxury, our physical enervation, the absence of great natures, the unavoidable contact with small ones, newspapers, cities, light profligate friends, moral desperadoes like Carlyle, our own selves, and the sickening consciousness of our own difficulties, but Arnold never attempted an assessment of a single contemporary English writer or of any contemporary movement in literature, and his inaugural lecture on Poetry at Oxford in 1869, *On the Modern Element in Literature,* had not a word about anything except Greece. He was preoccupied with the previous age, the Romantic period, with World Literature, with "Europe as being, for intellectual and spiritual purposes, one great confederation, bound to a joint action and working to a common result; and whose members have, for their proper outfit, a knowledge of Greek, Roman and Eastern antiquity, and of one another."

The seventeenth century, a period very much like our own, was much more concerned with what was happening, and a great critic like Dryden has a modernity we can appreciate in his awareness of living in a transitional age, under the towering shadow of the great Elizabethan period, and worried by the new literary standards of Baroque France. It was Dryden, in the last year of the seventeenth century, the year of his own death, who wrote the epitaph of the century in his *Secular Masque:*

> *All, all of a piece throughout: Thy chase had a beast in view; Thy wars brought nothing about. Thy lovers were all untrue. 'Tis well an old age is out, And time to begin a new.*

One of the reasons why the Victorians made no assessment was that they did not believe and could not believe that an age was coming to an end. It was only in the 'nineties that people became aware of a dissolution, which they called a decadence, and that was associated not with an epoch, but with a century — they spoke of *fin de siècle* literature. There is a curious mystical feeling about the end of a century, and by some accident or coincidence the ends of centuries have been rather wonderful. The end of the fourteenth with Chaucer's *Canterbury Tales* and *Troilus and Criseyde,* the end of the sixteenth with Shakespeare and Marlowe, and Spenser's Faerie Queene, the end of the seventeenth with Congreve, the end of the eighteenth with a new world beginning with Coleridge's Ancient Mariner and Wordsworth's Tintern Abbey. For our own satisfaction, we must try to impose a pattern on our time, which means a simplification, and inevitably an over-simplification. Can we pin our faith in dates, and does our age begin in 1901? Does it depend on the deaths of great men? Does our time begin with the death of Oscar Wilde in 1900, or would it be truer to say that the half-century which has a unity is that from the death of Carlyle in 1881 to the death of D. H. Lawrence in 1930, or must it really be the double death of Virginia Woolf and James Joyce in 1941; or does the break really come where Virginia Woolf said it did, in 1910?

Let us be bold and say that our period really begins in 1903 with the "Life Force" as displayed in Bernard Shaw's *Man and Superman* and ends with the death-force, that it moves from the age of biology, which is the legacy of the Victorians, to the atomic age, or that it begins as the sociological age and continues as the psychological era. The new century began on a new note. Victorian solemnity was replaced by an Edwardian, or perhaps more particularly a Shavian friskiness, no less serious but much less solemn. You remember Tolstoy's letter to Bernard Shaw about *Man and Superman:* "The first defect in it is that you are not sufficiently serious. One should not speak jestingly of such a subject as the purpose of human life, the causes of its perversion, and the evil that fills the life of humanity to-day." After Carlyle and Ruskin and Tolstoy a lighter touch was certainly necessary. The chief offence of Matthew Arnold in the eyes of the Victorians was not his attack on the Philistines — not his doctrine, but the tone of voice in which he pro -mulgated it. That too was Oscar Wilde's major offence. *The Importance of Being Earnest* was just as serious an attack on Victorian standards as Butler's *The Way of all Flesh,* but the deft, good-humoured tone was more damaging. Wilde's other offence was taking the art of criticism too seriously. The artist's raw material is life, experienced through the senses, patterned by the mind, and given divinity by that mysterious thing we know nothing about, the soul, intuition, the unconscious, or whatever we like to call it. The critic's raw material is the finished work of art, which he uses as a building brick in the larger architecture of criticism. The present age scarcely gives Oscar Wilde credit for the vast progress of criticism in our time.

It was in 1903 also that the first part of Thomas Hardy's *The Dynasts* appeared. The new century began by accepting what had been fought so bitterly in the nineteenth, the new view of the world as a mechanism, as a process rather than the work of a beneficent Deity, Heaven undermined by science. In his preface Hardy drew attention to "the supernatural spectators of the terrestrial action, certain impersonated abstractions, or intelligences, called spirits" and explained calmly that "The wide prevalence of the Monistic theory of the Universe forbade, in this twentieth century" (notice how Hardy insists on the new century) "the importation of Divine personages from any antique Mythology or ready-made sources or channels of Causation, even in verse, and excluded the celestial machinery of say Paradise Lost, as peremptorily as that of the Iliad or the Eddas. . . . And the abandonment of the masculine pronoun in allusions to the First or Fundamental Energy seemed a necessary and logical consequence of the long abandonment by thinkers of the anthropomorphic conception of the same." England had already experienced the scandal of Hardy's reference in Tess of the d'Urbervilles to "The President of the Immortals." That was in a novel and was noticed, but The *Dynasts* was in verse, and, as Hardy once said, "If Galileo had said in verse that the world moved, the Inquisition might have let him alone."

But the opening words of The Dynasts were startling enough for those who had eyes to read. The Shade of the Earth enquires:

What of the Immanent Will and Its designs?

And the Spirit of the Years replies:

It works unconsciously, as heretofore Eternal artistries, in Circumstance, Whose patterns, wrought by rapt aesthetic rote, Seem in themselves Its single listless aim, And not their consequence.

Here was the æsthetic legacy of the 'eighties and 'nineties casting its shadow from behind, and here was the unconscious casting its shadow before. In that same year, 1903, in Samuel Butler's The Way of All Flesh, the unconscious speaks with a very modern voice. It is the scene in the forty-second chapter, when young Ernest Pontifex is being tortured by his parents into betraying his schoolfellows' crimes:

> *"No matter how awful was the depravity revealed to them, the pair never flinched, but probed and probed, till they were on the point of reaching subjects more delicate than they had yet touched upon. Here Ernest's unconscious self took the matter up and made a resistance to which his conscious self was unequal, by tumbling him off his chair in a fit of fainting."*

The twentieth century was being dovetailed into the nineteenth, and striding across the join was the new figure who was to own the new century – the Common Man. The social historian of the literature of our time will be much concerned with the social origins and backgrounds of its contributors, the intruders into the old settled order of middle-class authorship, and one of his chief documents will be what is in many ways the most important of twentieth-century books, H. G. Wells's *Experiment in Autobiography,* because it is the autobiography, not merely of an individual, but of a process. It is an epic of ambition and a parable of modern civilization. It lays bare that strain of inferiority-feeling which may perhaps give this age its historical label, the uneasiness of an epoch of discontent, and that obsession with sex which is the hallmark of adolescent maladjustment whether in a man or in a generation. Wells describes it as "The adventures of a sample human brain in the latter phase of the Private Capitalist System," and more shrewdly as the portrait of "an individual becoming the conscious Common Man of his time and culture." Wells is Kipps and Mr. Polly. He is the Philistine, something far deadlier than Matthew Arnold's educated Philistine; he is the self-educated Philistine, two generations younger than the self-improvers of the nineteenth century. He is the forerunner of the products of the Education Act of 1870. It is the Philistinism of a *nouveauriche science* passionately condescending towards an ancient aristocracy of culture. He is the prophet of the half-baked and confused, the mirror of the growing-pains of the twentieth century, and his influence on the thought and the literature of the first third of the century is infinitely greater than he has been given credit for. He is transparent and unashamed, and confesses everything. "So much of my life," he says, "has been a prolonged and enlarged adolescence." And on the novel, on its substance and its scope, if not on its form and its art, his effect has been profound.

Early twentieth-century fiction owes two of its main directions to Wells's activity as a pamphleteer and a novelist – the incursion of the theme of sex, and the deliberate extension of the whole field of action of the novel. *In A Modern Utopia* in 1905 he discussed Free Love and Contraception – then called Neo-Malthusianism, and, as he says, "The book was popular with the young of our universities. . . . It played a considerable part in the general movement of release from the rigid technical chastity of women during the Victorian period." His novel *Ann Veronica* in 1909 caused a scandal. "Its particular offence was," Wells writes, "that Ann Veronica was a virgin who fell in love and showed it, instead of waiting, as all previous heroines had hitherto done, for someone to make love to her. It was held to be an unspeakable offence that an adolescent female should be sex-conscious before the thing was forced upon her attention. But Ann Veronica wanted a particular man who excited her and she pursued him and got him, with gusto." The book was banned by the libraries, and preached against by earnest clergymen, and so advertised into notoriety and influence. The familiar ring and animal imagery of the moral reviewer begins to be heard. *The Spectator* wrote that "the muddy world of Mr. Wells's imaginings is a community of scuffling stoats and ferrets, unenlightened by a ray of duty and abnegation." By the time *The New Machiavelli* came to be printed in *The English Review* in 1910 and 1911 a new world was born.

Wells is also one of the protagonists in the battle between the novel as an art form and the formless novel, which is by no means the same as the artless. It is really a battle between the ragged native form and the shapely and purposeful foreign product, what Arnold Bennett used to refer to as "the great Flaubert, Turgenev, Zola, Maupassant, Goncourt group." Wells's attitude was a challenge to the history of nineteenth-century fiction. He was fighting against the conception of the novel merely as a vehicle for character. "In the established novel," he said, "objective through and through, the characteristic exterior reactions of the character were everything and the conflicts and changes of ideas within his brain were ignored." in 1911 he issued his manifesto on the Novel of Discussion. "We are going to deal with political questions and religious questions and social questions. We cannot present people unless we have this free hand, this unrestricted field. What is the good of telling stories about people's lives if one may not deal freely with the religious beliefs and organizations that have controlled or failed to control them? What is the good of pretending to write about love, and the loyalties and treacheries and quarrels of men and women, if we must not glance at those varieties of physical temperament and organic quality, those deeply passionate needs and distresses, from which half the storms of human life are brewed."

Henry James, he said, had no idea of the possible use of the novel as a help to conduct, so, Wells bluntly said, "the novelist is going to be the most potent of artists, because he is going to present conduct, devise beautiful conduct, discuss conduct, analyse conduct, suggest conduct, illuminate it through and through. He will not teach, but discuss, point out, plead and display. We are going to appeal to the young and hopeful and the curious, against the established, the dignified and defensive. Before we have done, we will have all life within the scope of the novel." This passionate and youthful iconoclast, this youth leader, was then forty-five. And from that time the novel, as Wells shaped and taught it, was to be not character but discussion — it was to be "The Portrait of the Artist."

Three years later, in his famous articles on "The Younger Generation" in *The Times Literary Supplement* of 1914, Henry James in his turn was to sum up the situation of the novel, to make yet another of the age's conscious and deliberate assessments. He defines the new as "an appetite for a closer notation, a sharper specification of the signs of life, of consciousness, of the human scene and the human subject in general, than the three or four generations before us had been at all moved to insist on." He finds Jane Austen wanting in this very special matter. "Where her testimony complacently ends the pressure of appetite within us presumes exactly to begin." He finds in Wells and Bennett an inordinate possession of the worlds they present, a saturation, in the tradition of the great master, Tolstoy, but something essential is missing. Each is the temporary master of our sensibility. We are given the facts of the life of the Five Towns. "But is this all?" he asks. "These are the circumstances of the interest – but where is the interest itself, where and what is its centre?" As a student of form James was superb, as a tipster he was deplorable. In that assessment, among the recent writers he was frightened, respectfully frightened, by D. H. Lawrence, and plumped for – Hugh Walpole!

In the meantime, while Wells was talking, before Henry James summed up, something very important was happening. While Wells was writing in 1911, something indeed had already happened. In 1924 Virginia Woolf attempted yet another assessment, this time of the Edwardian and the Georgian novel, under the title of *Mr. Bennett and Mrs. Brown.* In it she made the startling statement that "on or about December, 1910, human character changed" – a statement very comforting to the student of modern literature, but very few people, we imagine, have the faintest notion what she really meant by it.

The statement is ostensibly about the nature of modern fiction, but in 1910 – in December, 1910, as Virginia Woolf exactly dates it – the most important event in England was the opening of the notorious Post-Impressionist exhibition at the Grafton Galleries, where the older work of Manet, including *The Bar at the Folies* Bergère, and the paintings of Van Gogh, Gauguin, Matisse, Picasso and, above all, Cézanne were seen with a fresh eye. Visitors roared with laughter, the donkeys brayed, as they still do at Picasso forty years later. Only one man was honest, one of the men to be cast aside by the new generation. In that same December, Arnold Bennett wrote: "I have permitted myself to suspect that, supposing some writer were to come along and do in words what these men have done in paint,we might conceivably be disgusted with nearly the whole of modern fiction, and we might have to begin again. This awkward experience will in all probability not happen to me, but it might happen to a writer younger than me; at any rate, it is a fine thought."We can only record the fact of this impact of Post-Impressionism, and of Cubism and Futurism and Expressionism, and in a different way, of the Russian Ballet. The actual process is too complicated, and to analyse it we need the still uncollected confessions of those who were influenced, the still unpublished letters and diaries, the records of conversations and discussions, and all the underground material of history.

More direct was the effect of Russian literature, acceptable because it was a spiritual antidote to the materialism of Flaubert and Zola and the De Goncourts. As early as 1909 Arnold Bennett welcomed Tchehov. "We have no writer," he said, "and we have never had one, nor has France, who could mould the material of life without distorting it, into such complex forms to such an end of beauty." *Without distorting it* — notice, this was before December, 1910. But it was the appearance of Mrs. Constance Garnett's translation of Dostoevsky, beginning with *The Brothers Karamazov* in 1912, which started a period of hysteria which lasted throughout the war and shook up English fiction as nothing native had clone hitherto. Something of that fever can be seen in Mr. Middleton Murry's biography of Dostoevsky in 1916, and in parts of his *Evolution of an*

Intellectual after the war, and something of the resistance can be seen in John Galsworthy, who represented the vested interests of the English tradition of the novel -modified strongly by the other Russian, the gentler Russian, the French Russian, Turgenev. In 1914 Galsworthy was not the fictional ambassador to Europe he became in 1922 with the completion of *The Forsyte Saga,* and another part of the battlefield can be seen in his letter to Edward Garnett about D. H. Lawrence's Sons and Lovers of 1913. Here was the Patrician rebuking the Plebeian, the Patrician who had sent Garnett "a list of one hundred and thirty upper-class men and women he had met and known" to prove that he really was at home with the aristocracy.

"I've finished *Sons and Lovers,"* he wrote in 1914. "I've nothing but praise for all the part that deals with the mother, the father and the sons; but I've a lot besides praise for the love part. . . . It's not good enough to spend time and ink in describing the penultimate sensations and physical movements of people getting into a state of rut; we all know them too well. There's genius in the book, but not in that part of the book. The body's never worth while, and the sooner Lawrence recognizes that the better – the men we swear by, Tolstoy, Turgenev, Tchehov, Maupassant, Flaubert, France, knew that truth; they only use the body, and that sparingly, to reveal the soul." But the cry from the heart comes in the Postscript: "PS. Confound all these young fellows; how they have gloated over Dostoevsky."

With Dostoevsky literature plunged into profundities hitherto unknown, instructive, intuitive profundities, below the surface of consciousness. The door to the unknown was being pushed open. The known surface of man had seemingly been explored to exhaustion – the naturalist approach, the realist approach, the sociological approach. The biological, the financial and political organization of man, the obvious springs oflove had been examined, and overcropping had produced a kind of dust-bowl in the landscape of fiction. It remained only for science to give its sanction to the exploration of the remainder of human feeling, the submerged iceberg of the unconscious.

If, as we have suggested, the twentieth century may be said in one way to begin with the "life-force" which Bernard Shaw compounded out of the theories of Bergson and of Samuel Butler, in another way it can be said to begin with the publication of Sigmund Freud's *Interpretation of Dreams* in 1900. But not yet in England. Once again the year 1910 becomes significant, when Freud's own account of the development and subjectmatter of psycho-analysis was published in *The American Journal of Psychology. The Interpretation of Dreams was* translated in 1913 and printed in three separate impressions, just in time for the War of 1914-18, and with it and with *Wit and the Unconscious in* 1916 *and the Psychopathology of Everyday Life,* which has sold we don't know how many thousands in its Penguin edition, came a tremendous enlargement of our understanding of the mechanism of the emotions, and of the mechanism of the imagination.

Psycho-analysis came in time for the war, and it joined the influence of Dostoevsky. Nobody who went through the war was quite the same person again, and many writers read Freud for the first time in the trenches. Nobody who read Dostoevsky was quite the same person again, and nobody who read Freud could escape the logical and convincing relevance of his theories of human nature and the secret springs of human motives. Where anthropology and Frazer's *Golden Bough* had raised doubts about the origin and nature of religion and the validity of modern social organization, Freud had imposed a pattern on the secret evolution of mankind.

D. H. Lawrence in *Sons and Lovers* in 1913 had written a Freudian novel without having read Freud, though he had heard something about him. Lawrence was being studied by the psycho-analysts, and his friend Dr. Eder translated Freud's shorter book *On Dreams* in 1914. It was all in the air. May Sinclair's novel *The Three Sisters* in 1914 had some tinge of it. After the war it was learnt that the treatment of shell-shock had confirmed Freud's theories beyond all question, just as the results of the eclipse were to prove Einstein's theories. Rebecca West's *Return of the Soldier* in 1918 was based on a cure by Freudian therapy. In 1920 J. D. Beresford the novelist pointed out "that of all theories of the nature of man ever put forward by a reputable scientist, that of Sigmund Freud is the most attractive and adaptable for the purposes of fiction."

In 1921 D. H. Lawrence wrote on *Psychoanalysis and the Unconscious,* and by 1922 its influence in the novel was on the wane, it was no longer a novelty, it had become an essential and natural part of the modern writer's equipment. Mr. G. M. Young has said that "the arrival of the New Psychology had much of the excitement that attended the arrival of the New Learning at the Renaissance," and Mr. Auden, in his fine poem on the death of Freud in September, 1939, at the end of an epoch, wrote:

> *To us he is no more a person Now but a whole climate of opinion.*

which means that he is now as important as Darwin or Karl Marx, even to those who have never read a line of any of them.

By 1922! 1922 was the *Annus Mirabilis* of the halfcentury. The incredible ferment of the years from 1910 to 1914 was bound to produce a remarkable vintage. In 1922 appeared Virginia Woolf's Jacob's *Room,* a "cubist" novel, and James Joyce's Ulysses, an "expressionist" novel, and T. S. Eliot's *The Waste Land* a "post-impressionist" poem, and for balance, Galsworthy's Forsyte Saga, as a control to measure the speed and direction of the new movement. Galsworthy's was a voice from the past. Virginia Woolf's was a change of direction; she had rejected Galsworthy and Wells and Bennett. In Joyce and Eliot a river had come to the surface which had been running underground for some time. Joyce's Dubliners was begun in 1900, but could not be published until 1914. *A*

Portrait of The Artist as a Young Man was begun in 1904 and published in America in 1916 because the English printers refused to print some of the words, and in 1917 H. G. Wells reviewed it. "Its claim to be literature is as good as the claim of the last book of *Gulliver's Travels,* and one conversation in the book . . . By then D. W. Griffith's films *The Birth of a Nation* and *Intolerance* had been made, and the cinema had become an art. Wells told Arnold Bennett about Joyce. When Bennett read fragments of Ulysses in the pages of The Little Review he was puzzled, but, he wrote, "recalling the time when I laughed at Cézanne's pictures, I wondered whether there might not be something real in the pages after all." When the complete work appeared in 1922 he was won over. "The best portions of the novel," he wrote, "are immortal. I single out the long orgiastic scene, and the long unspoken monologue of Mrs. Bloom which closes the book. The former will easily bear comparison with Rabelais at his fantastical finest; it leaves Petronius out of sight. It has plenary inspiration. The latter — I have never read anything to surpass it, and I doubt if I have ever read anything to equal it." This generosity by Wells and Bennett meant much to a struggling modernity.

If we are concerned with the process of assessment, it is just these things we must know, because in all the arts, but especially in literature, there is the producer and the consumer. All our literary histories concentrate on the producer, on the goods offered and the goods which sold and continue to sell. What we need very badly is a consumer's history of literature, of the tastes and salesresistances, of the crazes and fashions, of the state of the market, and of the publicity campaigns, the actual sales figures and the profits, and the mergers and manceuvres, of the fight between the multiple stores and the little men, between book societies and literature, of the cheap editions and floating opinion, and even of the crashes and bankruptcies and remainders.

Much of the material for this exists, unless it has been sent for salvage, in that phenomenon of the twentieth century, the *"Little Reviews."* They take their name from The Little Review of New York, which fought so fiercely for the publication of Joyce's Ulysses. There was the *English Review* under Ford Madox Hueffer, and The New Age under Orage. One of the earliest was Katherine Mansfield and Middleton Murry's Rhythm in 1911, the first to publish Picasso and to discuss Van Gogh and Gauguin and Croce. There was that most powerful of coterie papers, The Egoist, enlivened by Ezra Pound, and later by T. S. Eliot, which published Joyce's Portrait of the Artist in 1914 and 1915, and Wyndham Lewis's novel Tarr in 1917.

It was in The Egoist that May Sinclair praised Dorothy Richardson's novels in April, 1918. It was there that T. S. Eliot fought for the recognition that important things for English poetry were happening in France, and published his essay on *Tradition and the Individual Talent*. There was Wyndham Lewis's Blast, with its fierce mixture of Futurism and Expressionism, and after the war Art and Letters, with Herbert Read and Osbert Sitwell, and the swan-song of *The Athenæum* under Middleton Murry, with T. S. Eliot, Virginia Woolf, Aldous Huxley and Katherine Mansfield as contributors.

You cannot have assessment without standards, ruthless standards and ruthless principles, and that is what the new criticism was building up under the influence of Mr. Eliot, whose Sacred Wood in 1920 gathered up what had been appearing in *The Egoist and The Athenæum,* and the chapbooks of Harold Monro's Poetry Bookshop, and anonymously in *The Times Literary Supplement*. The chief critical organ of the period was Mr. Eliot's Criterion, founded in October, 1922. In its first number appeared *The Waste Land*. It spanned the 'twenties and the 'thirties and its death by 1939 was another sign of the ending of an epoch. It died, as Mr. Eliot wrote in a poignant farewell, of the shame and depression of Munich, but it enshrined the critical conscience and the critical consciousness of Europe for two decades.

The middle of the half-century saw the founding of Mr. Edgell Rickword's *Calendar of Modern Letters,* a much neglected and ungratefully forgotten periodical. It may be seen in sample in the volume edited by Mr. F. R. Leavis under the title of *Towards Standards of Criticism.* Its two volumes of *Scrutinies,* also edited by Mr. Rickword, are still valuable, if only for D. H. Lawrence's ruthless and piercing demolition of John Galsworthy. The name *Scrutinies* gave the title to Mr. Leavis's periodical *Scrutiny,* which began in 1932. Mr. Geoffrey Grigson's New Verse, which ran from 1933 to 1939, and Mr. Cyril Conolly's *Horizon,* which kept sensibility alive from 1940 to 1949, complete but do not exhaust the list. But we want to make a special mention of *World Review* during the past two years under Stefan Schimanski, whose tragic death in an aeroplane crash over Japan took place in 1950. We want to pay this tribute because because very few people realize how much they owe to his eager and puzzled search for truth amid the Apocalyptic and Existentialist movements of the last ten years.

We have mentioned these "Little Reviews" because they are the foundations of the literature of our time, the battlegrounds of new movements and new ideas, the seed-grounds of all new literature, sheltering the young writers while they are growing, bringing them, while they are new, to the audiences ready for them, and offering them to the commercial world, which will decide their fame or their fate. We have mentioned their editors because one ought always to know who was the literary editor of a paper at an important period, for he has a policy, he chooses the contributors and the critics and distributes the tasks, he provokes creative criticism. The function of such reviews, as Mr. Allen Tate says, is "not to give the public what it wants, or what it thinks it wants, but what, through the medium of its most intelligent members, it ought to have."

To look through a whole file of one of these reviews is to step into a kind of Time Machine. You see what was new and suggestive at the time, and if you look at your own marked copies you can see something even more valuable — you can see what has happened to yourself, for a quarterly number gave you enough ideas to last you three months until the next instalment. Your copies should be marked, with the code signs which indicated what was fresh to you at the time, and what you proudly knew already. How valuable were those chronicles of foreign periodicals and of foreign literature, how illuminating those generalizations which appeared in the midst of a review of a now-forgotten book, and which appear still in reviews by V. S. Pritchett or Philip Toynbee or Walter Allen or P. H. Newby or Alex Comfort or Edward Sackville-West — and only too rarely by W. H. Auden. That is how a climate of opinion is created, and the very fact that critics are struggling hard to make generalizations is in itself an important mark of our century.

From the picture we have so far presented, it seems as though the first quarter of the century was a period of achievement, and the second quarter a period of conscious stocktaking, not so much of the facts of the achievement as of its inner and essential nature. And we can see this better if we look at the progress of American criticism. In 1925 Mr. I. A. Richards published his *Principles of Literary Criticism,* a misleading title, because it was not about literary criticism at all, but only about the psychological and neurological study of poetry, and in 1930 Mr. William Empson, his disciple, published his *Seven Types of Ambiguity.* These two Cambridge casuists differ profoundly. So far as we can judge, Mr. Richards is not really interested in poetry at all, but Mr. Empson is passionately concerned about it. Between them they instituted an approach which made for the close and intensive analysis of the poetic mechansim; and after Mr. Eliot's essays on the Metaphysical Poets, and his insistence on the "mechanism of sensibility" in John Donne and his followers, and on the "dissociation of sensibility" which took place in the seventeenth century, the whole of serious criticism in England and America was centred on the problem of the poet's response to the civilization of his own epoch, and the function and deployment of poetical imagery. The poetry of John Donne has dominated the critical thought of the last twenty-five years, and even Shakespeare's poetry has been illuminated by these studies. It is probable that no age of English literature has produced such a high level of penetrating criticism, and America proudly claims a large share of it. During the past ten years this has penetrated back again to England, and whenever we see *The Southern Review* which died in 1942, or *The Sewanee Review,* or *The Kenyon Review* and perhaps the best of them all, the nearest we have to a successor to *The Criterion,The Hudson Review,* with the work of John Crowe Ransom, and Allen Tate and R. P. Blackmur and others, we are pulled pleasurably up on our toes. It is not merely a critical inbreeding, concerned only with the poetry and principles of to-day, but it goes back to Aristotle and Longinus and Coleridge and Arnold, and continues where they left off, always adding Mr. T. S. Eliot, who is in many ways the Aristotle of our day, or perhaps rather the Dryden, in his methodical formulation of the canons of any form he is exploring. Mr. Eliot's studies on *Dante,* on *The Music of Poetry,* and more recently on the problems of *Poetic Drama* are already part of the history of English criticism.

But what is more interesting and more important for the future of criticism in the coming second half of this century is the fact that the American critics are turning from the deep analysis of poetry to the deep analysis of fiction. There the master is Henry James, whose great Prefaces promise to be the Poetics of the novel ready for the commentators of the New Renaissance. John Crowe Ransom and Allen Tate have already done some remarkable explorations which deserve more attention than they have yet received in England. Collections of such criticism, whether of poetry or of the novel, are beginning to reach this country, and we wish we could have delayed this assessment another twenty-five years, because the writing of the second quarter of this century is still a tangled medley. We hope to clear up some of these tangles when we deal with the texture and the structure of the more recent fiction. Our perspective is clearer for the first half of the period, as is only natural. We are a little too near to the work of Henry Green and William Sansom, Joyce Cary and Graham Greene, Miss Compton Burnett and Miss Elizabeth Bowen, and even to the later work of James Joyce and Virginia Woolf and Aldous Huxley.

The pattern is clear up to 1930, and that year was in two senses the end of a literary epoch. It was the end of the half-century beginning in 1880, when the contemporary world split off from the Victorian world, and it was the end of the self-contained period of twenty years from the crucial changes of 1910, a period of investigation and probing, of uneasiness and unrest and creation, which closes with the death of D. H. Lawrence. Lawrence was concerned with nature as an all-pervading force; he was interested in the animal and vegetable layers of human consciousness. His acute sensitiveness to social atmosphere, his awareness of the subtleties of human relationships spoken and unspoken, avowed and unconscious, go far to justify us in calling the years from 1910 to 1930, "The Age of Lawrence." During the past twenty years Lawrence's influence has been somewhat in abeyance, many of the younger writers have had no occasion to study him, and it may have some significance for the history of the second half of this century that' in 1950 the reading public was presented with a million copies of Lawrence's works in the Penguin edition.

In assessing a period of literature it is always important to know what kind of book was available both to the reader and the writer, what new books entered and old books re-entered. We are inclined to forget how much happened in the 'thirties, that it was not, at first, a decline from the glorious 'twenties. In 1930 appeared Wyndham Lewis's *Apes of God*, a satirical epitaph on the æsthetic pretensions of the previous decades, a didactic novel of vast dimensions with something of the same fierceness of an expiring epoch as Byron's *Don Juan*. It was an important work, which he followed up with a critical attack on the new influences from America, Ernest Hemingway "the dumb ox," and William Faulkner "the moralist with a corn cob," whose novels The Sound and *The Fury and Sanctuary and Pylon* were the nearest to genius this century had seen. England became very much aware of the world outside, of the European consequences of the war, of the Russian Revolution, and of the great American slump. No decade of the half-century was so generally and universally alive, and for the younger writers there was contemporary stimulus as well as recent classics to catch up and assimilate.

In 1930 appeared a translation of the great comic epic of the war – Hašek's *The Good Soldier Schweik,* a comic masterpiece which many serious people rank with *Don Quixote*: and in 1931 Alfred Döblin's *Alexanderplatz,* a Joyce-like picture of German chaos. In 1930 Proust was available in a cheap edition, and in 1931 appeared Stephen Hudsonnnn's translation of Time Regained, the concluding and explanatory section of Proust's masterpiece. In 1930 Auden's poems initiated a new movement in poetry, away from the symbolist and towards social comment. John Das Passos, Robert Cantwell, Albert Halper and other American proletarian novelists explored social structure, man, not as an individual, but as part of the social process. A flood of translation from the Russian culminated in the inevitable best-seller, Sholokhov's *Quiet Flows the Donn,* which filtered the doctrines of socialist realism and softened them to the larger masses. Christopher Isherwood presented the debris of the fixed and ordered world of Berlinnnn which was soon to pass. Graham Greene dealt with the physical and spiritual shabbiness of the present world, and Aldous Huxley demolished even the hopeful future in *Brave New World.* Joyce's *Ulysses* was still proscribed, and was not published in this country until 1936, but in 1930 anybody with a shilling to spare could buy his *Anna Livia Plurabelle,* and in 1936 Faber's *Book of Modern Poetry,* edited by Michael Roberts, made it clear to the ordinary reader that a new movement in poetry had begun – three new movements, to be exact: the worlds of Auden, of Dylan Thomas, and of Surrealism. There was Franz Kafka's *The Castle* and *The Trial*. In drama there was T. S. Eliot's *Sweeney Agonistes*, *The Rock*, *Murder in the Cathedral* and *The Family Reunion*, and the plays of Auden and Isherwood. Hitler, Spain, Munich. *The Criterion* was dead by 1939. Finnegans Wake was published in 1939, and so ended another epoch. After that, all is confused. We are back where we began, with Matthew Arnold again, "the height to which knowledge is come, newspapers, cities, our own selves, and the sickening consciousness of our own difficulties."

3
Chapter

Poetry in Early Twentieth Century

INTRODUCTION

Poetry, by its very nature, has always reflected and at times augmented the spirit of its age. In the period from 1890 to 1914, poetry was especially responsive to the rapidly shifting environment which is part of the time-spirit. Although 1890 marks no upheaval in life and letters, nor even so much as the publication date of a significant literary work, it was in the closing decade of the nineteenth century that a perceptible disquiet began to manifest itself in the arts, including poetry. The disquiet of the *fin de siècle* was the result of many factors, not the least of which was the restlessness of an age grown tired of its own conventions. The Victorian Age had been long and fruitful. A great romantic tradition had been established at the start which flourished under the momentum of the works of Wordsworth, Coleridge, Byron, Shelley, and Keats. As the mid-century passed, however, with the industrial revolution well under way, and with the discoveries of the scientists and preachments of the philosophers casting doubt into what had for long been an unrippled pool of thought, there was an increasing tendency to use literature as a means to moral and didactic ends, and to bring it to the level of those who, it was believed, might profit most by its lessons. The major poets Tennyson and Browning, working in the great tradition, had by reason of strong individual genius brought it to new heights; but there were many prolific writers who gave to the period little of its greatness but much of its prevailing tone. As the century advanced, a monotony, or at least a lack of variety was evident in the art forms, with moral baggage burdening the vehicles which were designed especially to reach the vast middle classes. Verse patterns, diction, and imagery were standardized into conventions which suffered from overuse. Victorian literature has been immoderately praised and disparaged, but the fact remains that the age was weary of itself before it came to an end.

Even before the century was drawing to a close, in limited circles there was a recognition of a need for change. The Pre-Raphaelites, for example, had set out deliberately to try to respiritualize art by going to the past for themes in order to escape from moral and didactic purpose; and in the works of Rossetti and Swinburne, both poets of extreme talent, the romantic movement flamed anew. Other manifestations of unwillingness to follow the prevailing pattern appeared, although the instances were isolated and without a carefully deliberated effort to escape the conventions of the times. George Meredith in *Modern Love* (1862) and *A Reading of Earth* (1888) was clearly out of tune with an age which kept marital love on a pedestal from which it was to be hymned with epithalamia or regàrded with reverence, and which viewed nature from an ornate gazebo to see it only in its rose-bowers and unmixed benevolence.

By 1890 the disquiet had become so pronounced that organized movements began to flourish in which there was a calculated effort to break away from the themes and manner of the time-weary age. The so-called Yellow Nineties, a name derived from the once-notorious periodical which flourished in the early part of the decade, *The Yellow Book,* witnessed the rapid growth of what has been variantly termed the Art for Art's Sake School, the Aesthetic Movement, and the Decadence. Adopting the earlier PreRaphaelite conviction that art should be respiritualized, some of Walter Pater's precepts, and devices of manner from the French symbolists, the poets of the Aesthetic Movement created a revolt against the Victorian conventions which possesses both historical and literary significance. Manifestations of the revolt appeared in many forms, including the drawings of Aubrey Beardsley and Charles Conder, and the prose tales of Hubert Crackanthorpe and George Egerton; and in much of the verse of Ernest Dowson, Arthur Symons, and Oscar Wilde the most distinctive features of the decadence appeared.

Almost concurrently a group of Irish authors, becoming increasingly aware of the rich storehouse of themes which lay virtually untouched in the old Gaelic legends, and, like the poets of the aesthetic school, unsympathetic to the conventional refinements of recent British verse, set deliberately to work to revive the Gaelic tales, not only to bring the heroic age of Ireland into high relief, but also to find avenues of escape from Victorian confines. The movement which has been called the Celtic Renaissance was probably more the result of a new nationalistic spirit than a reaction against Victorianism, but in the development of the movement there was a conscious effort on the part of its leaders to remain independent of English and Victorian influence. The idea of a Celtic literary revival was so appealing, and the need for change was evidently so great, that during the early phases of the movement more than a few talented London writers who had little on which to base their claim to Irish ancestry were readily led to attach themselves to the "Celtic fringe" and seek inspiration in Gaelic themes. It was William Butler Yeats who was the pole-star of the revival, both as publicist and poet. *The Wanderings of Oisin* and *Other Poems* (1889) and the verses in *Poems* (1895) illustrated the uses to which Gaelic lore could be put, and gave momentum to a movement which flourished until after the First World War and continues to exist.

It was during the nineties that Thomas Hardy made his first bid for recognition as a poet, as did A. E. Housman. The gnarled and blunt manner of Hardy *Wessex Poems* (1898), with the recurrent theme of the preponderance of ill, came as something unsalutary to many readers who preferred to close their eyes to realities while reciting Pippa *Song in Browning's Pippa Passes*. The structural beauties in A. E. Housman *A Shropshire Lad* (1896) made his work more acceptable than Hardy's, although it was not only among the die-hards that the conviction was expressed that such verse should not be placed into the hands of the young. "The black, vicious melancholy" attributed to the poetry of Hardy and Housman was a deterrent to the reception of their works which was not overcome until the twentieth century was well advanced. It is interesting to note that Housman's *A Shropshire Lad*, published in 1896, reached only its fifth small printing in 1905, whereas Sir Henry Newbolt's *Admirals All* (1897) went through twenty-one printings in a few years. Hardy *Wessex Poems* fared even worse than Housman's volume in the ten years after its publication.

The turn of the century saw the aesthetic movement well spent; in fact, before the first decade of the new century had passed, a reaction set in which has been called the First Georgian Revolt. This revolt had few of the aspects of an organized movement, and the poets who made up the very loosely knit group often had aims other than that of avoiding the extremes to which the decadents had gone. Although there was a strict avoidance of an exploration of the nuances of sensation, especially that which suggested the sinister and the carnal, there was also an effort to keep away from the overused rhythms and lofty diction of the Victorians, and to reject themes which were didactic and hortatory. The works of this scattered group, who were essentially traditionalists, illustrate not a return to Victorian morality, but a return to wholesomeness. Some of the early works of W. W. Gibson, Lascelles Abercrombie, and J. Elroy Flecker belong to this reaction. These poets and others who have been somewhat arbitrarily identified with the First Georgian Revolt by reason of their appearance in Edward Marsh *Georgian Poetry* did their most distinctive work independent of any reaction or movement.

It was during the first decade of the new century that the realism and muscularity which were a part of Henley's manner were carried to new provinces and heights by John Masefield. *The Salt Water Ballads* (1902), *Ballads* (1903), and especially *The Everlasting Mercy* (1911) employed themes and diction which were more pronounced in their naturalism than anything which the earlier reactionaries had shown. When in "A Consecration," he declared, "Mine be the dirt and the dross, the dust and scum of the earth!" he warned his readers that here would be poetry different from the sweetness and light of most of his predecessors. Masefield's realism shocked many of his readers, who were resentful not only because the dirt and dross appeared, but that the poet had placed such stress on them. The advancing century was becoming more accustomed to colloquial and even gross diction in verse, for specialists in calling a spade a spade were beginning to appear on all sides; but in 1911 when *The Everlasting Mercy* appeared, Masefield's apparent satisfaction in using realism as an end in itself was not generally approved.

It was against the extremes of realism and the frequent slip-shod technique of its practitioners that a counter-reaction set in which is at times called the Second Georgian Revolt. These so-called Georgian Revolts were little more than the efforts of individual poets, all of whom were essentially traditionalists, to demonstrate the strength and beauty which can be achieved without forsaking the time-tested conventions. Ralph Hodgson and Walter de la Mare were identified with this movement, although their greatest works are the result of highly individualized genius rather than of a clearly defined reactionary spirit. It is with the lesser figures in the motley assortment which were brought together by Edward Marsh in his anthologies *Georgian Poetry* that the most reactionary tendencies appear. The "dust and scum" of Masefield become the moonlight and roses of John Drinkwater, John Freeman, and W. J. Turner. There is little vitality and strength in most of these Georgian poems—at least when they are compared with Masefield's-but in them there is a serene sort of beauty which is in part dependent on a rigorous stylistic discipline. Without becoming conspicuously fastidious in their attention to form, the better poets whom Marsh brought into his collections were perfectionists to whom the file was more essential than the sledge. It was not until the outbreak of the war that the realists and the Georgians were brought for a time under one banner, at least insofar as they both found inspiration in a common theme.

THE AESTHETIC MOVEMENT

Although the nineties were marked by a restlessness which manifested itself in literature at large, the aesthetic movement was the most calculated effort to break away from the main current of Victorianism. By 1890 there was sufficient sentiment against the utilitarian spirit which permeated much of the immediately preceding and current literature to constitute a revolt which, as the decade advanced, became a wide and productive movement. In such gathering places as the Crown—a latter-day Mermaid Tavern—groups of young artists and poets talked far into the night about art for art's sake, Walter Pater's dicta, and the necessity *pour épater le bourgeois.* It was a period of art cults and clubs of which the short-lived but famous Rhymers' Club, which had as its members such young poets as Ernest Dowson, Lionel Johnson, Arthur Symons, and William Butler Yeats, was outstanding. Fastidiously designed and illustrated periodicals such as *The Yellow Book* and later *The Savoy* were issued presumably to rescue art from what the editors and contributors felt was its increasing concern with practical ends. In spite of the fact that the nineties cannot be labeled prevailingly decadent, for there were countercurrents constantly at work, it was during this interval that the aesthetic movement reached its zenith and fell into sharp decline.

The poetry which emerged has often been called decadent, largely by reason of the fact that in its most characteristic expression it showed much of the strain for the unusual which is part of an age grown weary of its conventions. Decadence appears in any art which is the result of a complex and highly developed civilization, but the decadence of the nineties was the outgrowth of a definite aesthetic philosophy. As an essential declaration in its creed, the aesthetic school rejected all objectives which were didactic and hortatory. In addition to a rejection of all utilitarian purpose, the creed insisted upon a stress on form—not a carefully molded conventionalized form save in the fundamental principle of stress—but a form which must be first, last, and always richly musical, and the more unusual—one might even say exotic—the better. For this part of their belief the practitioners of the aesthetic group went to the French symbolists, and especially to Paul Verlaine who in his "Art Poétique" had stated:

> *Music above everything And odd music at that— Vaguer and more soluble than air, Without anything in it that burdens or is set.*

With beauty as its chief objective, the decadents explored the responses to the senses, which in themselves were exalted as the most fertile source for response to beauty. The senses, however, dulled by the commonplace, had to be stimulated, even agitated, by a deliberate search for subtle, unusual effects: the result should produce nuances of sensuous response. It was here that decadence began to take on an unhealthy visage. Tiring of the fragrance of new-mown hay and even attar of roses, the poet in quest of nuances of sensation turned to patchouli and the fever plants of the south. Arthur Symons pointed out in his once-provocative essay "In Defense of Patchouli" that stimulation often lay in the less obvious sensory responses, and Oscar Wilde, in both precept and example, indicated that nature was an unproductive field in which to find poetic content. The characteristics which appeared in the poetry thus motivated have been summed up by Holbrook Jackson in *The Eighteen Nineties* (1914): "Perversity, Artificiality, Egoism, and Curiosity . . . characteristics not at all inconsistent with a sincere desire 'to find the last final shade . . .'"

Obviously poetry motivated by a beauty drawn almost entirely from the senses cannot be robust; its roots cannot be strong, if it has roots at all. Preserving its creed, it cannot reconcile God's ways to man, nor can it provide man with a philosophy, substantial and abiding, which will reconcile him to life's ironies and nature's laws. But it can be beautiful, exquisite, and haunting; and the poetry of Ernest Dowson was all of these.

Ernest (Christopher) Dowson

Ernest (Christopher) Dowson was born in Lee, Kent, of parents of literary interests and connections, but neither of whom was physically strong nor temperamentally stable. Complete maladjustment, traceable to his lack of formal schooling and discipline, the atmosphere of despair in his home, and tuberculosis, was the essential tragedy in Dowson's life. When both of his parents committed suicide, the life-weariness which was part of his birthright became more pronounced; and in spite of his half-hearted efforts to find something to which to tie the frayed ends of his life in writing and his association with the Bohemian circles in London and Paris, he was never successful in making the right adjustments with circumstances which beset him relentlessly. Habits of irregularity were thrust upon him, and he, with little strength of body or will to combat ill fortune, was tired of the struggle long before his death.

He wrote two novels with Arthur Moore, *A Comedy of Masks* (1893) and *Adrian Rome* (1899), did much translating from the French for Leonard Smithers, the publisher, and produced a dozen tales in prose, most of which appeared in *The Yellow Book* and *The Savoy*. All of his prose, especially that in "The Princess of Dreams" and "The Visit," has distinction and beauty. Although Dowson, himself, gave support to the conclusion that his poetry was composed of "verses making for mere sound, and music, with just a suggestion of sense, or hardly that . . ." much of the spirit of the decadence and of his own personality can be read into the lines. The love poems, among which are the justly famous "Cynara," and the devotional poems, such as Extreme Unc-tion tion" and Nuns of the Perpetual Adoration, show Dowson's wavering "between heaping garlands upon the altars of Aphrodite and lighting candles to the Blessed Virgin." Although the devotional poems have more than their tonal beauty to commend them, for the essential voice of the poet one must go to the verses in which a life-weariness is expressed. Although such a sentiment was part of the decadent spirit, in the light of what is known about the circumstances surrounding Dowson life, poems such as *"A Last Word"* and "They are not long, the weeping and the laughter" must be regarded as the expression of sincere feeling. It is true that his volume and range are slight, and his voice is never strong. As a true decadent, he was unconcerned with conveying a message. In his darkly beautiful lyrics, however, there are imagery and phrasings which are consummate, and melodies which are haunting.

Verse: *Verses* (1896), *The Pierrot of the Minute, A Dramatic Phantasie in One Act* (1897), *Decorations: In Verse and Prose* (1899), *Poems, ed. Arthur Symons* (1905). *Poems, ed. Desmond Flower* (1934).

Prose: *Novels with Arthur Moore: A Comedy of Masks* (1893), *Adrian Rome* (1899), *Dilemmas: Stories and Studies in Sentiment* (1895), *The Stories of Ernest Dowson, ed. Mark Longaker* (1947).

Arthur Symons

Arthur Symons was a directing force to the aesthetic movement as editor, critic, and poet. Born in Wales of Cornish parents, he was trained in provincial schools under excellent masters before taking up residence in Paris where he became familiar with the current art movements and many of the leading poets. On his return to England, he wrote reviews of the performances at the better music halls, of concerts and operas, and contemporary continental literature. An habitué of the Crown, a member of the Rhymers' Club, well informed about all the arts, Symons was well equipped at the time of the demise of *The Yellow Book* to take on the editorship of the new art magazine *The Savoy* which Leonard Smithers and Aubrey Beardsley were ready to put out. He wrote a vast number of critical essays during the nineties and later, some of the best of which appear in *The Symbolist Movement in Literature* (1899) and *Dramatis Personae* (1923); and he added much to the volume and direction of decadent verse. Such pieces as "A Revenge" and "The Café Singer" in *Days and Nights* (1889) are both decadent and melodramatic, and virtually all the poems in *Silhouettes* (1892) have a heady scent about them which leaves the senses cloyed. "To One in Alienation" in *London Nights* (1896) treats the theme which Dowson used in the *"Cynara"* poem, but Dowson genuine delicacy and rich melody are absent. In some of Symons' later verse, however, notably in "Modern Beauty" and "Night" there is no longer a preoccupation with the nuances of sensation. His last poems show a restraint unusual for one who had written *Silhouettes,* but in spite of the fact that they are interesting pictorially and good technically, they lack the surge which carries poetry to the heights. As a critic, Symons will continue to have some value, and his influence in giving shape to the aesthetic movement can scarcely be overestimated.

Verse: *Days and Nights* (1889), *Silhouettes* (1892), *London Nights* (1895), *Amoris Victima* (1897), *Images of Good and Evil* (1899), *Lyrics* (1903), *The Fool of the World and Other Poems* (1906), *Wanderer's Song* (1909), *Knave of Hearts* (1913), *Lesbia and Other Poems* (1920), *Love's Cruelty* (1923), *Jezebel Mort and Other Poems* (1931), *Collected Poems, 3 v.* (1924). *PLAYS: Tragedies: The Harvesters, The Death of Agrippina, Cleopatra in Judea* (1916), *Tristan and Iseult* (1917), *The Toy Cart* (1919).

Critical Studies: *An Introduction to the Study of Browning* (1886), *Studies in Two Literatures* (1897), *The Symbolist Movement in Literature* (1899), *Studies in Prose and Verse* (1904), *Studies in the Seven Arts* (1906), *William Blake* (1907), *The Romantic Movement in English Poetry* (1910), *Dante Gabriel Rossetti* (1910), *Studies in Elizabethan Drama* (1919), *Charles Baudelaire: A Study* (1920), *Dramatis Personae* (1923), *Studies on Modern Painters* (1925), *A Study of Thomas Hardy* (1927), *Studies in Strange Souls* (1929), *A Study of Oscar Wilde* (1930), *A Study of Walter Pater* (1932).

Essays and Sketches: *The Loom of Dreams* (1901), *Cities of Italy* (1907), *London, a Book of Aspects* (1908), *Parisian Nights* (1926), *Confessions, a Study in Pathology* (1930), *largely autobiographical; Wanderings* (1931).

Oscar Wilde

Although much of his decadent poetry appeared before the nineties, *Oscar Wilde* (1856- 1900) was definitely of the aesthetic school. It was his literary philosophy as well as Pater's which gave momentum to the decadents, and it was his early poetry which illustrated and exalted the art-forart's-sake principle. A brilliant essayist, a clever playwright and writer of tales, and a versatile and talented poet, Wilde stands out as one of the most vivid figures of the nineties. Born in Dublin, the son of a distinguished surgeon and a talented mother, Oscar Fingal O'Flahertie Wills Wilde, after a pampered childhood was sent to the Portora Royal School, Enniskillen, and Trinity College, Dublin, before matriculating at Magdalen, Oxford. His early successes with writing supported his inclination to be regarded as an esthete; and his talent, which included a cynical, epigrammatic wit, helped him to apply his statement: "The first duty in life is to be as artificial as possible." *Poems* (1881) and the plays which he wrote in the nineties were widely acclaimed among those of fastidious and progressive tastes as the work of rare genius. It was at the height of his popularity in the theatre that

Wilde's unfortunate sexual maladjustment brought him into difficulty through the ill-advised suit which he brought against the father of Lord Alfred Douglas. After two years imprisonment, he left England to live on the continent, chiefly in Bernaval, Paris, and Naples. An outcast from England, but not without friends who recognized his talents and charm, Wilde died in Paris in 1900.

Although not so widely known as the plays and some of the verse, Wilde's prose is a strong illumination of the author and his precepts. His aesthetic creed, and, in fact, his general philosophy are to be found in *Intentions* (1891) and *De Profundis* (1905). Of the prose narratives, *The Picture of Dorian Gray* (1891) illustrates Wilde's skill at using the framework of a story for expressing his views on art and life. The plays, with the exception of the sensuous poetic drama *Salome* (1893), are cleverly designed examples of the Comedy of Manners. The problems presented in *Lady Windermere's Fan* (1892), *A Woman of No Importance* (1893), and the trimly turned trifle *The Importance of Being Earnest* (1895) are never seriously considered or answered, nor are the characters completely realized. The lines given to them, however, are sprightly and often scintillating. In his poetry, Wilde shows considerable range and varying degrees of emotional depth. The themes vary from political precept to devotional sentiment, and from the revelation of a mood to the sociological implications in "The Ballad of Reading Gaol." His manner, often derivative, ranges from the adjective-laden lines in "The Sphinx" to the delicately restrained style of "Requiescat." His last poem *"The Ballad of Reading Gaol"* stands apart from much of the earlier poetry in the real substance of its theme and the sincerity of its expression. There is small doubt that Wilde had genius, but after the passing of a half-century, it is even more strongly affirmed that some of it was misdirected.

Verse: *Poems* (1881), *The Sphinx* (1894), *The Ballad of Reading Gaol* (1898).

Plays: Vera, or the Nihilists (1882), *The Duchess of Padua* (1884), *A Florentine Tragedy* (1885), *Lady Windermere's*

Fan (1892), *Salome* (1893), *A Woman of No Importance* (1893), *An Ideal Husband* (1895), *The Importance of Being Earnest* (1895).

Prose Stories and Essays: The Happy Prince and Other Tales (1888), *Lord Arthur Saville's Crime and Other Stories* (1891), *The Picture of Dorian Gray* (1891), *A House of Pomegranates* (1891), *Intentions* (1891), *The Soul of Man Under Socialism* (1891), *De Profundis* (1905).

John Davidson

John Davidson was associated with the decadents, but his most mature work shows a complete severance from the spirit of the aesthetic school. He contributed poems to *The Yellow Book* and was a member of the Rhymers' Club, the later meetings of which he attended irregularly. His attachment to the art movements of the nineties was probably more the result of his desire for sympathetic understanding and companionship than of any conviction of the soundness of the objectives of the art-for-art's-sake movement. Even before he came to London, his mind was too speculative and rapacious to allow him to lose himself in responses to the senses, and as the decade advanced and turned into the new century, his philosophical inquiries engaged him to such an extent that they became his preoccupation.

Davidson wrote three novels, six plays, many essays, some of which served as prefaces to his volumes of verse, a considerable amount of journalistic hackwork, and twelve books of poems. The prose is often dated in both content and style. In his preferred medium verse, there are two main tendencies revealed: an occupation with romantic themes in which a four-line ballad stanza is often employed and in which the manner has some of the decoration of the decadents; and a philosophical speculation cast usually into blank verse in which there is little attempt at adornment. The well-known "Ballad of a Nun" and "Ballad of Hell" illustrate his best and most distinctive work in the first group, and the "Testaments" show his trend of thought and manner in the second. Some of his early poems, especially the ballads, and many of the pieces in *Fleet Street Eclogues* (1893), will continue to be read; and such reflections of a courageous mind and spirit as those in "The Unknown" should be read by those who are too readily inclined to dismiss the poet's philosophical works as zeal without intellect.

Verse: *In a Music Hall* (1891), *Fleet Street Eclogues* (1893, *rev. ed.*, 1909), *Ballads and Songs* (1895), *The Last Ballad* (1899), *The Testament of a Vivisector* (1901), *The Testament of a Man God Forbid* (1901), *The Testament of an Empire Builder* (1902), *The Testament of a Prime Minister* (1904), *The Testament of John Davidson* (1908).

Novels: *Laura Ruthven's Widowhood, with C. J. Wills* (1892), *The Wonderful Mission of Earl Lavender* (1896), *Miss Armstrong's Circumstances* (1896).

Sketchess: *A Random Itinerary* (1894).

Richard Le Gallienne

Richard Le Gallienne, although spending much of his time in the United States since 1918, did his most distinctive creative work while still in England. Born in Liverpool in 1866 and educated at Liverpool College, he was down in London during the nineties, already well established in literary circles. A reader for John Lane and Elkin Mathews, one of the founders of the Rhymers' Club, a prolific reviewer, Le Gallienne contributed to the stream of decadent verse which the age produced. His account of the period in *The Romantic Nineties* (1926) is an illumination not only of the spirit of the times but of the author at this stage as well. His *Poems* (1892) are definitely of the fin de siècle tone, although he was never so lyrical as Dowson or so deliberate with sensory effects as Symons and Wilde. His later work in verse including *The Lonely Dancer* (1913) and *The Junkman and Other Poems* (1921) is different from the poems written during the nineties in both theme and manner, but his voice was never strong. Poetry, when it came to him, came as a sort of digression. His chief talent was critical. In America, he was perhaps best known for his numerous reviews in which all literary forms are his province, and for such delicately told stories as *The Quest of the Golden Girl* (1896).

Verse: *My Lady's Sonnets* (1887), *Poems* (1892), *An Elegy, and Other Poems, Mainly Personal* (1895), *New Poems* (1910), *The Lonely Dancer and Other Poems* (1913), *The Junkman and Other Poems* (1921), *The Magic Seas* (1930).

Prose: *George Meredith: Some Characteristics* (1890), *Prose Fancies* (1894), *The Quest of the Golden Girl* (1896), *The Sleeping Beauty and Other Prose Fantasies* (1900), *Attitudes and Avowals* (1910), *Vanishing Roads and Other Essays* (1915), *The Romantic Nineties* (1926), *There was a Ship* (1930).

THE CELTIC RENAISSANCE

The nineties, characterized by revolts and literary movements, saw the rapid growth of the Irish literary revival. Although the ultimate sources of the movement probably can be traced back into the middle of the century, it was with Standish O'Grady works, especially *The History of Ireland: The Heroic Period* (1878) that interest in the literary past of Ireland was given new momentum. At the start, the movement had as its main objective the retelling of Celtic legends and stories. A new literary consciousness developed out of this purpose which was to find expression in a large number of prose and verse narratives in which the old Gaelic heroes were reanimated and given a new significance and in which the magic of the Irish imagination played a distinctive part. In its more advanced stages, the movement did not confine itself only to a recognition and use of Ireland's literary past, but it expanded into an exploration of the significance of the political scene, and became increasingly concerned with the sociological problems of peasant and laborer. Such concerns, according to some of the figures in the movement, were beyond the boundaries of the purpose of the revival, but they were a natural outgrowth of a recognition of a new national consciousness.

The natural magic of the Celt appeared in the expression of this consciousness, regardless of theme; but it was in the poetry and dramas which were unhampered by utilitarian baggage that a strangely lighted world, somewhere between myth and reality, began to emerge. The tenuous themes and moods, often expressed in symbols drawn from the imagination rather than from reality, and the atmosphere of otherworldliness, led Yeats and some of his associates to speak of the early phases of the movement as "the Celtic Twilight." A mysticism which was often without the mark of the Church appeared in the retelling of the old legends and in the literature which was concerned with mood. The general tone of the style was archaic, or at least quaint, in that Gaelic elements frequently were introduced in order to add to the atmosphere of a remote past and the mood of unreality. At the beginning and up until the First World War, the revival was given direction by authors of exceptional talent, with the result that the poetry and drama of the Celtic Renaissance have undoubtedly enriched contemporary literature and literature at large.

William Butler Yeats

The outstanding figure in the Celtic Renaissance was William Butler Yeats (1865- 1939). To identify Yeats with a movement, or even with a national literature, however, is inadequate and misleading, for his work, in spite of the distinctively Celtic quality of much of it, is so varied in theme and manner that it cannot be labeled by a sufficiently inclusive phrase. There are many sides of Yeats, some of them apparently anomalous, but all of them essentially poetic. He advanced steadily in intellectual scope and depth, but the lyric note he never lost. Although some of his later works seem heavy with thought and difficult of comprehension, his artistry can never be questioned. A masterful technician and a severe self-critic, he produced little which does not have on it the stamp of his finest talent. Fundamentally a romantic, he nevertheless applied the discipline of the classicist to his work, especially in his mature poems. There is apparent traffic with the modernists in some of the later pieces, but this is more of a reflection of his many-sided poetic personality than an expression of loss of faith in the objectives and manner of the traditionalists.

William Butler Yeats was born at Sandymount, a suburb of Dublin, in 1865, the son of John Butler Yeats, an artist of considerable talent. A younger brother, Jack Yeats, became well known as a painter, and one of the sisters was distinguished as a bibliophile and the founder of the Cuala Press in Dublin. From his own report the poet was unhappy as a boy. "I remember little of my childhood but its pain," he wrote. "I have grown happier with every year of life as though gradually conquering something in myself. . . ." Sensitive and probably a little stubborn, he found his early schooling under the tutelage of an elderly woman distasteful, and it was not until his father took him in hand that he learned to read. "I was always near the bottom of my class," he reported, "and always making excuses that but added to my timidity." Intermittently, however, he was an avid listener to the tales and legends which were told to him in the heavy brogue of northern Ireland where he was often sent for long sojourns with relatives while his parents moved back and forth between Dublin and London. When he was eight, he was taken by his parents to London where he attended the Godolphin School in Hammersmith. After seven years in London schools where he overcame much of his early timidity, he was taken to Dublin where his father then made his residence, and until he was eighteen he followed a classical training at the Erasmus Smith School. In spite of the fact that he showed much interest in literature, especially in the English poets, even to the extent of writing a considerable amount of verse in the manner of Spenser, it was decided that he enter the Metropolitan School of Art. Although he showed talent in art, he had developed a compelling interest in writing; and frequently, according to his own report, he neglected his sketching and reading in art history in order to write and destroy page after page of verse. Recognizing the seriousness of his interest in writing, and encouraged by the publication of some of his verse in the *Dublin University Review* and later in the *Irish Monthly*, he decided even against strong parental objection to abandon art as a profession and devote his energy and talent to writing.

During his twenties he spent most of his time in London which he believed was better suited than Dublin as an environment for a man of letters. London during the eighties and nineties was the scene of much literary activity; and Yeats, no longer the timorous schoolboy, became a zealous participant in the art groups which sat at the Crown and the Cheshire Cheese. He was active in the affairs of the Socialist League, he attended seances and joined clubs which were concerned with Theosophy and the arcana of the East, he rarely missed a gathering at the Fitzroy Settlement; and all the while he was contributing stories, articles, and poems to the London and Dublin journals. With his inborn and cultivated interest in Irish folklore, he was a major figure in founding the Irish Literary Society and in circulating the information that there was an Irish literary rebirth. Nor did his interest in Irish literature end with publicizing its significance. Already in 1889 *The Wanderings of Oisin* appeared, in which Celtic figures from the dim past move about "the Firbolgs' burial mounds." Although indebted to Standish O'Grady for some of the material in this poem, Yeats embroidered the tale with a richness of phrase and melody which led many readers to see at once the poetic resources of Irish legend. With *The Countess Kathleen and Various Legends and Lyrics* (1892) he gave additional momentum to the movement which was under way and to his own reputation as a poet. It was soon after the publication of *The Countess Kathleen* that the Rhymers' Club set aside "Celtic Nights," and Lionel Johnson began to affect a brogue. The time was ripe for a great poet to express the beauty of Irish legend and mood, and Yeats, with his energy and genius, was at hand.

Back and forth between London and Dublin, he helped to organize the Irish National Literary Society, and by 1900 he brought to fulfillment an idea which for long had been an increasingly vivid dream: the founding of an Irish National theatre. Assisted by Lady Gregory and Douglas Hyde, Yeats made possible the Abbey Theatre in Dublin from which there came some of the best plays and players of the present century. Yeats was not content to be only an organizer and for a time the manager: the creative impulse in him was too strong for him to be only a propagandist and critic. The Abbey Theatre had its ups and downs during its early years, but all along Yeats brought to it his enthusiasm, his skill at organization, and his splendid talent as a dramatist.

Although his love for Maud Gonne, the famous Irish beauty and zealous nationalist, was unrequited and left him disconsolate for long, after the First World War, Yeats's life was a progression of literary successes. Many distinctions were to come to him in recognition of his services to Ireland and his literary genius. The University of Dublin conferred degrees on him, and on his seventieth birthday, he was honored by a great banquet as Ireland's most celebrated figure.

From 1922 to 1928 he was a senator in the Irish Free State, in which role he maintained a discerning conservatism which served as a check and balance to some of the policies of his more outspoken colleagues. He married Miss Georgia Lees in 1917 out of which union a son and daughter were born. In 1923 he was awarded the Nobel prize for literature, Oxford presented him with the degree of Doctor of Literature, and on his visits to America he was given distinctions and honors. Already in the twenties he often referred to himself as an old man, for many of his contemporaries were gone; but there was little diminution in his intellectual curiosity and energy. He retained his enthusiasm for literature and life until his death in 1939.

In Yeats's personality there were combined the zeal of youth and the discipline of maturity. Always a poet, he existed in the land of faery, but he was endowed with an unusual amount of practical wisdom which gave balance to his life and works. Those who knew him intimately recall a man of great intensity, sensitive and bold in turn, with a pronounced eagerness of countenance and mind. One could not be in his presence without feeling something of his greatness.

Although his talent was essentially poetic, Yeats frequently employed the medium of the drama. He was one of the very few playwrights in recent times who could make poetry effective from behind the footlights. One of his earliest plays, *The Land of Heart's Desire* (1894), with its theme drawn from Celtic folklore of a girl whose soul is lured to "the land of heart's desire" by a fairy child, reaches a high poetic plane in both conception and in many of the lines. *Kathleen ni Houlihan* (1902), written in prose, has interest and power even when its symbolic significance is removed; and in the character of Michael Gillane, Yeats has drawn a memorable portrait. In *A Pot of Broth* (1902), written with Lady Gregory, he attempted farce which is obviously not his chief stock in trade. His later plays show an advance in design, occasionally at a loss to the lyric quality; but *The Shadowy Waters* (1904), one of his particular favorites, and *Deirdre* (1906) show his finest work as a dramatic poet. Both of them possess much lyric beauty, but it is in *Deirdre* in which he combines great dramatic effectiveness with the loftiest poetry.It was in the province of nondramatic poetry, however, that he did his most distinctive work. His creative period, extending over almost half a century, falls into more or less readily distinguishable intervals. The division indicated by Herbert Palmer in *Post-Victorian Poetry* (1938) is illuminating:

1. The period in which he was occupied with mythology and richly embroidered verse, when, though variable in technique, he concentrated mainly on wavering rhythms. It was the period of the Celtic Twilight.
2. A middle period, which commenced shortly before the War, when he wrote more intellectually and with

greater austerity. His rhythms harden, and are more in line with the Elizabethan texture of verse.

3. A later period which commenced some years after the War, when affected by the cult of the Modernists he becomes increasingly cerebral and obscure. He is still Yeats, but inclined to be academic and sometimes a little sour. The English poet who seems to have most affected him is John Donne.

The period in which he did his finest work is a question whose answer depends largely on one's preferences in poetry. There are critics of the traditionalist school who insist that Yeats's greatest contribution to literature was made before 1914, whereas those of modernist leanings are prone to disparage the earlier works as the product of an only relatively fruitful apprenticeship, and to point to *Later Poems* (1924) and "The Tower" (1928) as the full flower of his genius.

Fortunately the differences in his poetry are not so sharply pronounced as to make a middle ground in the judgment of his works untenable.

Certainly the early narratives in which Celtic legend is the theme are told with a beauty and grace which few readers can overlook or mistake for rhetoric. Nor can the richly descriptive passages in such an early poem as *"The Wanderings of Oisin"* be dismissed as eloquence. There are lines which are profusely embroidered and even purple, but their beauty is rarely obscured by the weight of decoration. *"The Rose of the World," "Into the Twilight," "The Song of the Faeries"* in The *Land of Heart's Desire*, and the much anthologized *"Lake Isle of Innisfree"* are representative of his early manner.

In the later works, the symbolism is often derived more from the mind than from the imagination and the emotions; and much of the decoration of the earlier poems gives way to compression of phrase. The rhythms of *"Down by the Salley Gardens"* and *"The Song of Wandering Aengus"* appear less frequently, and in their place more austere cadences are employed. His images, no longer highly colored, continue to retain an intensity which was a faithful part of his poetic temperament. "*The Tower*" (1928) affords a good example of the later Yeats. "The early rainbows" are gone, and if there was a romantic rhetoric in his poetry, it certainly is gone. If his imagination and mind led him at times into symbolism which is remote and obscure, the result cannot be traced to a conscious effort on his part to be ingenious, much less difficult. As an influence on his age, and as an author of range and depth, the stature of Yeats is undoubtedly that of a major poet.

Verse: *Mosada: A Dramatic Poem* (1886), *The Wanderings of Oisin and Other Poems* (1889), *Poems* (1895), *The Wind Among the Reeds* (1899), *In the Seven Woods* (1903), *Poems*, 1899-1905 (1906), *The Golden Helmet and Other Poems* (1912), *Responsibilities and Other Poems, The Wild Swans at Coole, Other Verses, and a Play in Verse* (1917), *Michael Robartes and the Dancer* (1920), *Later Poems* (1922), *The Cat and the Moon and Certain Poems* (1924), *The Tower* (1928), *The Winding Stair and Other Poems* (1933), *Collected Poems* (1933), *The King of the Great Clock Tower* (1934), *New Poems* (1938), *Last Poems and Plays* (1940).

Plays (*in verse and prose*): *The Countess Kathleen* (1892), *The Land of Heart's Desire* (1894), *The Shadowy Waters* (1900), *Cathleen ni Houlihan* (1902), *Where There is Nothing* (1902), *The Hour Glass* (1903), *A Pot of Broth* (1904), *The King's Threshold* (1904), *Deirdre* (1907), *The Unicorn From the Stars and Other Plays, with Lady Gregory* (1903), *Four Plays for Dancers* (1921), *Wheels and Butterflies* (1934), *Collected Plays* (1934).

Essays: *Ideas of Good and Evil* (1903), *Discoveries, a Volume of Essays* (1907), *Poetry and Ireland, with Lionel Johnson* (1908), *Synge and the Ireland of his Time* (1911), *The Cutting of an Agate* (1912), *Essays* (1924), *Letters on Poetry to Dorothy Wellesley* (1940).

Memories: *Reveries over Childhood and Youth* (1915), *Four Years* (1921), *The Trembling of the Veil* (1922), *Autobiographies, includes Reveries over Childhood and Youth and The Trembling of the Veil* (1926), *Estrangement* (1926), *Reflections from a Diary Kept in* 1909, *The Death of Synge and Other Passages from an Old Diary* (1928).

George Russell

George Russell better known as A.E., although not so widely read as Yeats, played an important part in the Irish Literary Revival as both publicist and poet. Stephen Gwynn, in writing about the contributions which Yeats and A.E. made to the movement, observed:

> *These two men were to dominate the entire literary revival, and affect the whole intellectual life of Ireland in their time . . . Both were mystics. But whereas in George Russell mysticism appeared inseparable from his being, with Yeats it had the aspect of an exotic cult. Russell was of service to Ireland through the philosophy which radiated through his nature. It was in part a love of beauty, but more truly a love of humanity, of the divine in human nature.*

Both poets drew much of their inspiration from the magic of Ireland's past, but whereas Yeats in his reanimation of tales from the Heroic Age was narrative and descriptive in manner, especially in the earlier poems, A.E. was always reflective. His effort in drama for the Irish Playhouse, a version of the Deirdre theme, although satisfactory, indicated that playwriting was not his most fruitful province. He lacked Yeats's ability to weave beautiful designs on a sustained narrative theme, and in spite of the fact that he was an admirable decorator in words, few of his poems were motivated to produce only vivid sensuous response. He shared with Yeats a fondness of symbolism, but the symbolic in A.E. was almost always remote and possessed of less warmth than that of his contemporary, for his symbolism was that of the soul striving to maintain communication with the eternal and divine. "I know I am a spirit," he wrote in the preface to *Homeward*, "and that I went forth from the self-ancestral to labours yet unaccomplished; but filled ever and again with homesickness I made these songs by the way."

Born in 1867 in Lurgan, County Armagh, George William Russell attended school in Dublin, and on account of his talent in drawing, he was sent to the Metropolitan School of Art at the age of sixteen. Although recognition came to him chiefly as a writer, he never forsook pictorial art, for there are more than six hundred paintings, chiefly in oil, which he gave away or sold for a pittance. When Yeats first met him at the art school, Russell was already interested in the cults of the East, Theosophy, and the Bhagavad-Gita. Recognizing in himself a dual personality, Russell allowed his real name to represent the practical side of his nature, and A.E. the mystic and poetic. The two distinct sides of his nature are plain, for the same man who wrote "Oversoul" and "Reconciliation" was the chief organizer of the Irish Agricultural Society, a competent authority on soil conditioning, and editor of *The Irish Homestead* from 1904 to 1923. Into both spheres he brought zeal, intellect, and talent. Many distinctions came to him in his late years, including honorary degrees from Dublin University and Yale; and he was offered a senatorship in the Irish Free State. This he refused, for he did not like the turn of political events in the twenties. It was his opposition to what was going on in Irish politics which led him to spend his last years in England where he died in 1935.

In addition to his play *Deirdre* (1902), written at the request of the Irish National Dramatic Company for their spring festival, Russell wrote a considerable amount of prose, some of which remains uncollected. *Some Irish Essays* (1906), *Imaginations and Reveries* (1915), and *Song and Its Fountains* (1932) which heightens an appreciation of his poetry, represent the most characteristic pieces of his literary prose. Although a prolific poet with nearly a dozen volumes of verse between *Homeward: Songs by the Way* (1894) and *The House of Titans and Other Poems* (1934), A.E. has never been widely read outside of Ireland. His mysticism, although deistic, contains Oriental and Celtic elements, and goes farther back than orthodox Christianity. The themes, often symbolic and abstract, are conveyed through measures which are melodic and strongly accented. Although his poetry is charged with meaning, some of it has an abiding appeal largely on account of its tonal quality. Such poems as "Carrowmore" and "The Twilight of Earth" afford ample proof that A.E.'s contribution to literature extends beyond the active part he played in supporting the Irish revival.

Verse: *Homeward: Songs by the Way* (1894), *The Earth Breath and Other Poems* (1897), *The Divine Vision and Other Poems* (1904), *By Still Waters* (1906), *Gods of War and Other Poems* (1915), *Voices of the Stones* (1925), *Collected Poems* (1926), *Midsummer Eve* (1928), *The, Dark Weeping* (1929), *Enchantment and Other Poems* (1930), *Vale and Other Poems* (1931), *The House of Titans and Other Poems* (1934), *Selected Poems* (1936).

Drama: *Deirdre: A Drama in Three Acts* (1907). *PROSE: Some Irish Essays* (1906), *The Hero in Man* (1909), *The Renewal of Youth* (1911), *Imaginations and Reveries* (1915), *The Candle of Vision* (1918), *The Interpreter.;* (1922), *Song and Its Fountains* (1932).

James Stephens

Some of the younger Irish poets looked upon A.E. rather than Yeats as their leader, and it was through his encouragement and help that a goodly number of talented young men and women were brought into the revival. Of these, none was more deserving of encouragement than James Stephens (1882-1950) . It is a familiar story of how Stephens, leading a life of penury and drudgery as a clerk in a solicitor's office, but writing stories and verse all the while, sent A.E. some of his poems with a wistful inquiry concerning their possible worth, and of how the older poet after reading the poems invited the young man to his home to read his verse before a roomful of authors already known to fame in Dublin. All Stephens needed was a start, for he had much to contribute to the later development of the revival and to literature at large. Irish to the core and a natural supporter of the purposes which underlay the revival, he was at the same time capable of showing the entire English-speaking world the charm of the Celt. Readers who have put the peculiarly Irish works of Yeats and A.E. aside as too local, and, as a result, too obscure for the uninitiate, have found Stephens' *The Crock of Gold* (1912) delightful. It is here, and occasionally elsewhere in Stephens'works, that the American and the New Zealander with no Irish background can readily see the quaint, the mystical, the comic, and the poetic which in various combinations give to Irish literature much of its appeal.

James Stephens was born in Dublin in 1882. His birthright and early environment were scarcely congenial to a literary career. It was not until he was in his late teens and already at work at a variety of unpromising jobs that he became an avid reader and attended the Abbey Theatre to witness the dramatized versions of tales from the Heroic Age. His early marriage and attendant obligations of rearing a family kept him from venturing far afield in search of inspiring employment, but in his spare time he wrote articles and verses. Through the help of A.E., Stephens found employment at the National Gallery of Ireland and receptacles for his writing. After his success with *The Crock of Gold* he made his residence in London and Paris, with occasional long sojourns in his native Dublin. Several times during the twenties and thirties he visited the United States to lecture and read his verse. In the years preceding his death in 1950, he continued to write, but his efforts showed little of the vigor and charm of his early work.

Although a versatile author, Stephens is known most widely for *The Crock of Gold,* an identification by no means unfortunate, for the story has an easily recognized worth.

The manner is beguiling, ranging from the comic to the wistful, and from bold to light, faery touches.His verse reveals a poet of many voices and varied moods. In *The Renaissance of Irish Poetry* (1929) David Morton says aptly: "He is in succession a poet of nature with quaint and smiling imaginings, a Paddy of coarse humor, and finally a romantic dreamer haunted with a passionate memory of his country's beautiful and legendary past." There is exuberance in much of his early poetry in which there is a reflection of his love for life and humanity. Although interested in Ireland's past as indicated in the free adaptations from the Gaelic in *Reincarnations* (1918), he is apparently as much concerned with what the lowly Thomas said in a pub as with trying to project himself into the spirit of Celtic heroes. The fine poem "The Shell" is a sort of transition between his interest in the real and human and his concern with the abstract and mystical, and the twenty-three cantos of *Theme and Variations* (1930), although not without melody, have little of the buoyancy of the verse in *The Rocky Road to Dublin* (1915). *Strict Joy* (1931), his most mature work technically, contains poems which indicate that Stephens was not only the observer of humanity and a reviver of old tales, but a poet of considerable insight as well.

Verse: *Insurrections* (1909), *The Lonely God and Other Poems* (1909), *The Hill of Vision* (1912), *The Rocky Road to Dublin* (1915), *Songs From the Clay* (1915), *Green Branches* (1916), *Reincarnations* (1918), *Collected Poems* (1926). *The Outcast* (1929), *Theme and Variations* (1930), *Strict Joy* (1931), *Kings and the Moon* (1938).

Prose: *The Crock of Gold* (1912), *The Demi-gods* (1914), *Deirdre* (1923), *In the Land of Youth* (1924), *Etched in Moonlight* (1928).

Seumas O'Sullivan

Seumas O'Sullivan was born in Dublin with a rich heritage of Celtic lore as part of his birthright. From youth he was bent on preparing himself for a literary career, and even in his middle teens he was seriously concerned with writing verse. Like Stephens, he came under the influence and encouragement of A.E., who printed some of his early poems in a collection he made from the verse of the younger writers. Zealously interested in the Celtic revival and one of its major supporters in the later phases of the movement, O'Sullivan has brought a fine intellectual vigor to the editorship of *The Dublin Magazine*, and critical and creative talent to a wide variety of work. He is well known in Ireland as an erudite bookman and a discerning critic, but his reputation has become more than local through some of his fine verse. Small collections of poems have appeared since *The Twilight People* in 1905, among which *The Earth Lover* (1909), *Mud and Purple* (1918) and the volume *Dublin Poems* (1946), in which many of the earlier poems reappear, are representative. Thus far he has had no traffic with Eastern mysticism in the manner of Yeats, A.E., and in a lesser way, James Stephens; and in the poem *"Credo"* he rejects the mysticism of the church in the first stanza. Devotional and pagan elements, the latter drawn from Celtic mythology, appear side by side in his volumes; but he was neither a devotional poet nor the singer of pagan rites. Much of his verse was the result of mood in which there was no occupation with the role of prophet and seer. In his poetry of Dublin, there was much which suggests the city of yesteryear, especially of the eighteenth century. In such poems as *"Nelson Street"* and *"Mer-rion Square"* he was scarcely the poet of whom A.E. said: "He is the literary successor of those old Gaelic poets who were fastidious in their verse, who loved little in this world but some chance light in it which reminded them of fairyland." O'Sullivan's works as a whole indicate that he had many loves other than the land of faery. When he does linger in scenes of twilight, however, there is something of Walter de la Mare's magic. In manner, he was of the traditionalists, employing for the most part diction and verse measures whose beauty and rhythms have stood the test of time.

Lennox Robinson

Lennox Robinson became an active figure in the Celtic Renaissance as a very young man, and he has been a sustaining force to interest in the revival for almost half a century. He has compiled anthologies of Irish verse, he edited Lady Gregory *Journals*, he was the stage manager of the Abbey Theater from 1910 to 1914, and he was an outstanding contributor to the Irish drama in the middle and later period of the revival. The son of a clergyman, Robinson from youth had decided that writing was to be his career; but it was not until he saw the Abbey Players that he considered the medium of the drama. He had barely turned twenty-two when his play *The Clancy Name* (1908) was produced at the Abbey Theatre. This was followed by *The Crossroads* (1909), *Harvest* (1910), and *Patriots* (1912). The themes in these plays are distinctively Irish, and to a certain extent they were aimed at correcting conditions in Ireland. The element of propaganda is there, especially in *Patriots*, but it does not become obtrusive, nor does it impair the value of the plays as human documents. Of the later plays, *The Whiteheaded Boy* (1920) and *The Far-Off Hills* (1931) are illustrative of the high plane to which Robinson can rise with realistic comedy.

Although the major part of Henley's work was done before the turn of the century, there are many qualities in his verse which are definitely un-Victorian and which anticipate the characteristics which are loosely labeled modern. With the issues which gave Tennyson and Browning much of their inspiration and theme, he was unconcerned; and against the deliberate aestheticism of the Pre-Raphaelites and the decadents of the nineties, he took a positive stand. For the man Henley, one must have considerable admiration, for this "booming, bursting, bumptious" personality, as Edith Sitwell called him, although a cripple from youth, was not an invalid in spirit.

In the sequence *"In Hospital,"* with the themes drawn from his bedfast days at Lister's Infirmary in Edinburgh,

Henley's stark realism was an innovation unpalatable to many Victorian readers. The poems in *London Voluntaries,* and *"A Song of Speed"* are more interesting for their venturesome metrics and diction than for their impressionistic effects. Henley's range was slight, and in spite of the fact that he is more than a one-poem author—the celebrated "Invictus"—G. B. Shaw was sound in his conclusion that "when Henley had such an experience as the Hospital to go on, he wrote well; otherwise, his case was one of manner without matter." His manner, however, illustrates a fine sense of pictorial values, virile words, interesting versification, and an unmistakable gusto.

> *A Book of Verses, including "In Hospital"* (1888), *London Voluntaries and Other Verses* (1893), *Poems* (1898), *Hawthorn andLavendar*(1901), *A Song of Speed* (1903), *Collected Works, including essays and prefaces,* (1908).

Thomas Hardy

Although Hardy's work in the novel was completed by 1897, most of his verse appeared after the turn of the century. His fiction is probably more widely known than his poetry, but had he been given to George Meredith's cleverness of phrase, he, too, might have said: "Fiction is my kitchen wench; poetry my muse." Hardy's verse is a more compact and illuminating revelation of the essential man than his prose. His wife and biographer, Mrs. Florence Hardy, observed: "Speaking generally, there is more autobiography in a hundred lines of his poetry than in all of the novels." As both novelist and poet, he has a secure place among the greatest authors of our times.

He was born June 2, 1840, on the border of Bockhampton Heath, about three miles from Dorchester, Dorset, the son of a mason and builder. There is little in his heredity to account for his genius and bent of mind. The environment in which he was born and reared, however, had a pronounced bearing on his novels and poems. His biographers have pointed out that it is almost impossible to think of Hardy without associating him with that part of southern England, Dorsetshire, which he called Wessex. Dorset has been retenanted with Clyms and Eustacias, Judes and Bathshebas; Puddleton Heath, near Bockhampton, has been identified with Egdon Heath; and Dorchester has Casterbridge as its second name. That Hardy, like his character Eustacia Vye, "imbibed much of what was dark in its tone" may account in some measure for what has been called his peculiarly twilight view of life.

For a time his parents thought that he might be trained for the clergy, and there was talk of his going to Cambridge. But he was not eager for university life, and even in his late teens he had no inclination toward dogmatic religion. At sixteen, he went to work with John Hicks, an architect of Dorchester, who taught him little, but who helped him to determine to follow the profession of architecture. At twentytwo he was in London, doing miscellaneous work in drafting rooms and taking evening courses at King's College under Sir Gilbert Scott, a Gothic expert. Although he himself said: "I was a child till I was sixteen; a youth till I was twentyfive; a young man till I was forty or fifty," during his twenties he had already pondered long and earnestly over the inner significance of life. His questionings and reflections he cast into verse; and the thought that they might have worth caused him to neglect his profession of architecture, and by 1869 to launch out into literature. He found his poems generally unsalable, but noting the success of Meredith with fiction when the latter had had little response from his verse, Hardy set to work on a novel. Meredith, recognizing his earnestness and talent, helped him considerably both with criticism and encouragement. From 1871 until 1897 he rose to one of the highest places in English fiction, starting with *Desperate Remedies* (1871) and ending with *Jude the Obscure* (1896). *The Well-Beloved* appeared in 1897, but Hardy's determination to forsake the novel dated from his distress over the bitter reviews which appeared on the publication of *Jude*. Volumes of verse began to appear before the close of the century, and by 1925 nine fairly large books had been issued. The *Collected Poems* (1931) contains virtually everything included in the earlier volumes, with the exception of the massive poetic drama *The Dynasts* which had appeared in three parts in 1903-6-8. Too much significance should not be attached to the dates of publication, for many of the poems were written much earlier. His last works were produced at Max Gate, Dorset, where he led a secluded life until his death in 1928.

Hardy's prose is of considerable volume: eleven novels and three collections of short stories. The novels vary in interest and merit, but even in the early works such as *Desperate Remedies* (1871) and *Under the Greenwood Tree* (1872), there is an unmistakable sense of design. With the culminating situation always in view, Hardy fitted his characters, settings, and plots into a well-centralized development in which all of the parts are skilfully integrated. His portrait gallery of characters is exceptionally wide, and in the principal figures there is always a three-dimensional quality which indicates a penetrating observation of the cause and effect of human action. His characters are shaped both by their inner natures and the external circumstances which surround them. They are not masters of their fate; in fact, circumstance plays a large part in the direction of their lives; but they often contribute to the outcome of events by forces which lie within their own natures. Eustacia Vye, Damon Wildeve, and Clym Yeobright in *The Return of the Native*; Bathsheba Everdene, Gabriel Oak, and Farmer Boldwood in *Far From the Madding Crowd*; Tess and Angel Clare in *Tess of the D'Urbervilles*; and Jude and Sue in *Jude the Obscure* are all memorable characters, not only for what they did but for what they were. They may antagonize the reader—in fact, they often do—and few of them can be called endearing; but they compel the reader's interest and sympathy by reason of their poignant reality. They represent universal types in their strength and weakness, but they are strongly marked individuals in their efforts to surmount the obstacles which their temperaments and circumstance put in their way.

Even finer than his characterization is his handling of setting. Although his backgrounds lack variety, for he deals almost exclusively with Wessex, there is ample latitude for a man of Hardy's penetrating observation to relieve any monotony. As a local colorist, he has few equals. Not only can he create atmospheres which in themselves become a powerful force in the motivation of the characters, but he can take specific events and places which are part of the background, and with a fine sense of graphic detail, create scenes which cause the reader to become an eye-witness to rural and community life in Wessex. The fine description of Egdon Heath in *The Return of the Native*, the insight into rural life in *The Woodlanders and Far From the Madding Crowd*, and the revelation of the inner spirit of the community in *The Mayor of Casterbridge* are only a few illustrations of Hardy's ability to create vivid settings.

It is Hardy's handling of plot which has aroused most discussion and antagonized many readers. The precept in one of his earlier poems "In Tenebris": "If a way to the Better there be, it exacts a full look at the Worst. . . ." finds expression in almost all of his novels. His characters are thrust into circumstances over which they can exercise small control, and from which they rarely escape. Jude, with his yearning for education, is beset by obstacles which Hardy makes insurmountable; Tess, with a chance for happiness, places a letter which might have given her peace from her past under the door of Angel Clare's room, to learn when it is too late that the letter was concealed under the carpet; and Eustacia, in her attempt to escape from the heath which has been her Hades, falls into the weir and is drowned. It is true that these characters are in themselves tragic figures who contribute much to the fate which finally overtakes them; but with the author's manipulation of circumstances, all controlled by the forces of ill, they have small chance to overcome the obstacles which confront them. The plots of the novels suffer by reason of the relentless application of his belief in the preponderance of ill in the world, but their poignancy as records of man's struggles remains unmitigated.

Not only are the novels masterpieces of design, but the style often rises to a high plane of poetic prose. It is true that the manner is at times heavy and cumbersome, as if the author is straining at the bonds of his medium; and there is nothing which can be called sprightly. With cleverness, there is no traffic, and there are passages which lack conciseness and finish. Some of the episodes are overwritten to such an extent that the effect approaches melodrama, and his belief in the forces of evil in the world gave support to a noticeable inclination to stress the bitter episodes in the lives of his characters. The suicide of Father Time in *Jude*, the aftermath of the burial of Fanny in *Far From the Madding Crowd*, and the killing of Alec D'Urberville in *Tess* are memorable on account of the explicit morbid detail with which they are described. Over and against such inadequacies are his sustained cadences in the chapter "Queen of the Night" in *The Return of the Native*, the fine restraint in the closing passages of *The Woodlanders*, and the artistic sincerity which marks all of his work.

Hardy's poetry is in large measure a continuation, an illumination and a distillate of the novels. In fact, many of his poems have been called condensed novels, for in their compact development there are themes and characters which might readily be put into the longer prose medium. Such poems as *"The Newcomer's Wife," "The Dance at the Phoenix,"* and *"The Turnip Hoer"* are made of the same stuff as the novels; and the outcome of the characters' struggles against the caprices of circumstance is the same. They are skilful in their compression of unstable situation; and by reason of their lean development, the climaxes and tragedies come with a suddenness that is often shocking. The last line of "The Newcomer's Wife" has a directness and force which cause the reader to wish for a few stanzas in preparation for it. The verse schemes in these pieces are simple; and the diction is unembellished by any rhetorical devices of imagery which might relieve their starkness. They are not great poetry, for their themes are limited to what the reader hopes are isolated experiences in the life of man; but in their plain, sturdy lines there are poignancy and power.

Hardy's greatest poetry is not that in which he traces in compressed form life's ironies, or in which he is the iconoclast in dogmatic religion, or even when he is crying out against the futility of war, as in his poem *"The Pity of It"*; he undoubtedly attains his greatest heights when he is seeking the reasons for life's wounds and anguish. Here he is no longer recording life's ironies through specific episodes, but attempting to penetrate the cause and to find "a way to the Better." Here he becomes not a prophet and seer, but a cosmic poet, dealing with the universal and ageless problems which beset men's minds and souls. To Nature's questioning, in the poem under that title, "We wonder, ever wonder, why we find us here!" he replies, "No answerer I"; but the struggle through which he has gone before making the admission is implicit in the poem; and in that struggle there are nobility and greatness. Such poems as *"Hap," "A Young Man's Epigram on Existence,"* and the long poetic drama *"The Dynasts"* are of cosmic theme, and *"The Dynasts"* is of cosmic scope. It is on a plane with *"Paradise Lost"* and "Prometheus Unbound" in its loftiness of theme, and certainly in its depth and sincerity of purpose. Its length, and its complexity of conception and design, keep it from being widely read; but it is one of the most magnificently conceived poems of our times. That it lacks the lyric beauty of Shelley's "Prometheus Unbound" is against its consummate greatness; and despite the elevated tone and unmistakable power in its entirety, there are passages which are heavy with the effort to convey his theme.

Hardy had not been "the idle singer of an empty day," nor had he created a dream world in which one is surrounded by the beauties of sight and sense and in which one is contentedly lost. He was not an opiate to the mind and soul, nor does he stimulate a desire to reform the institutions to which man was accustomed. He is, amongst the recent poets, one of the least musical. But as Siegfried Sassoon has said: "Men are alive only when they struggle. When they grow aware of the futility of their effort, and yet strive to fashion something from it, they become noble and tragic; such was Hardy."

Verse: *Wessex Poems and Other Verses* (1898), *Poems of Past and Present* (1902), *Time's Laughingstocks and Other Verses* (1909), *Satires of Circumstance* (1914), *Moments of Vision and Miscellaneous Verses* (1917), *Late Lyrics and Earlier* (1922), *Human Shows, Far Phantasies, Songs and Trifles* (1925), *Yuletide in a Younger World* (1927), *Winter Words in Various Moods and Metres* (1928), *Collected Poems* (1931).

Poetic Drama: *The Dynasts: A Drama in Three Parts* (1903-6-8).

Novels: *Desperate Remedies* (1871), *Under the Greenwood Tree* (1872), *A Pair of Blue Eyes* (1873), *Far From the Madding Crowd* (1874), *The Hand of Ethelberta* (1876), *The Return of the Native* (1878), *The Trumpet-Major* (1880), *A Laodicean* (1881), *Two on a Tower* (1882), *The Mayor of Casterbridge* (1886), *The Woodlanders* (1887), *Tess of the D'Urbervilles* (1891), *Jude the Obscure* (1896), *The Well Beloved* (1897).

Alfred Edward Housman

The age which reflected on Thomas Hardy's "In Tenebris" with its forthright line: "If a way to the Better there be, it exacts a full look at the Worst," was given additional incentive to question life's unmixed benevolence in the slender volumes of A. E. Housman. But whereas Hardy sought to find the ultimate sources of the world's ills, Housman was largely concerned with a recognition of them and a way to ease their pain; and whereas Hardy was often gnarled and rugged in expression, with little in his verse that can be termed melodic, in Housman there is a constant song quality. Although in much of their verse there is a common theme, there is nothing to indicate that either influenced the other.

Alfred Edward Housman was born March 22, 1859, at Bournheath, Worcester, the son of Edward Housman, a solicitor, and one of seven children among whom were Laurence Housman, the poet and playwright, and a sister

Clemence whose talents were recognized by editors and publishers of the nineties. Shropshire, the county with which he has become associated by reason of the settings and place names in many of his poems, and the title of one of his volumes, was never his home. It was an adjacent county, the land beyond the horizon. After learning the rudiments of Latin and Greek at the Bromsgrove School, he went up to St. John's College, Oxford, on a scholarship where he remained from 1877 to 1882. Although qualified for a degree, he did not receive it until 1892, at which time he forsook his work as a Higher Division Clerk in the British Patent Office to become Professor of Latin at University College, London. In 1911 he became Kennedy Professor of Latin at Trinity College, Cambridge, where he remained until his death in 1936.

Authorities in classical literature agree that Housman was a scholar of considerable note, not only for his contributions to the *Classical Quarterly* and *Classical Review*, but also for his excellent editions of Juvenal, Lucan, and the five books of the *Astronomica* of Manilius. Although the point need not be labored, there seems to be ample evidence that Housman went to school under the Latin poets, for in his works there are the qualities of conciseness, lucidity, and restraint, qualities usually associated with the classical manner.

In 1896, four years after he had become Professor of Latin at University College, London, when he was thirty-seven, a small volume of sixty-three poems appeared under the title *A Shropshire Lad*. Twenty-six years later, in 1922, forty-one poems appeared under the significant title Last Poems. A few months after his death in 1936, forty-eight poems were issued by his brother Laurence entitled *More Poems*. The appearance of this volume came as a surprise to his readers, for in the preface to the volume Last Poems, he had said: "I publish these poems, few that they are, because it is not likely that I shall ever be impelled to write much more. I cannot be expected to be revisited by the continuous excitement under which in the early months of 1895 I wrote the greater part of my other book, nor could I well sustain it if came." Although there is nothing strikingly different in either theme or manner from the poems of the earlier collections, the pieces which Laurence Housman collected for *More Poems* are not inferior to the average of the already published poems; in fact, they add to Housman's stature as a poet and to the reader's enjoyment. Many of them belong essentially to the same time as that at which the poems in *A Shropshire Lad* were written; and although the name Terence does not appear, they often express a young man's concern with the preponderance of ill in the world.

In spite of the fact that Housman's province is limited, there are many classifications of his poems to invite the reader; but the most illuminating division, and one that often goes unrecognized, is that there are poems not only of darkness but poems of light.Mr. Charles Williams in *Poetry at Present* (Oxford, 1930) writes to the point when he says: "Not every poem is explicitly concerned with the 'much less good than ill.' A reader who opened *A Shropshire Lad* at the beginning could read the first sixteen poems without finding in it more than an occasional stanza of darkness, and without necessarily holding it to be more than dramatic or semidramatic. For those sixteen contain love songs, a ballad lyric, and one or two of as exquisite nature poems as any in English, especially the famous 'Loveliest of trees, the cherry now'. . . ." A fairly long list of poems could be compiled from the three volumes in which life's ironies have little part. "Reveille" is a sinewy call for action and courage; "Oh, When I Was in Love with You" tells of the ennobling power of love; "Epithalamium" points out the blessings of friendship; and "The Chestnut Casts its Flambeaux, and the Flowers," with all of its lamenting of man's sad lot, is poignantly insistent that trouble can be borne. The poet offers no solution for escape, but in many of the poems there is the comforting assurance that in the face of the misery in the world there are beauties in nature, in friendship, and in love which give man courage to bear his unfailing burdens.

Although "the hemlock fascination of the poet's self-centered, self-pitying, and abject pessimism" has been overstressed by a generation of readers who needed support for their own misgivings about the world's goodness, there is no doubt that the poems of darkness outweigh in both quantity and intensity the poems of light. The allegory in the closing lines of "Terence, This is Stupid Stuff" leaves one fully aware of the poet's recognition of life's ills; and such poems as "When Smoke Stood Up From Ludlow," "Bredon Hill," and "The Culprit," among many others, have a sombreness which cannot be escaped. Frustration, futility, hopelessness all play a part in the quietly bitter resignation out of which these poems take shape. Despair and tragedy, often made more bitter by abrupt anticlimax, are the end of many a rose-lipt maiden and light-foot lad. The impermanence of youth and beauty becomes the sentiment for laments in which there is little to suggest Herrick's advice of "Gather ye rosebuds while ye may." No doubt, as his brother Laurence observed: "He would have liked the laws of God and man to be kinder than they are; and a great deal of the anger and bitterness of his verse is due to the fact that they are so much the other way."

It is probable that the sentiments of the poems would have attained only a mild response had they been presented with less grace and melody. To the mature poetry reader who has been made completely aware of life's ills through experience, Housman's themes exercise little fascination, but the manner is so compelling that in many instances the thought becomes secondary in arousing and sustaining interest. Even the most bitter themes are made palatable as the poet in an apparently effortless way expresses his mood. The manner is consistently appealing by reason of its seeming simplicity and artlessness. The diction and stanzaic patterns are always in keeping with the changing moods of youth beset by the contemplation of life's scheme. Although the manner is always simple and direct, there is ample evidence to indicate that it was cunningly deliberated and painstakingly revised. Only a perfectionist in style could achieve such effects with the simplest words and verse measures. The note is seldom strong and resonant; rather it suggests a shepherd's pipe heard at a distance in autumn.

In spite of the fact that many of the poems were designed to reflect the moods of troubled youth, in them there are an unfailing dignity and restraint. Bitter as they sometimes are, they are never vituperative, and one never feels that the poet is consciously straining to give emphasis to his sentiment. The dignity and restraint of the diction are often put to severe tests in the many instances in which everyday language and colloquialism are introduced as a realistic part of the presentation, but in no instance do the colloquial and the poetic get in each other's way. The two stanzas which begin, "The fairies break their dances" in *Last Poems* are an example of the poet's remarkable skill at blending two apparently hostile levels of diction. To a lesser artist, the effect could readily descend to parody and jingle, but with Housman the results are always poetic.

In the Leslie Stephen Lecture, delivered by Housman at Cambridge in 1933 under the title "The Name and Nature of Poetry," the poet compared his art to a secretion: The creative process in Housman, it would seem, was the result of his sympathetic understanding of the troubles which beset all "ill-treated fellows" to which mankind at large belongs. Pessimistic, but not misanthropic, he set out as a sort of self-deliverance to reflect the moods of an imaginary character who had, as he observed, "something of my temper and view of life." To this reflection he brought a severely disciplined economy of phrase, simplicity of diction and verse, and a haunting music.

Verse: *A Shropshire Lad* (1896), *Last Poems* (1922), *More Poems* (1936), *Collected Poems* (1939).

Prose: *The Name and Nature of Poetry* (1933).

SOME DEVOTIONAL POETS

A considerable amount of devotional poetry has been written in England since 1890. Oscar Wilde, Ernest Dowson, and Lionel Johnson found some of their inspiration in the Church, as did Katharine Tynan Hinkson, Dora Sigerson Shorter, and Alice Meynell; and more recently Alfred Noyes, Roy Campbell, and T. S. Eliot have found compelling themes in religion. Although the major part of his work was done before 1900, Francis Thompson (1859- 1907) became widely known as a devotional poet after the turn of the century. Born at Preston in Lancashire, the son of a physician who had become a zealous convert and a woman who had had the intention of becoming a nun, the boy was reared in an atmosphere congenial to his parents' wish that he become a priest. After seven years of preparation at St. Cuthbert's at Ushaw, he was told by his advisers that he should withdraw and undertake a different career. His failure to qualify for the priesthood was a source of acute and lasting grief to him and his parents. Since his father was a physician, it was decided that he go to Owens College, Manchester, to prepare himself to become a doctor. Physically and temperamentally ill-suited to such a profession, and with his ideal of becoming a priest shattered, Thompson became addicted to drugs, left medical school after successive failures, and went to London to sink in time to the level of a tramp. When he was still presentably clad, he sought warmth in the public library where he read poetry and occasionally wrote on paper he had salvaged from the streets.

It is a familiar story of how Wilfrid Meynell and his wife Alice, coeditors of *Merry England*, received early in February, 1887, some tattered manuscripts on blue wrapping paper. The unpromising appearance of the manuscripts caused Meynell to put them aside, and it was not until nearly a year had passed that he glanced at them, to be at once impressed by the contents, especially the stanzas entitled *"The Passion of Mary."* After much difficulty, he arranged for a meeting with the writer which was the beginning of Thompson's rescue and his real beginning as a poet. The Meynells gave him courage and hope, inspiration, and a receptacle for his verse. They sent him to a hospital to be treated for his affliction, and from there to the priory at Storrington. Later, after staying with the Meynells in London, Thompson went to the Capuchin Monastery at Pantasaph, Wales, where he mingled with the monks, and where he often saw Coventry Patmore who offered him guidance and encouragement. By 1896 he returned to London to work occasionally at journalism until his death in 1907.

His most widely known poem *"The Hound of Heaven,"* first printed in *Merry England* in July, 1890, is autobiographical in that it records the poet's experiences in the years following his rejection for the priesthood. While trying to find peace through all the well-known channels—in science, in nature, and in an apostleship to beauty—his soul was being pursued by the Hound of Heaven, a daring symbol for God's search for the souls of men. As a devotional document the poem may have only a limited usefulness to some readers; but for power of theme, intensity of purpose, artistry of conception, and rapture of ultimate realization, *"The Hound of Heaven"* has a high place in English poetry.

The shorter poems such as *"Lilium Regis"* in which the lily of the king is God's Holy Church; the sonnet *"Ad Amicam,"* the first in a sequence of fifteen, in which the poet expresses the peace which comes to those whose souls have been found; and *"In No Strange Land"* in which his mystic relationship with the divine becomes very real, are characteristic of Thompson's finest work in the devotional lyric. For an illumination of the poet's belief in the sanctifying grace which attends the innocence of children, *"Daisy"* has deservedly found its way into most of the anthologies.

Thompson is neither a poet of thought, nor a poet of melody and beauty for their own sake, although melody and beauty of imagery are pronounced characteristics. He is essentially an inspired devotional poet in whose works can be found an authentic mysticism, an intensity of purpose and feeling, and lyric rapture. At times this lyric rapture found expression in a beautiful simplicity: in such poems as *"Daisy," "Little Jesus,"* and *"In No Strange Land"* there are directness and ready comprehensibility in diction and imagery. In the

"Sister Songs" and some of the sonnets, however, his expression often lacks discipline, with the result that extravagances of imagery appear which border on the turgid. Despite his easily recognized lack of restraint, amongst devotional poets and poets at large, Thompson has a secure place.

Verse: *Poems* (1893), *Songs Wing to Wing* (1895), *Sister Songs: an Offering to Two Sisters* (1895), *New Poems* (1897), *The Hound of Heaven, Selected Poems, Youthful Verses* (1928), *Terence Connolly, Collected Poems* (1932).

Prose: *Health and Holiness* (1905), *Shelley* (1909), *St. Ignatius Loyola* (1909), *Selected Essays* (1927)

Alice Meynell

The importance of Alice Meynell is two-fold: she presided over a generation of writers and she wrote verse and prose in which there is considerable distinction. To George Meredith she presented "the image of one accustomed to walk in holy places." Of Thompson's mysticism, however, there is little, and the variety of themes indicates that she was not exclusively a devotional poet.

Born Alice Thompson in 1847 into a serene home of parents interested in the arts, she possessed literary inclinations as a part of her birthright. Sojourns with her parents in Italy, tutors of more than average capabilities and culture, an atmosphere of refinement in her home, and her conversion to Catholicism at the age of twenty, were the background out of which her personality and talent developed. Even in her teens she wrote poetry, but it was not until 1875 that a small collection *Preludes* appeared in which she was perceptibly influenced by Mrs. Browning and Christina Rossetti. In 1877 she married Wilfrid Meynell, a young man occupied with editing conservative periodicals, a man of undoubted taste and literary perception whose talent was more largely critical than creative. With him she became the coeditor of *Merry England*, and for years she shared his work, helping with reviews and submitting essays and poems. Her writing was not confined to the periodicals which she and her husband edited, for Henley printed some of her work in the *National Observer*, and some of it appeared in the *Spectator* and the *Saturday Review*. In addition to all the activity as editor and contributor, she became the mother of eight children, most of whom were to show considerable talent; and she was a source of inspiration and encouragement to those who sat in her drawing room at Palace Court in London and her hospitable home in Sussex. Richard Le Gallienne said of her: "The touch of genuine asceticism about her seemed but to accent the sensitive sympathy of her manner, the manner of one quite simply and humanly of the world, with all its varied interests, yet not of it. There was the charm of a beautiful abbess about her, with the added *esprit* of intellectual sophistication. However quietly she sat in her drawing room of an evening with her family and friends about her, her presence radiated a peculiarly lovely serenity, like a twilight gay with stars." Although in her late years her speech became slow and without its earlier keenness of phrase, she was never pedantic. She died at her home in Sussex in 1922.

A glance at a list of her published works indicates that she was more fluent in prose than verse. Her critical standards, illustrated in many reviews, reveal her insistence on discipline and moderation. Nimbleness of phrase for its own sake she deplored, and she was quick to detect any sort of artificiality of manner. Sentimentality and overwrought effects were high on her *index prohibitorum*, along with any inclination away from the precise and discriminating. Her essays in which the purpose was other than critical show a careful application of the discipline she advocated in her reviews. They are subjective without becoming really personal, and in spite of their easy, informal air, they are always dignified. In them there is nothing of Lamb's delight in the confession of human frailty, and nothing which approaches the boisterousness of Stephen Leacock. There are light passages, to be sure, in which a fresh and, at times, unexpected humor comes to the reader; but there is no deliberate attempt to be whimsical, much less coy. Without becoming austere, Mrs. Meynell's essays reflect her serene personality and her intellectual and stylistic discipline.

Although the greater volume of her work was in prose, at intervals—some of them long—little volumes of verse, much of which had appeared in magazines, were issued. In the collected edition of 1923, which contains little more than a hundred pages, there is more variety in theme and manner than is implied in Edith Sitwell's description of her poems as "limp exhortations to virtue." The assurance and dignity of the manner can scarcely be called limp; and although Mrs. Meynell no doubt wanted the world to be a better place than it often is, she was not a reformer. Were it not for the delicate richness of feeling in many of her poems, she might have become a victim of her own restraint and selfimposed discipline. There are no great emotional surges, and there is no lavish imagery as one encounters in Thompson. In such a poem as *"Renouncement"* she escapes from the charge of lack of warmth, but generally the reader has the impression of emotion well leashed. The intensity of her religious emotion appears in such well-known poems as *"The Shepherdess"* and *"Christ in the Universe,"* but it is a serene, intellectualized emotion rather than rapture. A perfectionist in form, Alice Meynell illustrated in her poetry the quiet richness of her spiritual life in a fashion which appeals to readers of the most exacting tastes.

Verse: *Preludes* (1875), *Poems* (1893), *Other Poems* (1896), *Later Poems* (1901), *The Shepherdess and Other Verses* (1914), *Poems of the War* (1915), *A Father of Women* (1917), *Last Poems* (1923), *Collected Poems* (1923), *Complete Poems* (1940), *The Poems of Alice Meynell* (1947).

Prose: *Colour of Life and Other Essays* (1897), *Second Person Singular and Other Essays (nd)*, *Spirit of Place and Other Essays* (1899), *Childhood* (1913), *Essays* (1914), *Selected Essays* (1926).

Rudyard Kipling

A conclusive judgment of Rudyard Kipling's worth is still to be made. Some indication of his popularity is afforded by the estimate that more than 3,500,000 copies of his books were sold by his American publishers between 1895 and 1935. The critical disparagement which is at times implied in such notices of an author's popularity is not always applicable to Kipling, for in spite of the fact that his works have appealed to many classes of readers, he cannot be dismissed as only a prolific and clever writer who gave the public what it wanted.

Joseph Rudyard Kipling was born December 30, 1865, in Bombay, India, the son of John Lockwood Kipling, a sculptor and authority on the Hindu plastic arts, and Alice Kipling, the daughter of a distinguished Wesleyan clergyman. Kipling's birthright augured well for the future; and when at an early age he showed a fondness for all manner of stories and displayed a lively imagination, his parents agreed that he was marked for a career with his pen. When he was six, he and a younger sister were sent to England to school, to live at Southsea with an elderly relative whose manner was austere and whose home Kipling was to call "the House of Desolation." It was relief for him to be sent to the United Services College at Westward Ho where he remained for four years. His stories in *Stalky and Co.* (1899) afford a pleasant picture of the school and its life at the time, and one can detect in the character Beetle lineaments of the author. Although the training he received at Westward Ho was no great contributing factor in his development, he edited six numbers of the school paper and contributed stories to it. As early as 1881, he had published *School Boy Lyrics.*

At seventeen, he returned to India where through his father he obtained congenial work on the staff of the Lahore *Civil and Military Gazette* to which he brought enthusiasm and energy, combined with a talent for writing lively articles and stories. The Gazette in turn provided him with a receptacle into which to place his writing and a rigorous apprenticeship in giving readers what they want. By the time he was twentytwo he was adequately trained to fill the post of assistant editor of the *Pioneer* at Allahabad, at the time the greatest of the Anglo-Indian papers. Because he was not always submissive to editorial policy, he was in time given "more assignments at a distance than in the immediate vicinity of the office"; and after several years of moving about India procuring good copy, he was sent by the Pioneer as correspondent-at-large to England, and later to Australia, New Zealand, and South Africa. Soon after his arrival in England he sent some of the verses which he later collected for *Barrack-Room Ballads* to W. E. Henley who was enthusiastic about their merit and issued them promptly in the National Observer. On his return to London in 1892 after extensive travel for the *Pioneer,* Kipling was ready to give up professional journalism, and collect some of his stories and verse for publication in book form.

While looking after the issue of his books, Kipling met Wolcot Balestier, a young American critic, whose sister Caroline he married in 1892. He came with his wife to live at her home in Brattleboro, Vermont, until 1896. According to report, "He adopted Vermont, but Vermont never adopted him," and, not without bitterness, he and his wife left America to search for a good place for a permanent home. After an interval of travel, they settled at Rottingdean, Sussex, which Kipling grew to like to such an extent that in his later years he rarely went far from the boundaries of his garden. In 1907 he won the Nobel Prize for literature, not for any particular or recent work, but on account of his achievements over a period of years. There was a perceptible falling off of volume after 1910, but his vigor of manner persisted and he was by no means written out. To the end he produced valuable additions to both his verse and prose, especially during the First World War; and his autobiography, *Something of Myself,* written late in life, is full of his characteristic strength. He died at his home in Sussex in 1936.

Although Kipling is more widely known through his verse than his prose, in the tales and novels there is much which is characteristic of his talent and which continues to appeal to a wide class of reader. The pieces in *Soldiers Three* (1888), though an engaging anticipation of what he was later to do for the soldier in his verse, are not so finely written as the stories in *Plain Tales From the Hills* (1888). These tales reveal much of the author's understanding of Anglo-Indian life and his sense of vivid pictorial detail as well as his talent for compelling narrative. Of the stories which have an Indian background, "Without Benefit of Clergy" and "The Man Who Would be King" are among the best. *The Jungle Book* (1894) and *The Second Jungle Book* (1895) are classics in a sense, for these stories, designed largely for children but appealing to all ages, are excitingly and delightfully told. *Wee Willie Winkie* (1888), though agreeable, is not so compelling to the imagination as are many of the stories in the Jungle Books, nor does it have the fine narrative artistry of *Puck of Pook's Hill* (1906).

The novels *The Light That Failed* (1890), *Captains Courageous* (1897), and *Kim* (1901) are entirely plausible in character and plot, but *The Light That Failed* lacks the force of great tragedy. *Captains Courageous,* though appealing as a story and illuminating in its description of the background of the fishing fleets of the North Atlantic, is undistinguished by any really memorable passage of prose. *Kim,* with its setting in India, has striking passages of description; and although the plot is loosely woven, Kim and the old lama are a picturesque, endearing pair as they move through the bazaars and along the Grand Trunk Road.

Kipling's verse reveals a writer of many themes, moods, and manners. There are poems, for example, in which he is the romanticist of modernity and the machine age. In *"M' Andrew's Hymn"* he shows very persuasively that the drama and glamor of the sea did not disappear with the advent of the steamship. "The Bell Buoy," with its onomatopoetic refrain, dramatizes vividly the struggles between the forces of the sea and a product of man's mechanical ingenuity. In *"The King"* he gives the most eloquent expression to his belief of the presence of romance in the here-and-now of reality. In much of his verse, especially in *"The Rival," "La Nuit Blanche," "The Explorer,"* and *"Mary, Pity Women,"* he demonstrates a remarkable talent for projecting himself into different types of character, thinking their thoughts and using their idiom. In *"Mary, Pity Women"* the manner in which the poet expresses the anguish of the poor, disillusioned girl whose lover is leaving her an expectant mother goes beyond clever mimicry. In such well-known pieces as *"The Ladies," "Pink Dominoes,"* and *"Tommy"* he seeks not only a skilfull imitation of a point of view and the idiom of his characters, but an expression of his own shrewd wisdom. In many of these pieces the wisdom is of a practical worldly sort, with its application limited to particular circumstances, and with cleverness rather than profoundness in the manner and tone. "The Recessional," *"If,"* and *"L'Envoi"* are still recited, at times probably more for their rhetoric which is not too well concealed than for their lofty sentiment. Unfortunately some of Kipling's finest lyrics are ignored for those in which there is something the reader mistakes for greatness, but what is in reality only a tuneful jingle conveying a clever theme. The poems *"A Nativity"* and *"My Boy Jack"* have a dignity and beauty which puts them into a different class from the overworked measures in *"Boots"* and the cleverness in "Pink Dominoes." Many of Kipling's themes have already been put aside as dated, but his versification, generally vigorous and martial, exercised at times at the expense of consummate tonal effects, continues to give pleasure; and his diction and imagery, comprehensible and usually down to earth, delight readers who prefer the explicit to the subtle and cerebral.

Verse: *Departmental Ditties* (1886), *Barrack Room Ballads and Other Verses* (1892), *The Seven Seas* (1896), *Recessional and Other Poems* (1899), *The Five Nations* (1903), *Rewards and Fairies* (1910), *prose and verse; Songs From Books* (1912), *The Years Between* (1919), *Sixty Poems* (1939), *Rudyard Kipling's Verse* (1940), *The Novels, Tales, and Poems of Rudyard Kipling* (1939).

Prose: *Plain Tales From the Hills* (1888), *Soldiers Three* (1888), *The Light That Failed* (1890), *Many Inventions* (1893), *The Jungle Book* (1894), *The Second Jungle Book* (1895), *Captains Courageous* (1897), *The Day's Work* (1898), *Stalky and Co.* (1899), *Kim* (1901), *Just-so Stories* (1902), *Puck of Pook's Hill* (1906).

Autobiography: *Something of Myself* (1937).

SOME WOMEN POETS

Charlotte Mary Mew

Of the women who have written verse in this century, none is more genuinely poetic than Charlotte Mew (1869-1928) . Although her volume is slight, doubtless because of her severe self-criticism, her two small books of verse, *The Farmer's Bride* (1916) and *The Rambling Sailor* (1929), show more range in both theme and manner than is commonly supposed. Occasionally she has handled conventional themes in a conventional manner, as for example in *"In the Fields,"* and the prettily turned *"Song"* which begins "Love, love today, my dear," but she is never trifling. At times there is a rustic theme and manner, as in *"Old Shepherd's Prayer,"* but she is no imitator of the prettiness of the pastoral mode. Although she is best known for her compressed narratives such as *"The Farmer's Bride,"* it is invariably the lyric manner of recording her theme rather than the story element which is outstanding.

Charlotte Mary Mew was born in 1869, the daughter of an architect who bequeathed to his family little more than an artistic strain. Evidently illness and want were part of Charlotte Mew's lot, and both rumor and internal evidence in her verse hint at an unhappy love affair. Although it is likely that she wrote verse even in her girlhood, Miss Mew's first published work was in prose narrative, the story *"Passed"*which appeared in the July issue of *The Yellow Book* in 1894. It was not until 1916 that Alida Klemantaski, who became the wife of Harold Monro of the Poetry Bookshop, persuaded Miss Mew to submit some of her poetry for publication. Although recognition was given to her work in both England and America (where in 1921 the poems in *The Farmer's Bride* were published under the title Saturday Market), her acute critical sense kept her from releasing any verse which would merely add volume to her work. Thomas Hardy was sufficiently impressed by some of the poems in *The Farmer's Bride* that he named Miss Mew the best woman poet of her time. And it was Hardy, along with De la Mare and Masefield, who was instrumental in securing for her a Civil List Pension. But recognition from such men as Hardy and a widening audience, and the meagre pension, were not enough for her troubled spirit. With the death of her mother and her sister, an increasing life-weariness beset her which left her with little on which to build a plan for her declining years. On March 24, 1928 she committed suicide in a nursing home in London. The year following her death, a small volume of poems which she had been revising for the press was brought out by her friends at Monro's Bookshop under the title *The Rambling Sailor*.

There is no doubt that something of Miss Mew's own troubled life found its way into her poetry. Without being somber, the themes are often touched with premonitions of death and a yearning for the peace which comes with death. Even *"The Farmer's Bride"* has the sere tone of autumn in it; and the farmer's lament in the closing lines is a poignant cry, full of the heartache of mankind. In her longer narratives such as "The Changeling," in which the theme like that in *"The Farmer's Bride"* is carried through in monologue, there is the haunting plaintiveness of the child who understands too well her lot.

In all of the narratives there is a fine compression which permits the inclusion of only the barest essentials of the situation and its development. And still the manner is always warm and intense. Although some of the verse lines exceed twenty syllables, one is constantly aware of the melody. The tones are generally muted, as if they came from a distance, without losing distinctness. The sixty-odd poems which

Charlotte Mew saw fit to prepare for the press, although varying in quality, are a small but precious addition to contemporary poetry.

> *The Farmer's Bride* (1916), *reprinted in the United] States as Saturday Market* (1921), *The Rambling Sailor* (1929), *Collected Poems* (1949).

Sylvia Townsend Warner

Well known in both England and the United States, She was probably more widely known for her novels and short stories than for her poems, for her novel *Lolly Willows: or the Loving Huntsman* (1926) was the first selection of the Book-of-the-Month Club; and some of the stories in *The Museum of Cheats* (1947) first appeared in the New Yorker. In her prose narratives she was a realist when such an approach suits her ends, as was plain in "View Halloo" and "Rosie Founders" in *The Museum of Cheats*; her realism was often pointed with irony, as in the "Story of a Patron"; and again she could deal effectually with the fanciful as in *Lolly Willows*. The novelist T. S. Powys said to the point: "The secret of Sylvia Warner's success in literature is that she understands exactly how much flavouring to put into a dish—and she never lets the cake burn." It is true that she used her flavouring—especially irony—with a master hand, and there is no instance in her use of satire in which she loses restraint.

Sylvia Townsend Warner was born in Middlesex in 1893, the daughter of a schoolmaster. There was evidently a background of music in the home, for she had composed music; and from 1916 to 1926, she was one of the editors of the monumental ten-volume work *Tudor Church Music*. Even before her part of this work was completed, she had printed a volume of poems, *The Espalier*, in 1925. This was followed by the novel *Lolly Willows* in 1926, which brought wide recognition to her on both sides of the Atlantic. Almost every year between 1926 and 1935 she was ready with another volume of either prose narratives or poems. Her work might seem to indicate that she was no longer concerned with the world of fancy, but rather with themes and issues which belong to that time. Although the stories in *The Museum of Cheats* (1947) had power and a fine mastery of style, they were not able to survive so well as some of the poems in *Time Importuned* (1928). *Opus* 7 (1931), and *Whether a Dove or a Seagull* (1933), written with Valentine Ackland.

Such poems as *"Nelly Trim"* and *"The Rival"* remain more vividly in the memory than anything Miss Warner had done in her short prose narratives. The former, in a haunting ballad measure, is a fine illustration of Miss Warner's talent for blending the unreal with the real, and for handling a blunt theme in a delicate and lyric way. *"The Rival"* takes on the form of a monologue in an interesting five-line stanzaic pattern in which the farmer's wife laments her lot of being wed to a man who is more attached to the soil than to her. In these poems there was a faint suggestion of the Wessex poems of Hardy; and in the *"Four Epitaphs"* the suggestion becomes more pronounced. In spite of the fact that Miss Warner was capable of profound thought, in her work there was little of Hardy's concern with the cosmic plan. Her manner varied from the simple and rugged in both diction and verse to the most subtle refinements of basic stanzaic patterns. She was at her best, however, in the compressed narrative poems in which her apparently simple themes conveyed meanings which were far-reaching, and in which her manner, although bold and direct, is consistently poetic.

Verse: *The Espalier* (1925), *Time Importuned* (1928), *Opus 7* (1931), *Rainbow* (1932), *Whether a Dove or a Seagull: Poems, with Valentine Ackland* (1933).

Prose: *Lolly Willows; or the Loving Huntsman* (1926), *Mr. Fortune's Maggot* (1927), *The True Heart* (1929), *Elinor Barley* (1930), *A Moral Ending and Other Stories* (1931), *The Salutation* (1932), *After the Death of Don Juan* (1935), *The Museum of Cheats* (1947), *The Corner That Held Them* (1948).

Anna Wickham

Anna Wickham is a striking antithesis to the Victorian "poetesses." Emancipated, resourceful, outspoken, she had little in common with the mild-mannered ladies who wrote conventional verse in the last century. In some measure she resembles the American Dorothy Parker, although she has nothing of the latter's smart sophistication. What she lacks in urbanity and clever phrase, however, she compensates for in forthrightness and strength. She is fearless in the expression of her thoughts, and she has thought much. Poetry is evidently the only fairly satisfying outlet for her, for in "Self-Analysis" she has written that the tumult of her mind gives her a sort of expression which is faulty and harsh, and in which there is some of "the incompetence of pain."

Anna Wickham was born in Wimbledon, Surrey, in 1884 of Australian parentage. At the age of six she went to Australia where during her formative years she led a life less restricted than that of girls in the English provinces. She was educated at the Sydney High School, and along with her classical studies she took lessons in music. At twenty-one she returned to England determined to prepare herself for a career in opera. After studying opera in Paris for a time under De Reszke, she gave up her intention to become a prima donna on account of the endless and exacting discipline such a profession involved and in order to marry Patrick Hepburn. It was soon after her union with Hepburn that her creative energy found a medium in verse. It has been reported that she wrote nine hundred poems in four years, some of which were later collected for *The Contemplative Quarry* (1915) and *The Man with a Hammer* (1916). During the years immediately following the First World War she continued to write much for a widening audience, but during the thirties there was a perceptible falling off of creative energy, accompanied by a blunt and prosaic manner.

Although there is little in her work which shows consummate workmanship, for she was never a meticulous craftsman, there is a robustness of manner which is almost universally appealing. She herself said in "The Singer" that were her mind and spirit less troubled, she could doubtless make a lovely poem:

But I am stung with goads and whips So I build songs like iron ships.

The nearest she came to true lyric beauty is in *"Divorce"* in which her yearning for freedom from her "little-love's warm loneliness" rose to a fine crescendo in the refrains. With no concern for prettiness of manner, her approach to the thoughts which beset her was arresting in its freshness and forthrightness. The sentiment in *"To a Crucifix"* is interesting in its attitude toward religious symbols and is representative of the poet's unwillingness to take the old conventions for granted. Although there is considerable variety in her several volumes, Anna Wickham's principal theme is the struggle of a sensitive, idealistic woman brought face to face with the realities of woman's lot. Her protests are uttered incisively and sincerely; and although her phrases are at times striking in their compactness, she never seeks mere cleverness. Even in the verses in a lighter vein such as *"Dedication of the Cook,"* there are no rhetorical embellishments. In spite of the fact that her robust manner is responsible for much of Anna Wickham's appeal, it is the poetic way in which she apprehends her themes that is most important in judging her verse.

The Contemplative Quarry (1915), *The Man With a Hammer* (1916), *The Little Old House* (1918).

Ruth Pitter

Although Ruth Pitter reported that she started to write verse in 1902 at the age of five, and had volumes of verse published in 1920, 1927, and 1930, it was not until Alida Monro's anthology *Recent Poetry:* 1923-1933 appeared in 1933 that she became known outside a very limited circle. And the curious piece *"Digdog"* through which she attracted attention is in small way representative of the nature and quality of her verse. Whereas the anthology-piece is almost impossible to understand, the larger part of Miss Pitter's work is lucid and unusually well disciplined; and instead of being an experimentalist in verse measures, as some readers were easily led to believe, in her volumes after 1930 she was essentially a traditionalist who, as Herbert Palmer observed, "walks around in borrowed clothes."

Ruth Pitter was born at Ilford, Essex, the daughter of a school teacher. Her education at the Coburn School, London, according to her own report, was somewhat sketchy, but it was evidently adequate to encourage her to wide reading and to continue her education at college. At the outbreak of the First World War, she interrupted her studies in the middle of the Intermediate year to work for almost two years in the War Office. Later she started a small shop where she made and sold hand-painted trays. Poetry, however, was more than an avocation, and by 1920 she had issued a small volume of verse. It was not until the publication of *A Mad Lady's Garland* (1935), however, that her talent became known in other than limited circles. Many distinctions came to her in the thirties: she won the Hawthornden Prize for Poetry; she had Hilaire Belloc, A.E., and Walter de la Mare commended her work highly in the reviews; and James Stephens , in writing the introductory note to her volume *A Trophy of Arms* (1936), stated perhaps extravagantly that as a companion poet to William Butler Yeats at his best, Ruth Pitter should be named. Such a statement need not be taken too literally, but in the light of what she had done in *The Spirit Watches* (1940), she might be considered one of the most important and promising of the contemporary women poets.

There are many moods and themes in her verse, among which the poems which deal with the grotesque, those which reveal her fine observation of nature, and those of mystical insight are most distinctive. In the poems in *A Mad Lady's Garland* there is much which indicates a curious occupation with the incongruous and even repulsive. Of this aspect of her work, A.E. wrote: "I would shrink from the grotesque poetry in *A Mad Lady's Garland* with all the shuddering with which we remove ourselves from the vicinity of cockroaches and earwigs, only Miss Pitter makes the creatures of her fantasy—spiders, fleas, cockroaches, worms, mice, or whatever else—speak so classically, and with so exquisite an artifice, that I am stayed to listen to them, and admit into my house of soul thoughts I would have closed the door upon if they had not come dressed in so courtly a fashion." In The Coffin-Worm, for example, the poet develops a monologue by a grave-worm to his worm-love in which, for all of the specific morbid detail as the worms settle down to their grisly business, there is an unusual effect of dignity. Miss Pitter's occupation with coffin-worms and their kind is a striking part of her work, but she dealt with the more beautiful manifestations of nature in a fresh and richly imaginative way. In *"The Swan Bathing"* and *"Time's Fool"* she brings authentic observation into the descriptive lines which form the background for the development of meditative themes. With nature as such she is not particularly concerned, but she makes certain to keep her images drawn from nature vivid and accurate. Although one feels that Miss Pitter's feet are on the ground and that she sees clearly and honestly what lies about her, there is also the impression that her world is essentially a spiritual world. *"The Eternal Image"* is a poem of pure vision, with mystical insight, in which there are resemblances to A.E. and the seventeenth-century Vaughn, and in which there is a fine use of terza-rima.

A Mad Lady's Garland (1935), *A Trophy of Arms* (1936), *The Spirit Watches* (1940), *The Bridge* (1945). *Sully-André Peyre, "Ruth Pitter," Marsyas* (April, 1935), 804-813.

Victoria Sackville-West

After reading about the spiders and coffin-worms in Ruth Pitter's *A Mad Lady's Garland,* one finds the pastorals of Victoria Sackville-West refreshing in their forthright, healthy treatment of English country life. Although Miss Sackville-West did not confine her content to only the agreeable aspects of nature, for she sees the tiger's claw as well as the full-blown rose, she much prefered to see nature's beauty instead of its cruelty. That she is not nature's eulogist is clearly stated in an early passage of *The Land* (1926), and still one feels that she understands and glories in "the sweat, the weariness, the care," and that she is not speaking idly when she says, "The country habit has me by the heart." It is a mistake, however, to identify Miss Sackville-West with only the pastoral mode, for she has written about Persia, Sans Souci, and South Carolina; and even in *The Land* she is as much concerned with human nature as with orchards and bees. *Her Collected Poems* (1933) and her more recent work in both prose and verse indicate a considerable latitude and variety of interests and themes.

Victoria Sackville-West was born at Knole Park, Kent, in 1892, the daughter of Baron Sackville whose name and estate go far back into English history. Although essentially of the same generation and tradition as Edith Sitwell, she was entirely satisfied with the old established order in spite of the fact that in she years following the First World War she realized that the English aristocracy and the old estates could not expect to remain unchanged. In *Pepita* (1937) she engagingly illuminates her attitude toward her ancestors and her birthright, and while indicating the practical inadequacies of the system of bountifully-landed aristocracy in the *twentieth century*, she was always aware of the nobility and charm which belonged to those who established and sustained the old order. She travelled widely and had seen England from the outside, with the perspective that comes from a long-range view, but with little diminution of her fondness for the English countryside. As the wife of Harold Nicholson, biographer and diplomat, she had no doubt been concerned with England's policies at home and abroad, but her interests were not essentially political. In 1927, she won the Hawthornden Prize with her poem *The Land*, and since that time she wrote much verse on varied themes and a considerable amount of prose, including her venture in murder-mystery, *The Devil at Westease* (1947).

Although she wrote poetry as early as *Poems of West and East* (1917), it was not until The Land was issued in 1926 that her work attracted real attention. No doubt the then current Georgian interest in the English pastoral scene was an incentive to the wide reception of the poem, but the fact remains that long after the Georgian revival of nature as a theme was spent, *The Land* continued to give pleasure to many readers. In spite of its length, the poem is unpretentious in purpose and manner. In design it suggests James Thomson's The Seasons: the poem is divided into four parts, each part devoted to a season of the year. The themes within the seasons range from how to spray against minor pests in "Spring" to how to make cider in "Autumn." At times the piece becomes a sort of versified "Practical Hints on Gardening," but the manner rarely descends to a prosaic level. Of the many other themes she treats, those with a reflective, philosophical tone and those which have only a piece of filigree for substance are outstanding. "Insurrection" is not only self-illuminating, but it shows an understanding and sympathy for the verities of life, and a genuine intensity of feeling. "Full Moon" is a dainty little poem, with something of De la Mare's witchery, and a very fine last line. The verse is almost invariably deftly spun, and in such a poem as *"Fear"* she demonstrates talent as a versifier of fine virtuosity. The novels, including the once popular *The Heir* (1922) and the recent *The Devil at Westease* (1947), show an author of well-disciplined technique, animated and reflective in turn, and satirical without being cynical. She can turn phrases trimly without any suggestion of smartness. The themes and characters show variety and depth of observation, but in them there is little compelling emotional attachment for the reader. It is as a poet of varied moods and themes, with a style that has warmth beneath its serene reflectiveness, that Victoria Sackville-West did her finest work.

Verse: *Poems of West and East* (1917), *The Land* (1926), *Collected Poems* (1933).

Prose: *The Heir* (1922), *The Edwardians* (1930), *All Passion Spent* (1931), *Pepita* (1937), *The Devil at Westease* (1947).

Lady Dorothy Wellesley

Lady Dorothy (Ashton) Wellesley is not only difficult to place in any of the recognized categories, but also difficult to judge. Her chief experiences and associations have been literary. Were it not for the enthusiastic praise which William Butler Yeats bestowed on her verse, one might conclude after reading any one of her volumes that she has something of the poet in her, but that it never became quite articulate. The panegyrical Introduction by Yeats to *Selections from the Poems of Lady Dorothy Wellesley* (1936)—with a frontispiece drawing of Lady Dorothy by Sir William Rothenstein—gives the one who is inclined to dismiss her work as that of a minor experimentalist at least momentary pause. Yeats's admiration was further demonstrated in the disproportionate amount of space he allotted to her work in *The Oxford Book of Modern Verse*. She is at her best—or at least her most comprehensible—in her verse which deals with nature, in which there is a suggestion of V. Sackville-West. In the poems in which she is apparently exploring what has been called her "Dream World," however, there is little on which the reader can get a grip, for the reality of unreality with which Coleridge and De la Mare caught the illogical and bizarre images of dreams is missing. Her early work represented in *Genesis, An Impression* (1926), and *Poems of Ten Years,* 1924-1934 (1934), so highly praised by Yeats, seems without direction, and the manner shifts capriciously from the conventional to the experimental, with richly decorated phrases standing out from a vocabulary which is generally down to earth. In her later volumes, *Lost Planet, and Other Poems* (1942), and *The Poets, and Other Poems* (1943), there is a clearer indication of purpose, especially in the title-poem of the earlier book; and a more unified and deeper tone is evident.

Genesis: An Impression (1926), Poems of Ten Years, 1924-1934 (1934), Lost Planet, and Other Poems (1942), The Poets, and Other Poems (1943).

Frances Cornford

Frances Cornford had written five small volumes of verse, all of which show distinction. She was born in 1886, the daughter of Sir Francis Darwin and granddaughter of Charles Darwin. It was not until after her marriage to Francis

Cornford, Lecturer of Trinity College, Cambridge, that her first volume *Poems* (1910) appeared, although poetry had occupied much of her time in her early twenties. *Spring Morning* (1915) was followed by *Autumn Midnight* (1923) and *Different Days* (1928); and in 1935 *Mountains and Molehills* appeared. In these volumes there is little which can aptly be called either a mountain or a molehill in poetic worth. The themes are varied, to be sure, ranging from the lightly ironic and well-turned triolet "To a Fat Lady Seen From the Train" to the more sombre and searching sestet which begins "My brain is like the ravaged shores . . .", but she was never trifling. Mrs Cornford was a flawless craftsman whose expression of feeling never got beyond the limits of restraint, and her sense of melody and tone never failed. "Mutely comforting" nature was one of her favorite themes, which she treated in a manner that is both delicate and warm.

Lillian Bowes Lyon

Lillian Bowes Lyon produced small volumes of verse since 1934 when *The White Hare* appeared. *BrightFeather Fading* Feather Fading (1936), *Morning is a Revealing* (1941), *Evening in Stepney* (1943), *A Rough Walk Home* (1946), and *Collected Poems* (1948) with an introductory note by C. Day Lewis represent her bid for recognition, which up to the present has not been wide. Although she employed irregular measures and free association of images through emotional rather than logical sequence, especially in her later verse, she can scarcely be called an experimentalist since her aims and methods are those with which the reader of contemporary poetry has been long familiar. In her early verse, particularly in the poem which provides the title for the volume *The White Hare,* in both imagery and the use of the short line she suggests Ralph Hodgson. Her most satisfactory work is concerned with what she sees in nature in her region, Northumbria. Here her images are clear and never falter. "The White Hare," although somewhat heavy with adjective, is memorable for the vividness and poignancy with which the theme is developed. In the later pieces such as "Evening in Stepney" and "A Rough Walk Home," in which nature and its metaphors are only incidental to the illumination of emotion in the abstract, Miss Bowes Lyon is not altogether articulate. That some of her latest work, according to C. Day Lewis, "was written under circumstances which would have silenced most poets" may provide a clue to the emotional urge which sought expression in these poems, and a perspective for critical judgment as well.

THE GEORGIANS

During the first two decades of the new century the tendencies which were at odds with Victorianism continued to flourish, but with increasing discipline and restraint. The excesses of the aesthetic school and the more graphic realism of the early Masefield began to show signs of moderation. Extremes in literary reactions are generally most prevalent at the start, and as the first decade of the century passed into the second, English poetry began to strike a balance which led a few of the critics to believe that a golden age in poetry was in the making. In 1912, Edward Marsh brought out his first anthology of *Georgian Poetry* in the Introduction of which he stated: "This volume is issued in the belief that English poetry is now once again putting on new strength and beauty . . . we are at the beginning of another 'Georgian period' which may take rank with the several great poetic ages of the past . . ." The appearance of Marsh's anthology, almost concurrent with the accession of George V, led the reviewers to label those who had contributed to its contents Georgian poets. Additional volumes of *Georgian Poetry* were compiled by Marsh and issued from Harold Monro's Poetry Bookshop in 1915 and 1917; and in 1919 and 1922 two more volumes appeared but without Monro's support and favor. The miscellany *Neo-Georgian Poetry:* 1936-1937 (1937) edited by John Gawsworth was only in small part a revival or continuation of the series compiled by Marsh.

To try to list the tendencies which appeared in this series of anthologies is like trying to catalogue the characteristics of a whole generation of poets. The Georgian poets had no pole-star or directing hand: poems by such widely different and highly individual authors as James Elroy Flecker, Walter de la Mare, Lascelles Abercrombie, Gordon Bottomley, John Drinkwater and John Collings Squire were included; and even John Masefield was represented despite the fact that bold realism was high on the *index prohibitorum* of the editor. Although the Georgian poets were all at least presumably devoted to common aims, the results were so heterogeneous when the poets' works at large are considered that one wonders at the editor's ability to select poems from the varied group which would best fit into his definition of Georgian verse. In his efforts, he was not entirely successful, for certainly much which was included only bears out more strongly the fact that poets do not travel in groups, singing their songs according to group standards.

There were, however, several objectives which the Georgian poets had in common and which at least at the start were recognizable. First, there was an unmistakable concern with form. The unevenness of the experimentalists, and the apparent formlessness of the early modernists were deplored as being alien to the poet's craft. Discipline and restraint in diction and imagery were primary requisites, even to the extent of the avoidance of symbolism. Although the lines were to be faithful to observation, especially of nature, realism was suspect, particularly as it applied to the sordid or ugly. In the postwar collections there was a deliberate effort to avoid the issues of the here-and-now, to forget the war and its aftermath, and to return to nature. Were it not for the well-calculated avoidance of the didactic, the poetry in the Georgian anthologies would seem to indicate an attempt to revive the Wordsworthian tradition. In the light of the passage of time and what the individual poets who were identified with the Georgian anthologies did in their more mature work, the term Georgian as it applies to a well-unified group or movement is woven of very thin fabric; but the fact remains that during the early decades of the century there were forces at work in poetry to curb the excesses of the reactionaries and to explore more fully the province of the great tradition.

Walter de la Mare

Identified with the Georgians chiefly on account of the appearance of some of his verse in Marsh's anthologies, but independent of any group or movement, and borrowing little from his predecessors or contemporaries, Walter de la Mare had written some of the finest poetry in recent literature. "If there were such a thing as 'pure poetry,'" said Charles Williams, "Mr. de la Mare would seem to be our greatest poet." He had written some thirty-odd volumes, many of which are in prose, including fiction and criticism; and although his work in prose had much merit, it is in poetry that he had done his greatest and most distinctive work.

Walter John de la Mare was born at Charlton in Kent in 1873 of Huguenot, Scotch, and English ancestry. He was educated at St. Paul's Cathedral Choir School in London, after which he was employed in the English branch of the Standard Oil Company for eighteen years. Such employment evidently hampered his essential interests very little, for as early as 1901 he was writing poetry and miscellaneous prose, and after 1908 he had literature as his profession. In *Songs of Childhood* (1902), his first volume, he used the *nom-de-plume* "Walter Ramal," an anagram of part of his name; but in 1904 with the appearance of his novel *Henry Brocken*, he began to use his own name. In 1910 he won the Edmond de Polignac prize with his poem *"The Return,"* and his reputation as a poet was assured with the publication of *"The Listeners"* (1912). A sizable two-volume edition of his collected verse was issued in 1928, to which a third volume was added in 1934. His later work was more largely in prose, which falls into two main categories: the fiction, of which *The Memoirs of a Midget* (1921) attained a very wide circulation; and the criticism, of which his *Lewis Carroll* (1932) and his expanded essay *Poetry in Prose* (1935) are representative. In his poetry there are three somewhat varied tendencies which may be labelled the verse about and for children, the versified characterizations from Shakespeare, and the shadow poetry. When one considers the poems about and for children, one must recognize that these pieces, for all their apparent jingle and trifling, are always poetic. It has been said that "De la Mare is the singer of a young and romantic world, understanding and perceiving as a child." Such poems as "The Mocking Fairy" and "The Song of Finis" in *Peacock Pie* (1913) have a beauty which removes them completely from nonsense jingles. It is true that some of Lewis Carroll's influence is apparent in such lines as "The Fairy nimbling mambling in the garden," but most of de la Mare's comings have captured in their combinations of vowels and consonants sounds which have a lyric rather than a ludicrous tone. In the small and difficult province of child vision and expression, the poet in a seemingly artless way has captured scenes of delicacy and beauty, and a song quality which often suggests the far-away voices of children.

In the "Characters From Shakespeare" group, there are interest and merit, especially to the reader who is familiar with Shakespeare's gallery. There are lines such as those at the end of the "Hamlet" which seize upon the very essence of the character and give it a new vitality. The "Mercutio" is exceptionally well turned; in fact, none of them is without discernment and grace of portrayal. As a group, however, they are not representative of de la Mare's most distinctive talent, and in spite of their appeal to those who enjoy association with the characters from Shakespeare's plays, they cannot take a place as poetry with many of his more purely subjective and lyrical pieces.

It is in the poems which deal with the world of shadows and half-lights that de la Mare rose to supreme heights. There is magic which suggests at times the chilly pale blue light of Coleridge *"Christabel,"* but the parallel cannot be sustained for long. It is not a world of brightness and cheer into which one is cast, nor is it a land of bleakness and despair. Of excitement and passion there is nothing; the emotions and senses are lulled rather than stimulated, for the roses are always fading and the musk has long been blown. But there are roses, and there are birds and children, although their voices are sleepy and far away. The poet is not lamenting the impermanence of beauty; rather he is feeling the passage of twilight into night, and the mood is one of soul drowsiness. In that strange stage between sleep and consciousness, there is a meeting place where past and present, unreality and reality join for a time. It is only natural while lingering in such a sphere that the poet should create something of the ominous and sinister, and although these qualities appear, they are never terrifying. Under his witchery the sinister in the fading light takes on a rare beauty; and in spite of the chill of approaching night, in de la Mare's shadows there is nothing oppressive. Poems such as "Shadow," "The Dark Chateau," "The Dwelling Place," "The Empty House," and "The Listeners" are fine examples of an expression of a world of shadow. "The Listeners" is sheer magic which leaves the reader subdued long after the poem has been put aside.

Walter de la Mare's poetry is that of mood, and as a result his range cannot include a wide variety of themes in which stylistic virtuosity is a primary concern. As with every great poet, however, it is the style as well as the theme which gives his work permanence; and de la Mare's manner has in it the qualities which are ideally suited to his moods. To make articulate a mood such as that in "The Listeners" is the result of nothing short of genius. He did not hesitate to employ extra syllables for some of his lines, and he used rime only when it suited his purpose. Never diffuse, his word usage, even when he employed the unusual and archaic, is rich with suggestion. Although his poetry as a whole varies in texture, it is of a consistently high level; and in the poems which deal with shadows around old houses he captured moods in a fashion which is truly great.

Verse: *Songs of Childhood* (1902), *Poems* (1906), *The Listeners and Other Poems* (1912), *A Child's Day: A Book of Rhymes* (1912), *Peacock Pie: A Book of Rhymes* (1913), *The Sunken Garden and Other Poems* (1918), *Motley and Other Poems* (1918), *Poems: 1901 to 1918* (1920), *Story and Rhyme* (1921), *The Veil and Other Poems* (1922),

Down-adown-Derry: A Book of Fairy Poems (1922), *Ding Dong Bell* (1924), *prose and verse, Selected Poems* (1927), *Stuff and Nonsense* (1927), *The Captive and Other Poems* (1928), *Poems for Children* (1930), *Old Rhymes and New* (2 v., 1932), *The Fleeting and Other Poems* (1933), *Poems: 1919 to 1934* (1936), *Memory and Other Poems* (1938), *Bells and Grass* (1941), *poems for children, Collected Poems* (1941), *Inward Companion: Poems* (1951).

Prose: *Henry Brocken, His Travels and Adventures in the Rich, Strange, Scarce-imaginable Regions of Romance* (1904), *The Return* (1910), *Memoirs of a Midget* (1921), *At First Sight: a Novel* (1928); *the critical studies Some Thoughts on Reading* (1923), *Desert Islands and Robinson Crusoe* (1930), *and Lewis Carroll* (1932); *and the tales in The Scarecrow and Other Stories* (1945).

Lascelles Abercrombie

Acquainted with most of the writers included in *Georgian Poetry* and himself an occasional contributor, Lascelles Abercrombie (1881-1939) cannot be strictly identified with any group, movement, or tradition; and although he has been called a latter-day Robert Browning, the resemblances are superficial. At times he is as formless as the most ingenious of the modernists, but his themes and the objectives controlling them are largely those of the traditionalist. His most frequently employed medium is a form of verse-drama which by reason of its compression of manner and complexity of thought is better adapted to rereading in the library than to stage presentation.

Born at Ashton-upon-Mersey in 1881 in an atmosphere congenial to theological and literary interests, Abercrombie was educated at Malcolm College and Manchester University. In his twenties, while reviewing for the *Liverpool Courier*, he issued his first volume of poems, *Interludes and Poems* (1908) which was commended by Alice Meynell and Thomas Hardy. By 1910 he made his home at "The Gallows," Ryton, Gloucestershire, where he busied himself by supplying reviews to four of the leading periodicals and by writing verse. Rejected for service in the First World War on account of deficient sight, he became an inspector in a shell factory in Liverpool where he worked twelve hours a day. After the War he was given a Lectureship in Poetry at Liverpool University in which he acquitted himself with such distinction that he was soon sought by other institutions. From Liverpool he went to the University of Leeds, then to London University, and finally to Oxford; and he also lectured at Queen's University, Belfast, the Sorbonne, and Harvard. In spite of the obstacles to creative work after his round of lectureships started, he continued to write poetry until shortly before his death in 1939.

Abercrombie's most characteristic province is narrative verse in which dramatic dialogue and often monologue play a large part. The themes are strikingly varied and unusual. It is true as Herbert Palmer observed that "he takes pleasure in out-of-the-way subjects—especially the weird, the mystical, the horrific, the macabre . . . Witchcraft, the end of the world, a legend concerning St. Thomas, the death vision of a friar, Judith's murder of Holofernes . . . are among the strange themes which he treats at length and from an individual angle." Although the narrative thread is always there, Abercrombie's chief interest is not in the story he has to tell but rather in the speculations which the situation provokes and the emotional intensity of the theme. In these poems lines are given to the characters which are often out of keeping with their background and attainments, but this lack of realistic treatment is outweighed by the rich poetry in many of the passages.

Emblems of Love (1912), his most ambitious and complex nondramatic poem requires intent application if the meaning of the whole or many of the parts is to be grasped, nor can its theme be reduced to a brief statement without losing the real essence of the poem. Occasionally, as for example in the passage called "Woman's Beauty" from the Vashti section, the reader is led to believe that something of Coventry Patmore's *The Unknown Eros* is about to emerge; but the woman's beauty of which Abercrombie writes is not only the meeting place between God and man, but "the flame within the lantern" by which man recognizes the manifold facets of beauty. The emblems include virtually all forms and stages of love, and their manifestations are approached through history, mythology, and the real and the symbolical. Although the poem represents Abercrombie's loftiest objective, he will probably be read more for his dramatic narratives of which "The Death of a Friar," "The Sale of St. Thomas," and "The New God" reveal a poet of exceptional talent.

Verse: *Interludes and Poems* (1908), *The Sale of St. Thomas* (1911, expanded 1930), *Emblems of Love* (1912), *Deborah* (1912), *FourShort Plays Short Plays* (1922), *Phoenix* (1923), *Twelve Idyls* (1928), *Complete Poems* (1930).

Prose: *Thomas Hardy, a Critical Study* (1912), *The Theory of Poetry* (1924), *The Idea of Great Poetry* (1925).

James Elroy Flecker

It was James Elroy Flecker (1884- 1915), often named as one of the central figures in the Georgian group, who gave expression to one of the more striking dicta of the authors represented in Marsh *Georgian Anthology*: "The poet's business," he said, "is not to save the soul of man, but to make it worth saving." Realism, especially that which was used to illuminate the ugly aspects of modern life, he deplored; his poetry almost all deals with themes remote from the here-and-now, and it generally suggests a primary concern with form. But the complete Flecker eludes neat labeling, in spite of the fact that in his preface to *The Golden Journey to Samarkand* (1913) he called himself a Parnassian. It is true that he shared the Parnassian interest in technique, but there are many sides to Flecker's work—some of them great.

James Elroy Flecker was born at Lewisham in 1884, the son of the Headmaster of Dean Close School. As a youth he was an avid reader and showed talent in writing; and at Trinity College, Oxford, from which he took his degree in 1906, he wrote a considerable amount of verse. For a year after his graduation from Oxford he taught school at Hampstead, but his eagerness for life and variety led him to enter the diplomatic service. He studied Arabic at Cambridge University, and by 1910 he was sent to Constantinople as viceconsul, later to be transferred to Beirut, where he remained until 1913. He married a Greek woman whom he called Hellé and who was an engaging companion and a source of help and inspiration to him. Advanced tuberculosis caused him to leave his post in Syria for Davos, Switzerland, where after two years he died at the age of thirty-one. His friends found him a man unusually gifted, a good scholar competent in the classical languages and Levantine tongues and lore, and a brilliant talker. During the decade following his death, his work was widely read and commended, and in spite of a perceptible falling off of interest in recent years, his poetry has in it characteristics of permanence.

In his brief though full life, Flecker wrote a remarkably large amount of prose including the well-received novel *The King of Alsander* (1914), a brightly colored romantic drama, *Hassan: The Story of Hassan of Bagdad* published after his death in 1922, and the less colored *Don Juan* (1925); and seven volumes of verse of which *The Golden Journey to Samarkand* (1913) and *The Old Ships* (1915) are representative. J. C. Squire's edition of Flecker *Collected Poems* (1916), although not inclusive, is an excellent collection of the finest and most distinctive verse. In these poems there is generally an admirable fusion of romantic theme and classical discipline. "The Old Ships" is well-nigh consummate in attaining its rich effect with simple diction and verse scheme. There is something of the sensuousness of Keats in this poem, as in others such as "Gates of Damascus." A more tranquil but equally poetic side of Flecker is to be found in "To a Poet a Thousand Years Hence." Here the simplicity and precision that the poet so much admired but not always attained are in evidence. Although some of the judgments of his poetry which appeared in the years immediately following his death were overenthusiastic, there is small doubt that with Flecker's death there was removed from English poetry one of its greater spirits.

Verse: *The Bridge of Fire* (1907), *Forty-two Poems* (1911), *The Golden Journey to Samarkand* (1913), *The Burial in England* (1915), *The Old Ships* (1915), *Collected Poems* (1916), *Complete Poems* (1923).

Plays: *Hassan: The Story of Hassan of Bagdad* (1922), *Don Juan* (1925).

Prose: *The Last Generation: A Story of the Future* (1908), *The King of Alsander* (1914), *Collected Prose* (1920), *Letters of J. E. Flecker to Frank Savory* (1926).

John Drinkwater

Although John Drinkwater (1882- 1937) is probably better known in America for his plays *Abraham Lincoln* (1919) and *Robert E. Lee* (1923), he was one of the mainstays in Edward Marsh's *Georgian Poetry*. In fact, he has often been referred to as the typical Georgian pastoral poet, with all the connotations, good and bad, that the label conveys. To identify him with a few biographical plays and a series of pastoral poems, however, is by no means an indication of the volume and variety of his work. Drinkwater was one of the most prolific and versatile of the recent men of letters: playwright, biographer, anthologist, critic, journalist, and verse-writer were some of his roles. In only a few instances did his work attain true distinction, but on the other hand, there is little in his vast output which can be called really bad.

John Drinkwater was born at Leytonstone, Essex, in 1882. After completing the prescribed studies at the Oxford High School, he tried many jobs before settling down with an insurance firm with which he remained for twelve years. Facility in writing and encouragement from his friends, however, led him to give up his work in insurance in order to write reviews and miscellaneous articles for a Birmingham paper. In 1907 he helped to organize the Pilgrim Players, which later became the Birmingham Repertory Theatre of which he became manager in 1913. A half-dozen plays of fair quality grew out of this association, among which the one-act *Cophetua* (1911) and the three-act *Rebellion* (1914) are representative. As early as 1903 he had written verse, some of which was collected and published under the title Poems; and by the time Marsh was selecting verse for his *Georgian Poetry*, a great many of Drinkwater's poems were available in periodicals. With a thorough apprenticeship in the theatre behind him, he wrote a long series of biographical dramas including *Mary Stuart* (1921), *Oliver Cromwell* (1921), *Robert E. Lee* (1923), and *Robert Burns* (1925). During the late twenties and early thirties he wrote a number of biographies, and continued to write verse. His two volumes of autobiography, *Inheritance* (1931) and *Discovery* (1932) are agreeable reading in their illumination of the man and his times. Drinkwater died in 1937.

As a playwright, he did his most distinctive work in the field of the biographical drama. His plays appeared at a time when biography was flourishing under an unprecedented vogue. They all make for a pleasant and fairly instructive evening, either in the theatre or the library; and in spite of the author's obvious heightening of episode for effect, the spirit if not the letter of the plays is adequately faithful to history. But even in the best of them, *Abraham Lincoln* and *Oliver Cromwell*, the playwright is more of a popularizer than a discerning interpreter of his subjects; and the lines given to the characters too often take on an inflated quality which makes the effect more theatrical than real. The biographies, including studies of *Byron* (1925), *Charles II* (1926), *Cromwell* (1927), *Pepys* (1930), and *Shakespeare* (1933), although not suffering from the overwrought lines of the plays, are without any particularly searching illumination of character, but they are well unified and informational in a general way. The poems are of wide variety of mood and manner in spite of the fact that they never forsake the conventional. The *Collected Poems* (1922) contains most of Drinkwater's verse which is worth preserving. As a pastoral poet, he represents the detachment from the issues of the present which was a part of the Georgian creed, and his verse has a conventional sort of beauty in which occasionally there is an apparent strain for rapture. He lacks the fine observation of Edmund Blunden; in fact, the inaccuracies in "Pike Pond" led some of the British critics to call him a weekend naturalist. Perhaps his finest verse is that in the series entitled *Preludes*, narrative love poems in which there are choiceness of phrase and an easy, supple rhythm. In general, however, Drinkwater's verse suffers perceptibly by its thinness of theme and its failure to rise sufficiently often to true lyric intensity.

Verse: *Poems* (1903), *The Death of Leander and Other Poems* (1906), *Poems of Men and Hours* (1911), *Poems of Love and Earth* (1912), *Preludes*, 1921- 1922 (1922), *Collected Poems* (1923), *Summer Harvest: Poems*, 1924-1933 (1933).

Plays: *Cophetua: A Play in One Act* (1911), *Rebellion* (1914), *Abraham Lincoln* (1919), *Mary Stuart* (1921), *Oliver Cromwell* (1921), *Robert E. Lee* (1923), *Robert Burns* (1925), *Laying the Devil* (1933), *A Man's House* (1934).

Biographies: *The Pilgrim of Eternity, Byron* (1925), *Mr. Charles, King of England* (1926), *Charles James Fox* (1928), *Pepys: His Life and Character* (1930), *Shakespeare* (1933).

Autobiography: *Inheritance, Being the First Book of an Autobiography* (1931), *Discovery, Being the Second Book of an Autobiography* (1932).

4
Chapter

Poetry in Late Twentieth Century

THE MODERN POETS

It was in the interval between the wars that the aims and standards of the established order in poetry were challenged by an increasing number of young writers whose literary ideals were at variance with those of the traditionalists, and especially those of the Georgians. The two world wars were not responsible for everything which has been indiscriminately attributed to them, but there is no doubt that much of the spirit of revolt in recent literature can be traced to the shifting political and social standards which appeared during the First War and its aftermath. The old avenues which for long had been accepted as the only means to the highest civilization and culture began to be regarded with mistrust, and much which had heretofore been considered the only media for expression in the arts, especially in painting and poetry, began to appear conventionalized and restricted. In both subject-matter and form, poetry sought to widen its scope by breaking away from what the practitioners of the new art considered artificial and confining.

The theories and principles of the so-called new poets had their roots in many soils, and there are scores of in stances in which some of the principles of the modernists were employed with varying degrees of conviction and skill long before the turn of the century. It has even been pointed out that the free rhythms and irregular metrical patterns of the modernists are more truly in line with the Biblical and Anglo-Saxon traditions than all of the stylized metrics of Swinburne and Tennyson. Although there are fundamental similarities between the old traditions and the manner of the modernists, the new poets are often plainly experimentalists. New media and modifications of the old have been attempted in order to try to make articulate the themes which have grown out of the marked changes of the times. Writers who were impressionable to the influence of two great wars, progressive political ideologies, the rapid strides of the machine age, and the psychological precepts of Jung and Freud sought new forms which, they felt, were more appropriate to their themes than the strictly patterned manner of the traditionalists. Although some of the changes of the past thirty years were only a natural reaction against Victorian standards, the revolt of the modernists has its chief roots in the spirit of the times.

Groups and cults have sprung up, often ephemeral and without organization, which have been at cross purposes not only with the traditionalists but with one another as well, which bear on their standards such names as imagists, futurists, dadaists, surrealists, and apocalyptics. Among them there have been the leftists and the rightists, the Marxists and the conservative laborites. Concise differentiation among the various groups is impossible, for there has been an exasperating overlapping in the aims and works of most of the exponents of these schools. There are some who hold to familiar stanzaic patterns and regularity of line but who avoid conventional poetic themes and diction. Others retain poetic themes and diction but insist on complete freedom in matters compositional, including design of line, logical sequence, and even syntax. And there are instances in which a poet has started out zealously in one camp and ended up in another, or even back with the traditionalists.

In a general sense, however, modernist poetry has shown the characteristics indicated by Selden Rodman in *A New Anthology of Modern Poetry.*

imagery patterned on everyday speech. absence of inversions, stilted apostrophes, conventional end-rhymes, "poetic" language generally, except where used deliber-ately for incantatory effect.

freedom from the ordinary logic of sequence, jumping from oneimage tr the next by association rather than by the usual cause-effect method.

emphasis on the ordinary, in reaction against the traditional poetic emphasis on the cosmic.

concern with the naked consciousness and the newly identified "unconscious" as against the "soul."

concern with the common man, almost to the exclusion of the "hero" or the extraordinary man.

concern with the social order as against "heaven" and "nature"

Although concern with the social order, especially that which derived from Russian communism, has declined sharply with the increasing concern with man as an individual who must work out his destiny independent of social agencies, most of the modernists continue to view skeptically the old pathways of nature and religion in which the traditionalists have found guidance and inspiration.

A notable exception in this respect is T. S. Eliot (1888) who as early as 1928 stated that he was "an AngloCatholic in religion, a classicist in literature, and a royalist in politics." The skeptical and cynical Eliot of "The Hippopotanius" has indicated after his sojourn in the wasteland a profound desire for the emotional and spiritual security of religion in the *Quartets* (1943). The emptiness which he had outlined so insistently in *The Waste Land* (1922) was a near approach to nihilism; and with a temperament and background such as his it was almost inevitable that he should try to find something in traditional religion as a way to spiritual calm.

Thomas Stearns Eliot was born in St. Louis, Missouri, in 1888. His paternal grandfather, after graduating from Harvard College, established the first Unitarian Church in St. Louis, and was Chancellor of Washington University, which he had helped to found. Eliot's father was a successful businessman with some reputation as a bookman. After preparing for college at the local schools, Eliot entered Harvard in 1906, there to earn both his bachelor's and master's degrees. While at Harvard he wrote poetry, some of which appeared in the *Harvard Advocate,* of which he was the editor. His interest in languages and literature led him to continue his education at the Sorbonne, where he amassed much of his store of information about French literature. Upon his return to America he resumed his work at Harvard and for a time was an assistant in the department of philosophy. After being awarded a traveling scholarship, he went to Europe again, to study in Germany for a time before settling down at Merton College, Oxford. During the First World War he taught school near London for a year before becoming associated with Lloyds Bank. Before the end of the war, however, he gave up his work with the banking firm to become assistant editor of *The Egoist.* After 1920, he devoted his time exclusively to editing periodicals, including *The Criterion,* lecturing on literature, and writing critical essays and poetry. Although he spent considerable time in his native America, he adopted England as his home. He married an Englishwoman, Miss Vivienne Haigh, in 1915, became a member of the Anglican Church, and in 1927 became a subject of the Crown. He had the Order of Merit conferred on him, and in 1948, he won the Nobel Prize for poetry.

As early as 1917, Eliot impressed a small audience with a sample of his extraordinary talent in " *The Love Song* of J. Alfred Prufrock." In the development of the theme of a sensitive man's sense of futility in the stratum of society to which he belongs, there is nothing of the usual logic of sequence; and the images, many of which are susceptible to different levels of interpretation, are thrust into the irregular lines with little by way of transition. The poet's remarkable talent for attaining effects with words and images of totally different pitch appears at times in "Prufrock," but its poetic force is more fully realized in the well-unified "Portrait of a Lady," and in the shorter poems such as "Sweeney among the Nightingales"—a title in itself rich in suggestion of the sharp contrasts which may be expected. *The Waste Land* (1922), if not "a center for the poetic achievement of the first quarter of the present century," created more discussion and exercized a wider influence than any recent literary work. The five parts are related rather than connected by the prevailing mood suggested in the title. The spiritual and moral emptiness of the present generation and of the trend of civilization is the background out of which the theme emerged. Miss Jessie L. Weston *From Ritual to Romance* provided a key to the plan of the poem, but many of the passages depend for satisfactory explication on a familiarity with a wide field of culturehistory including mythology, Oriental literature and religion, Dante *Divine Comedy*, and Frazer *The GoldenBough.*

Eliot's negative approach in *The Waste Land* began to give way to a somewhat more positive attitude in the socalled "Ariel Poems," but it was not until "Ash Wednesday" (1930) appeared that he indicated a path away from desolation in what in his Essay on Dante he called "a coherent traditional system of dogma and morals." The positive assertion emerges only after a long conflict in which the poet prays that he can forget:

These matters that with myself I too much discuss
Too much explain . . .

The four long poems which make up *Quartets* (1943) are in a sense a continuation of the assertion, although these poems have much in them which is not directly concerned with the necessity for an abiding religion. "The Dry Salvages" and "Little Gidding" are not so full of arresting and ingeniously contrived images as the early poems, nor are the contrasts in association and tonal quality so pronounced. They have some of the subdued and flowing tone of meditative poetry in which at times a mystical element is part of the mood. In fact, it has been aptly observed that "the poet who was regarded as the spokesman of a disillusioned generation has become the poet of Christian mysticism."

The plays *The Rock* (1934), *Murder in the Cathedral* (1935), *The Family Reunion* (1939), and *The Cocktail Party* (1949) have themes and characters which lend themselves to dramatic rendering, but Eliot's dramaturgy, like his versification, is not confined to the more conventional patterns. Although his people attain an adequate reality, they are essentially symbolic: Becket, for example, in *Mur-der in the Cathedral* der in the Cathedral is memorable more as a symbol of conflict than as a biographical portrait. These plays have been successfully produced, but their real power is not in dramatic situation, suspense, and climax, but in the frequently recurrent poetry of the lines.

Eliot's critical essays are erudite and provocative. In For *Lancelot Andrewes* (1929), *Selected Essays,* 1917-1932 (1932), *Essays Ancient and Modern* (1936), and *Notes Toward the Definition of Culture* (1948), there is an indication that some sort of system of aesthetics is evolving, although there is no clearly defined pattern. His familiarity with many literatures, even the more obscure phases of them, is plain in the wide variety of his subjects and in his occasional comparative approach. He was at constant pains to define his terms in order to clarify his judgments, most of which were provocative and searching. His forthrightness in modifying some of the statements in his earlier essays in later works supported rather than impaired his reputation as a discerning critic. Among his finest achievements are his essays *"The Metaphysical Poets"* (1921), *"Religion and Literature"* (1935), and especially *"Dante"* (1929), all of which appeared in the new edition of *Selected Essays* (1950). His precepts are widely discussed and quoted, and many of the essays posses a stylistic merit which makes his criticism in itself a form of creation.

Verse: *Prufrock and Other Observations* (1917), *Poems* (1919), *Ara Vos Prec* (1950), *The Waste Land* (1922), *Poems, 1909-1925* (1925). *Journey of the Magi* (1927), *A Song for Simeon* (1928), *Animula* (1929), *Ash Wednesday* (1930), *Marina* (1930), *Triumphal March* (1931), *Sweeney Agonistes: Fragments of an Aristophanic Melodrama* (1932), *Collected Poems:* 1909-1935 (1936), *Old Possum's Book of Practical Cats* (1939), *Four Quartets* (1943), *includes "Burnt Nortoa," "East Coker," "The Dry Salvages," and "Little Gidding."*

Plays: *The Rock: A Pageant Play* (1934), *Murder in the Cathedral* (1935), *The Family Reunion* (1939), *The Cocktail Party, produced in Edinburgh* (1949).

Prose: *The Sacred Wood* (1990), *Homage to John Dryden* (1924), *For Lancelot Andrewes: Essays on Style and Order* (1928), *Selected Essays,* 1917-1932 (1932), *The Use of Poetry and the Use of Criticism* (1933), *After Strange Gods: A Primer of Modern Heresy* (1934), *Elizabethan Essays* (1934), *Essays Ancient and Modern* (1936), *Points of View* (1941), *Notes Toward the Definition of Culture* (1948), *Selected Essays* (1950), *Poetry and Drama* (1951).

The Sitwells

In spite of the small grain of truth in F. R. Leavis comment that "the Sitwells belong more to the history of publicity than to the history of poetry," Edith, Osbert, and Sacheverell Sitwell are interesting figures in literature. They were the talented offspring of Sir George Sitwell who traced his ancestry back to the Angevin kings, and who felt that strict conventionality was the proper environment for his family. He was the sort of Englishman who "would appear for dinner even in a sordid wayside *trattoria* dressed in white tie and tails." To his daughter Edith he once remarked that the best kind of Englishwoman was one who should be bad at nothing and good at nothing. The young Sitwells obviously found much in the old order, which was stifling, and once started on their career of rejection of the old, they gloried in their new freedom.

Of the three, Edith Sitwell is best known and the most prolific poet. As a child she startled her parents by the pronouncement that she wanted to be a genius. She wrote verse in her teens, but it was not until she made her residence in London and began to edit the progressive periodical-anthology *Wheels* in 1916 that her talent took shape. *The Mother and Other Poems* (1915) failed to attract much notice; it was with *Clowns' Houses* (1918) and *The Wooden Pegasus* (1920) that she attracted an increasingly wide and curious audience; and by the time *Façade* (1922) was presented at the Aeolian Hall in London, "Sitwellism" became a part of the vocabulary of the literati. Four small volumes appeared between 1922, and *Gold Coast Customs* (1929), to be followed by an interval in which she devoted her time to prose studies of which *Alexander Pope* (1930) and *The English Eccentric's* (1933) are representative. She returned to verse during and after the Second War to produce some of her best work.

There are essentially two Edith Sitwells, the early and the late. In her early work there is a considerable amount of toying with verse patterns and tonal effects, and what seems at least on the surface to be nonsense verse. It is unfortunate that the virtuosity of the poet blinds some readers to the fact that in the earlier pieces including *Façade* she is doing little more than playing with tonal patterns and ingenious imagery. It is scarcely possible that Miss Sitwell had anything important to say in such dexterously turned pieces as "Hornpipe" and "Fox Trot." She said that she disliked simplicity, but such a statement should not mislead anyone into the notion that her word playing is always the medium for portents and profound readings of life. Although she herself had given support to the conclusion that *Gold Coast Customs*, written as early as 1929, was a definite prophecy of the imminence of the Second World War, the verses which appeared in the collection are more noteworthy for their rhythms than for any clear demonstration of prescience. Among the earlier volumes, however, there are poems which are not always exercises in verbal and tonal virtuosity, for there is much in *The Sleeping Beauty* (1924) and *Troy Park*

(1925) which shows emotional depth. In the latter collection, *"Colonel Fantock,"* with its nostalgic note and the implication that the times are out of joint, maintains a high poetic level. Of the shorter poems, *"The King of China's Daughter"* and *"Panope"* have more genuine feeling and authentic poetic phrase than the much-anthologized *"Aubade."* As an example of shifting of sense-impressions *"Aubade"* has interest, for "light creaks," "flowers cluck," and the light which "creaks" also "whines." In another verse-exercise, *"Trio for Two Cats and a Trombone,"* 'light is braying like an ass."

In her later work, although she has not forsaken artifice entirely, she is less the virtuoso and more the poet. She herself has observed that by the forties, her "time of experiments was done. " *The Song of the Cold* (1945), *Green Song* (1946) and *The Shadow of Cain* (1947) show a perceptible deepening of feeling, which can be traced probably to her consciousness of the tragedy of war. The awfulness of the atomic bomb, and the penalty man is paying for his unwillingness to try to cultivate what is good in his own nature and nature at large, have become themes to which she responds with profound feeling. The title-poem of her collection, *The Canticle of the Rose* (1949) reaffirmed her belief in the existence of elements of good in man if he would recognize them and follow them. There is a softening of tone in these poems, with a frequent use of a long line, which eliminates the abrupt, staccato effects in much of her early verse. The symbols, although arresting, are more plainly integrated in the fabric of the theme, and their recurrent use in different contexts is limited to recognizable poetic ends. Without losing her deftness in the manipulation of images and tones, Miss Sitwell demonstrated in her later work far more than the sheen of virtuosity.

Osbert Sitwell was born in London with the advantages that belong to an aristocratic heritage. He was educated by private tutors until he entered Eton. In one of his volumes of memoirs, *The Scarlet Tree,* he reported that he liked Eton, except for the work and the games, and for the boys and the masters. During the First World War he saw service in France as an officer in the Grenadier Guards, out of which he emerged with some of Sassoon's bitterness toward war and its instigators. Such pieces as *"Babel"* and *"Tears,"* written out of his wartime experience, are as forceful as anything he has done in verse. Although marked for a public career, since his late twenties he has devoted his chief time to writing. He contributed verse to *Wheels,* and later issued small volumes of poems under the titles *Argonaut and Juggernaut* (1920) and *Out of the Flame* (1923). The prevailing tone of the verse in these collections is satiric. Although his manner showed many of the characteristics of the modernists, in his verse he was never particularly concerned with form. He is generally more compressed and comprehensible than his sister; in fact, by comparison, his verse makes for easy reading. His later work has been done chiefly in prose, in which he works with considerable felicity. The four volumes of memoirs—*Left Hand, Right Hand* (1944), *The Scarlet Tree* (1946), *Great Morning!* (1947), and *Laughter in the Next Room* (1948)— are engaging illuminations of his heritage and the environment in which he was reared. Sir George Sitwell, the father of the triumvirate, for all of the satirical thrusts of the author, emerges, if not the hero of the memoirs, a very personable and likeable figure. Besides being a persuasive account of the Sitwells, these memoirs are a well-mellowed record of Edwardian England.

Sacheverell Sitwell , the youngest of the trio, and the Peregrine of *Colonel Fantock,* showed a striking versatility in interests and talents. Like Osbert, he was sent to Eton, and later he attended Balliol College, Oxford. After the First World War in which he served as an officer in the Grenadier Guards, he submitted verse to the literary *Wheels* on which his sister and others of the new schools were riding. The verse in *The People's Palace* (1918), *The One Hundred and One Harlequins* (1922), and *The Thirteenth Caesar* (1924) seems plainly experimental. There is a conscious and at times clever use of image and tonal effect in which dissonance is frequent, but there is no real depth of theme, nor are there any really memorable lines. *"Doctor Donne and Gargantua,"* which the reader is led to believe is to be a poem of serious intent has some of the design of a great poem, but the final result is fragmentary and disappointing. The poems in *The Cyder Feast* (1927), although without loftiness of purpose or design, present their themes more simply and directly. His later work had been done largely in prose in which he employed a lucid and engaging style in treating a wide variety of subjects in the arts, especially architecture and music.

Edith Sitwell: Verse: *Clowns' Houses* (1918), *The Wooden Pegasus* (1920), *Façade* (1922), *The Sleeping Beauty* (1924), *Troy Park* (1925), *Rustic Elegies* (1927), *Gold Coast Customs* (1929), *Collected Poems* (1930), *Poems Old and New* (1940), *Street Songs* (1943), *The Song of the Cold* (1945), *Green Song* (1946), *The Shadow of Cain* (1947), *The Canticle of the Rose: Poems* 19171949 (1949).

Prose: *Poetry and Criticism* (1925), *Alexander Pope* (1930), *Bath* (1952), *The English Eccentrics* (1933), *Aspects of Poetry* (1934), *Victoria of England* (1936), *Trio: Dissertations on Some Aspects of National Genius, with Osbert and Sacheverell* (1938), *I Live Under a Black Sun, A Novel* (1938), *A Poet's Notebook* (1944), *Fanfare for Elizabeth* (1946).

Sir Osbert Sitwell: Verse: *Argonaut and Juggernaut* (1919), *Out of the Flame* (1923), *England Reclaimed* (1927), *Collected Poems and Satires* (1931), *Penny Foolish* (1935). Prose: *Before the Bombardment* (1926), *The Man Who Lost Himself* (1929), *Miracle on Sinai* (1933), *Left Hand, Right Hand* (1944), *The Scarlet Tree* (1946), *Great Morning!* (1947), *Laughter in the Next Room* (1948), *Noble Essences* (1950).

Sacheverell Sitwell: Verse: *The People's Palace* (1918). *The One Hundred and One Harlequins* (1922), *The Thirteenth Caesar* (1924), *The Cyder Feast* (1927), *Doctor Donne and Gargantua* (1930), *Collected Poems* (1936),

Selected Poems (1948). Prose: *Southern Baroque Art* (1924), *German Baroque Art* (1927), *The Gothick North* (1929), *Spanish Baroque Art* (1931), *Mozart* (1932), *Liszt* (1934), *The Hunters and the Hunted* (1947), *Morning Noon and Night in London* (1947).

Harold Edward Monro

Harold Monro was a modernist more in theory than in practice. As the editor of *Poetry* and *Drama,* he tried to make plain to his readers that he and his contributors were striking out into new and unexplored fields of poetic expression, but by far the larger part of his verse has an easily recognized attachment to the established order. There are elements in his verse which are definitely modernistic, to be sure, especially in such poems as *"London Interior"* and *"Bitter Sanctuary,"* in which the measures are irregular and the imagery and diction are drawn from everyday speech; but these elements are not frequent or pronounced in his work at large. They seem to be rather well-deliberated devices which are employed to give his verse additional latitude, and to demonstrate the author's feeling of necessity for escape from the conventional manner. Certainly *"Everything," "The Earth for Sale,"* and *"Midnight Lamentation,"* among many others, belong essentially to the main current of English poetry. A careful reading of his prose criticism and his verse would seem to indicate that he was convinced of some of the principles of the modernists, but that he was unable to cut completely free from the traditionalists.

Harold Edward Monro was born in Brussels, Belgium, the son of a well-to-do civil engineer of Scotch descent. The boy was schooled in England, chiefly at Radley, before matriculating at Caius College, Cambridge, where he received his degree in 1901. While at Cambridge he was known as an assiduous poetry reader and a dilettante in the arts. After his graduation, he studied law for a short time before becoming engaged in a variety of occupations which included selling real estate and operating a poultry farm. Such occupations were evidently not to his liking, for his interests had long been literary, and finally he turned to literature as a profession. He was later to describe himself as an "author, publisher, editor, and book-seller," in all of which roles he became well known in London. As early as 1908, he had issued a small sheaf of verse entitled *Judas*. The Samurai Press, his first venture in publishing, had only an ephemeral existence; and his *Poetry Review*, founded in order to consider "poetry in its relation to life," was also short-lived. But in 1912, with the founding of the Poetry Bookshop and the quarterly *Poetry and Drama*, Monro became a London institution. Many of the younger poets carried their wares to him for publication, and the room above his bookshop became a gathering place for the more progressive of the literati where verse was read and judged. The First World War interrupted Monro's efforts, but upon his return, after serving in the War Office and as an officer in the antiaircraft corps, he reopened the Bookshop and launched a new periodical, *The Chapbook*, in which much of the spirit of *Poetry and Drama* was preserved. In 1920, he married Alida Klemantaski, herself a poet, who assisted him as both bookseller and editor. The same year he issued his concise and at times oversevere critical analysis of some of his contemporaries under the title *Some Contemporary Poets*, and in 1929 he brought out *Twentieth Century Poetry*, an anthology in which his tastes are clearly indicated. From 1908 until 1928, he wrote verse, much of which appeared in his periodicals and in chapbooks. His death in 1932 left a void for many of the younger poets who had found him and his Bookshop a source of encouragement and inspiration.

Although Monro has been called "a drab poet," and a "poet by intention" rather than "a singer by intuition," there is a considerable body of his verse in which he has handled worth-while and unusual poetic themes in a skilful and beautiful way. Furthermore, the song quality which in his defense of the modernists he insisted was unnecessary appears again and again in his verse. *"Solitude," " The Nightingale Near the House,"* and *"Midnight Lamentation"* are rich in melody and tonal effect. The last-named poem, for all of its artful manipulation of pronouns in the closing lines of the early stanzas, cannot be dismissed as mere rhetoric. Pieces such as "*The Dog*" have wide appeal, but they are not great poetry in either theme or manner, nor is the graphic "*Bitter Sanctuary*" of lasting quality. The poems which make up *Real Property* are uneven, some of them lacking in poetic substance; and in Part I especially, there is little that the reader wishes to retain. His finest and most characteristic theme is that which appears in many of the poems: a sort of mystic relationship between the poet and inanimate objects which he recognizes as a part of him. His feeling of association with the furnishings of his room, especially those which have served him well, becomes almost an expression of obligation. Thus a candle, the bed, an old copper basin all have "little cries," and become animated with the poet's sensitive response to their presence. In "*Everything,*" and in many of the stanzas in *Strange Meetings*, this relationship finds its choicest expression. Although definitely a minor poet, and one who profits greatly by selection, Harold Monro is nonetheless a true poet in a considerable part of his work.

Verse: *Judas* (1908), *Before Dawn* (1911), *Children of Love* (1914), *Trees* (1915), *Strange Meetings* (1917), *Real Property* (1922), *The Earth for Sale* (1928), *Collected Poems* (1933).

Prose: Some Contemporary Poets (1920).

Richard Aldington

Born in 1892 in Portsmouth, England, Richard Aldington, the son of a middle-class lawyer, grew up with an unwavering devotion to literature. After reading Keats's "Endymion" at fifteen, he spent two years absorbing major English poets and the complete canon of Elizabethan drama. A sudden decline in his family's fortune in 1911 forced Aldington to select his career path at an early age. Leaving the University of London after one year, Aldington began to actively pursue a literary career.

Getting his start as a sports reporter, Aldington soon made friends and contacts in the literary world. He wrote reviews and essays, worked on translations, and finally began selling his own poems. He soon made friends with a group of three other young poets: Ezra Pound, Hilda Doolittle, and Harold Monro, editor of the *Poetry Bookshop*. Aldington married Hilda Doolittle, or H.D. as she was known, in 1913, and in the years before World War I, they traveled to Paris and Italy and made themselves known to the larger literary world. During this period, Aldington became associated with the burgeoning "modernist" movement, largely through his association with Ezra Pound. His poetry appeared in Pound's 1914 anthology *Des Imagistes* and in Amy Lowell's annual anthology *Some Imagist Poets,* (1915, 1916, 1917). He published his first volume of poetry, *Images* (1910-1915), in 1915.

In 1916 Aldington enlisted in the British Army, saw active combat, and emerged in late 1918 with a captain's commission and severe shell-shock. Shortly after his return to London in 1919 he divorced Doolittle and by the end of the same year had left the hustle and bustle of city life for a more aesthetic lifestyle in a Berkshire village. He continued to write poetry, publishing *Images of Desire* (1919) and *Exile and Other Poems* (1923) but with a changed style expressing his negative experiences during the war.

By 1928 Aldington's writing provided him with enough income to allow him to leave England and lead a life of expatriatism, mostly in France and Italy. During the 1930s he turned his energies away from poetry and towards fiction and satire. With World War II looming at the end of the decade, Aldington found satire to be ignoble and wrote his memoirs, *Life for Life's Sake* (1941).

Aldington waited out the war in the United States, settling first in Connecticut and then in Hollywood where he wrote film scripts. In 1946 he returned to France and turned his pen to biographies, writing about his good friend D.H. Lawrence in *Portrait of a Genius, But...* (1950) and producing a blunt volume about T.E. Lawrence named *Lawrence of Arabia: A Biographical Enquiry*(1955). Both of these volumes were controversial and offended many readers and the reaction to the T.E. Lawrence book left Aldington bitter towards the English literary establishment. However, he continued to write and encourage other writers. In 1962 he visited Russia at the invitation of the Soviet Writer's Union, an invitation by which he was deeply honored. Two weeks after his return to France from Moscow, Aldington contracted an undiagnosed illness and died suddenly.

Verse: *Choricos* (1912), *Images* (1915), *Images Old and New* (1916); *The Love Poems of Myrrhine and Konallis: A Cycle of Prose Poems Written after the Greek Manner* (1917), *expanded and issued as The Love of Myrrhine and Konallis* (1926), *Reverie: A Little Book of Poems for H.D.* (1917), *Images of War* (1919), *Images of Desire* (1919), *War and Love* (1919), *Exile and Other Poems* (1923), *A Fool in the Forest: A Phantasmagoria* (1925), *Collected Poems* (1928), *Hark the Herald* (1928), *The Eaten Heart* (1929), *A Dream in the Luxembourg* (1930), *Poems* (1934), *Complete Poems* (1949).

Prose: *Death of a Hero: A Novel* (1929), *The Colonel's Daughter: A Novel* (1931), *All Men are Enemies: A Romance* (1933), *Women Must Work* (1934), *At All Costs* (1930), *Last Straws* (1930), *Two Stories: Deserter and The Lads of the Village* (1930), *A War Story* (1930), *Stepping Heavenward* (1931), *Soft Answers* (1932).

Studies: *The Poet and His Age* (1922), *Literary Studies and Reviews* (1924), *French Studies and Reviews* (1926), *Remy de Gourmont: A Modern Man of Letters* (1927), *D. H. Lawrence: An Indiscretion* (1927).

Memoirs: *Life for Life's Sake* (1941).

W. H. Auden

Auden, W. H. (Wystan Hugh Auden), 1907-73, Anglo-American poet, b. York, England, educated at Oxford. A versatile, vigorous, and technically skilled poet, Auden ranks among the major literary figures of the 20th century. Often written in everyday language, his poetry ranges in subject matter from politics to modern psychology to Christianity.

During the 1930s he was the leader of a left-wing literary group that included Christopher Isherwood and Stephen Spender. With Isherwood he wrote three verse plays, *The Dog beneath the Skin* (1935), *The Ascent of* F6 (1936), and *On the Frontier* (1938), and *Journey to a War* (1939), a record of their experiences in China. He lived in Germany during the early days of Nazism, and was a stretcher-bearer for the Republicans during the Spanish Civil War.

Auden's first volume of poetry appeared in 1930. Later volumes include *Spain* (1937), *New Year Letter* (1941), *For the Time Being a Christmas Oratorio* (1945), *The Age of Anxiety* (1947; Pulitzer Prize), *Nones* (1951), *The Shield of Achilles* (1955), *Homage to Clio* (1960), *About the House* (1965), *Epistle of a Godson and Other Poems* (1972), and *Thank You, Fog* (1974). His other works include *Letters from Iceland* (with Louis MacNeice, 1937); the libretto, with his companion Chester Kallman, for Stravinsky's opera *The Rake's Progress* (1953); *A Certain World: A Commonplace Book* (1970); and *The Dyer's Hand and Other Essays* (1968).

In 1939, Auden moved to the United States, he became a citizen in 1946, and beginning that year taught at a number of American colleges and universities. From 1956 to 1961 he was professor of poetry at Oxford. Subsequently he lived in a number of countries, including Italy and Austria, and in 1971 he returned to England. He was awarded the National Medal for Literature in 1967.

Verse: *Poems* (1930), *The Orators: An English Study* (1932), *The Dance of Death* (1933), *Poems* (1934), *Look, Stranger* (1936), *On This Island*(1937), *Spain* (1937), *Letters from Iceland, with Louis MacNeice* (1937), *Journey to a War, with Christopher Isherwood* (1939), *Another time* (1940), *Some Poems* (1940), *New Year Letter, For the Time Being* (1945), *The Age of Anxiety* (1946), *Nones* (1951).

Plays, *with Christopher Isherwood: The Dog Beneath the Skin* (1935). *Ascent of F* 6 (1936), *On the Frontier* (1938).

Stephen Harold Spender

Of the new voices which sounded during the early thirties, none showed more promise of high poetic attainment than that of Stephen Spender The reviews which followed the publication of his Poems in 1933 were generally enthusiastic: in some sources he was compared to Shelley as a rebel-lyrist. This promise has in some measure been fulfilled, although there are aspects of his craftmanship which are still somewhat removed from consummate artistry. Like many of the poets of his generation, he recognized the need for social change; but like most of them, he, too, has become disillusioned about the efficacy of the communist system as the road to man's salvation. He is still acutely sensitive to man's plight, but in the poems of his recent volumes, *Poems of Dedication* (1947) and *The Edge of Being* (1949) his approach to his themes is so highly subjective that there is little room for suggestions of means by which mankind at large can be relieved of distress.

Stephen Harold Spender was born in London in 1909, the son of Harold Spender, a journalist of considerable note. In his youth he showed a talent for painting, but he never considered it as a career. From his poems and autobiography, one can gather that his boyhood was sheltered, and that he regarded with mingled envy and fear the young rowdies who moved about his neighborhood. Even before he entered University College, Oxford, in 1927, he recognized the greatness of the poet's calling and had written verse, some of which was published as *Nine Experiments* (1928). Although sensitive and retiring, at Oxford he became familiar with some of the young poets who were in attendance, among whom Auden was the dominating figure.

Even before Oxford, he was well aware of prevalent social injustices and need for change, but it is likely that his associations at the University did much to help him crystallize the sentiment in the poem, "No man shall hunger: Man shall be man." After leaving Oxford, he travelled on the continent, chiefly in Germany where he became intimate with

Christopher Isherwood who had taken up residence in Berlin; and in 1937 he attended the International Writers' Conference in Spain where he was attentive to the preachments of André Malraux, the French antifascist author. Back in London he devoted much of his talent to writing pieces which were largely propaganda and to helping Cyril Connolly edit the progressive magazine *Horizon*. During the war, in an official capacity he helped to preserve morale on the home front. After 1945, he sojourned for a time in Germany, according to his own report "to inquire into the lives and ideas of the German intellectuals, with a particular view of discovering any surviving talent in German literature." The result was *European Witness* (1946), a series of travel essays in which a political note predominates. In the autumn of 1946 he came to the United States. He held a guest professorship at Sarah Lawrence College and lectured at many of the colleges in the east.

He was one of the preeminent English poets of the 1930s and a member of the "Oxford generation," a small group of youthful literary aesthetes whose innovative, socially committed work in that decade gave a new direction to English literature and left a lasting effect on later generations. While Spender was an undergraduate at University College, Oxford, he developed lifelong friendships with C. Day-Lewis and W.H. Auden, whose first collection of poems Spender printed in 1928. He also coedited *Oxford Poetry* (1929) with Louis MacNeice, and he lived with the novelist Christopher Isherwood for several months during a sojourn (1930-33) in Germany. *Poems* (1933), Spender's first important verse collection, was followed in quick succession by another, *Vienna* (1934); a volume of literary criticism, *The Destructive Element* (1935); and a collection of short stories, *The Burning Cactus* (1936). Although he remained a committed liberal, Spender joined the Communist Party but quickly left after becoming disenchanted with Marxism. He was coeditor (1939-41) of the literary journal *Horizon* and of *Encounter* (1953-67) until he learned of that periodical's links to the CIA. His total output included fiction, essays, plays, criticism, journals, translations, and several volumes of poetry, notably *Dolphins* (1994), which was published on his 85th birthday. He also held several academic positions, in particular as a professor of English at University College, London (1970-77, emeritus from 1977). Spender was the first non-American to serve (1965) as consultant in poetry in English to the U.S. Library of Congress. He was made Commander of the Order of the British Empire in 1962 and knighted in 1983.

Verse: *Nine Experiments* (1928), *Twenty Poems* (1930), *Poems* (1933), *Vienna* (1935), *The Still Center* (1939), *Poems of Dedication* (1947), *Returning to Vienna* (1947), *The Edge of Being* (1949).

Prose: *The Destructive Element* (1935), *Forward From Liberalism* (1937), *The New Realism* (1939), *European Witness* (1946), *World Within World* (1951), *an autobiography.*

Dylan Thomas

Dylan Thomas was born in the coastal town of Swansea, Wales. His father David, who was a writer and possessed a degree in English, brought his son up to speak English rather than Thomas's mother's native Welsh. He attended the boys-only Swansea Grammar School, (later known as Bishop Gore Grammar school, now reincarnated as Bishop Gore School), at which his father taught English Literature. It was in the school's magazine that the young Dylan saw his first poem published. Dylan Thomas's middle name, "Marlais", came from the bardic name of his uncle, the Unitarian minister, Gwilym Marles (whose real name was William Thomas). Thomas's childhood was spent largely in Swansea, with regular summer trips to visit his mother's family on their Carmarthen farm. These rural sojourns, and their contrast with the town life of Swansea, would inform much of his work, notably many short stories and radio essays and the poem "Fern Hill".

In 1937, Thomas married Caitlin Macnamara (1913-1994), and would have three children with her, throughout the relationship, littered with affairs. January of 1939 saw the birth of their first child, a boy whom they named Llewelyn (died in 2000). He was followed in March of 1943 by a daughter, Aeronwy. A second son and third child, Colm Garan, was born in July, 1949.

Thomas wrote half his poems and many short stories when he lived at 5 Cwmdonkin Drive—"And death shall have no dominion" is one of the best known works written at this address. By the time he left the family home in 1934 he was one of the most exciting young poets writing in the English language. He collapsed on November 4, 1953 at the White Horse Tavern after drinking heavily while in New York City on a promotional tour; Thomas later died at St. Vincent's hospital, aged 39.

The primary cause of his death is recorded as pneumonia, with pressure on the brain and a fatty liver given as contributing factors. His penultimate words were: "I've had 18 straight whiskeys, I think this is a record." His final words were to Liz Reitell, to whom he said "I love you, but I am alone". Following his death, his body was brought back to Wales for burial in the village churchyard at Laugharne, where he had enjoyed his happiest days. In 1994, his widow, Caitlin, was buried alongside him. Their former home, the Boat House, Laugharne, is now a memorial to Thomas.

Verse: 18 *Poems* (1934), 25 *Poems* (1936), *The Map of Love* (1939), *The World I Breathe* (1939), *New Poems* (1943), *Deaths and Entrances* (1946), *Selected Writings* (1936), *In Country Sleep* (1952).

Prose: *Portrait of the Artist as a Young Dog* (1940).

Hugh MacDiarmid

Hugh MacDiarmid was the pen name of Christopher Murray Grieve (August 11, 1892, Langholm - September 9, 1978), perhaps the most important Scottish poet of the 20th century. He was instrumental in creating a truly Scottish version of modernism and was, perhaps, the leading light in the Scottish literary Renaissance of the 20th century. Unusually for a first generation modernist, he was a communist. Unusually for a communist, he was a committed Scottish nationalist. He wrote both in English and in literary Scots (Lallans).

After leaving school in 1910, MacDiarmid worked as a journalist for five years. He then served in the Royal Army Medical Corps during the First World War. After the war, he married and returned to journalism. His first book, *Annals of the Five Senses* (1923) was a mixture of prose and poetry in English, but he then turned to Scots for a series of books, culminating in what is probably his best known work, the book-length *A Drunk Man Looks At The Thistle*. This poem is widely regarded as one of the most important long poems in 20th century Scottish literature. After that, he published several books containing poems in both English and Lallans.

As his interest in science and linguistics increased, MacDiarmid found himself turning more and more to English as a means of expression so that most of his later poetry is written in that language. His ambition was to live up to Rilkes dictum that 'the poet must know everything' and to write a poetry that contained all knowledge. As a result, some of the later work is a kind of found poetry reusing text from a range of sources. This led to accusations of plagiarism, to which the poet's response was 'The greater the plagiarism the greater the work of art.' The great achievement of this late poetry is to attempt on an epic scale to capture the idea of a world without God in which all the facts the poetry deals with are scientifically verifiable.

MacDiarmid wrote a number of non-fiction prose works, including *Scottish Eccentrics* and his autobiography *Lucky Poet*. He also did a number of translations from Scottish Gaelic, including Duncan Ban MacIntyre's *Praise of Ben Doran*, which were well received by native speakers including Sorley MacLean.

Verse: *Sangschaw* (1925), *Penny Wheep* (1926), *To Circumjack Cencrastus or The Curly Snake* (1930), *Penny Wheep to Stony Limits and Other Poems* (1934), *The Present Age* (1940), *A Kist of Whistles* (1947).

Prose: *Lucky Poet, autobiography* (1938).

5

Chapter

Fiction in Early Twentieth Century

VICTORIAN FICTION

The Three greatest novelists of the waning nineteenth century had all ceased to write by the middle of its last decade. In 1894, Stevenson died at Vailima at the age of forty-four, leaving unfinished *Weir of Hermiston,* which even as a fragment shows that he was just entering the maturity of his power. In 1895, Meredith, having won a late and somewhat grudging recognition from the public he despised, published his last novel *The Amazing Marriage*. In 1896, Hardy, disgusted with the abuse that had greeted *Jude the Obscure,* likewise retired from fiction. Meredith and Hardy thereafter devoted themselves to the poetry that from the first had been their love. At the same time the young men who were to be the vanguard of the new century, were publishing their first books. *Almayer's Folly* by Joseph Conrad and *The Time Machine* by H. G. Wells appeared in 1895, *From the Four Winds* by " John Sinjohn"—John Galsworthy—in 1897, and *A Man From the North* by Arnold Bennett in 1898. These four were to dominate fiction through the Edwardian to the close of the First World War.

The link between these two generations was formed by a number of writers who began to be noticed in the eighties and with years of creation ahead of them had the misfortune to belong neither to the old century nor the new. Often considered dangerously advanced in their early work, they were, with one or two exceptions, outrun by literary taste so that in their maturity they seemed hopelessly old-fashioned.

,The scrupulous naturalism that had been established in France by Flaubert and Zola was represented by several writers of whom George Gissing and George Moore were the best. Gissing after six years of bitter struggle won recognition with *Demos* in 1886, and became the leading portrayer of the world of shabbiness and poverty. Moore, a young Irishman fresh from Paris, appeared first as the author of *A Modern Lover* in 1883 and achieved a success of both estimation and scandal when, in 1894, *Esther Waters* shared the moral censure of Hardy's later novels. The bitter poverty and criminality of London's East End was strikingly presented by Arthur Morrison in *Tales of Mean Streets* (1894) and *A Child of the Jago* (1896), and in Somerset Maugham first novel, *Liza of Lambeth* (1897). Equally realistic studies of the Jewish quarter by Israel Zangwill began to appear in 1893 with *Children of the Ghetto.*

The life of the Scottish poor, sentimentalized yet not wholly unrealistic in treatment, was the subject of the Kailyard School of which J. M. Barrie was the leader, with *Auld Licht Idylls* (1888) and the various "Thrums" stories that followed them. Ian Maclaren (Rev. John Watson) wrote half a dozen novels of this school of which *Beside the Bonnie Briar Bush* (1894) is the best known, and S. R. Crockett *The Stickit Minister* (1893). They capitalized the interest in Scotland revived by Stevenson and in the humors of rustic character created by Hardy, making much of local color and quaint dialect. Together with the East End writers they did a great deal for the vogue of the regional novel.

Among cultivated readers Mrs. Humphrey Ward, and for a couple of years, Gerald Du Maurier, led the .popular novelists; among the uncultivated Hall Caine and Marie Corelli. Mrs. Ward had startled her contemporaries in 1888 with *Robert Elsmere,* a story of religious doubt and struggle and the most controversial novel of its day. Like her uncle, Matthew Arnold, believing that "conduct is three fourths of life" she dealt with problems of conduct in upper class, and often political, society, occasionally as in *Marcella* (1894) and *Bessie Costrel* (1895) entering the world of the poor. Although considered passé by some critics in the late nineties she continued to hold readers well into the nineteen-hundreds. Du Maurier, an artist who did not discover his literary talent until the end of his life, had a brief hour of glory with the appearance of *Trilby* in 1894. Its vivid picture of art-student life in Paris captured the popular imagination as very few novels do, and formed, with the opera *La Bohème,* which appeared two years later, the basis for a romantic illusion of the Latin Quarter firmly believed in by a whole generation of English and Americans. Richard Le Gallienne had an equally brief popularity as a novelist with *The Quest of the Golden Girl* (1896). Hall Caine appealed through his eloquent Christian socialism and a strain of Celtic mysticism that covered, for the uncritical, his grave defects as a writer. He reached the height of his popularity with *The Manxman* (1894) and *The Christian* (1897). The quality of Marie Corelli's flashy "spiritual" romances may be indicated by the titles *The Soul of Lilith* (1892) and *The Sorrows of Satan* (1895). Mrs. Ward, Hall Caine, and Miss Corelli—different as they were in quality—were all prolific "best sellers," continuing to write until the nineteen-twenties, though with a faded glory and without the spectacular sales of their brief prime.

Stevenson's legacy of romance was shared by a number of minor writers who though never approaching his stature, produced a large body of adventure stories of real merit and vitality. They were fortunate readers whose youth stood beside Allan Quartermain to meet the shock of the Zulu charge, or crossed swords with Black Michael, or felt the cold horror of the Copper Beeches. There was no sophistication in these adventures, but neither was there a more than allowable quantity of fustian—far less than in their modern counterparts—and the authors knew their subjects and how to tell a story. Henry Rider Haggard had begun in the eighties to exploit the romance of Africa, where he had spent some years, and as his work coincided with the increasing interest in South Africa that reached its peak during the Boer War, enjoyed tremendous popularity. *King Solomon's Mines* (1885), his best and one of the best of its kind, has become a juvenile classic; *She* (1887), which was even more popular, has not lasted so well. The energy of Haggard's work was exhausted by the early nineteen-hundreds but new books of his continued to be published for some years after his death in 1900. Anthony Hope (Hawkins) who aspired to be a serious novelist, is remembered only for that pleasant mélange of *Henry Esmond* and *The Three Musketeers, The Prisoner of Zenda* (1894) and its sequel *Rupert of Hentzau* (1898). These tales of state intrigue and royal romance in the kingdom of Ruritania are saved from absurdity by the author's good breeding and real knowledge of European society. They have outlasted any number of cheap imitations. More thoroughly in the tradition of Dumas were the cloak-and-sword novels of Stanley Weyman. Set chiefly in France of the sixteenth and seventeenth centuries, they were well plotted but weak in characterization. The best was *Under the Red Robe* (1894). Much better than these were the historical romances of A. Conan Doyle, *Micah Clarke* (1888), The White Company (1890), and Rodney Stone (1896). In 1897 appeared the most successful of all modern "gothic" novels, *Dracula,* by Bram Stoker, a horror classic that in fifty years has lost none of its power to excite and chill.

In the short story Kipling was pre-eminent. Since the amazing year 1888 when he had published in Allahabad and London no fewer than seven volumes (*Plain Tales from the Hills, Soldiers Three, The Story of the Gadsbys, In Black and White, Under the Deodars, The Phantom Rickshaw,* and *Other Tales, Wee Willie Winkie* and *Other Child Stories*) he had produced, besides other matter, *Life's Handicap* (1891), *Many Inventions* (1893), and *The Day's Work* (1898). His versatility seemed inexhaustible; his vivid local color and crisp journalistic realism were new and accordant with the high spirits of the years of imperial pageantry. There was much more to him than these superficial qualities, of course, but it was they that gave him his unrivalled popularity. His only successful novel *The Light that Failed* appeared in 1890. Next in popularity to Kipling stood Conan Doyle whose creation of Sherlock Holmes began an era in modern popular fiction. With the appearance in "The Strand Magazine" of the stories that were to become *The Adventuresof Sherlock Holmes* of Sherlock Holmes (1892) and *The Memoirs of Sherlock Holmes* (1894) the first, and greatest, detective of modern English fiction emerged as a character far more subtle, intelligent, and interesting than such simply conceived policemen as Inspector Bucket and Sergeant Cuff. Though the detective story did not attain its full popularity for some years, its first great success was in the cases admirably recorded by Dr. Watson. Another innovation was the early "scientific" stories of H. G. Wells—*The Stolen Bacillus and Other Stories* (1895), *The Plattner Story and Other Stories* (1897), and *Tales of Space and Time* (1899)—appealing especially to those "New Century" minds that looked forward eagerly to an era of realized marvels.

EDWARDIAN FICTION

From 1900 until the close of the First World War English fiction was dominated by Conrad, Wells, Galsworthy, and Bennett. Except Conrad they were promptly recognized and the appearance by 1910 of *Nostromo, Tono Bungay, The Man of Property,* and *Clayhanger* seemed to justify the belief that England now had her strongest group of novelists for half a century. The ironic detachment of Conrad's revelations of human weakness, the trenchant criticism and satire of Wells, the skill of Galsworthy in characterization, and Bennett's brilliant regionalism showed abundant variety of power. A new strictness of technique was evident in their work; they were familiar with Russian as with French fiction and had discarded the provincialism and easy going amateurishness that were the blemishes of so many Victorian writers. They were comparatively young men with their best work, presumably, yet to be done.

In view of this great promise, the sudden withdrawal of esteem in the twenties that caused all but Conrad to outlive their reputations and the neglect into which they have since fallen are at first hard to understand. In part it is traceable to a particular defect in each of them. Conrad wrote from within a professional ideal that passed with the sailing ship. Wells and Galsworthy were propagandists who repeatedly sacrificed their art to their causes, and Galsworthy had the added vice of sentimentalism, unforgivable to the following generation. Bennett's irrespressible commercialism would not allow him to write for long at his best, so that at the last his real achievement was clogged with much that was cheap and trashy. More than all this, however, they had all worked in a literary tradition that was passing. As soon as a sufficient body of postwar fiction had appeared for its character to become defined, it was apparent that they did not belong to it. Wells had no marvels or terrors for those who had been in the war, it was clear that Galsworthy did not understand the younger generation as he had understood the older, Bennett *Pretty Lady* seemed absurdly timid, and no one was going to learn the ropes of Conrad's ships. Moreover whatever the quality of their fiction they had made no innovation in technique, and this to a day in which all forms of literature were being radically overhauled was enough to condemn them.

Among the minor Edwardian novelists Maurice Hewlett occupies a high place; in fact at one time he promised to be a major novelist when his romances of the middle ages *The Forest Lovers* (1898) and *Richard Yea and Nay* (1900) were the literary sensations of their day. His reputation fell, however, when he attempted novels of contemporary life, and though his later Norse romances were good, they did not wholly fulfil the promise of his beginnings. Another disappointment was Gilbert Cannan whose social novels from 1910 to 1915 showed great distinction. A mental breakdown at the end of the war forced him to give up writing, although his books continued to be published until 1924. Robert Hichens enjoyed a decade of great popularity beginning with the tremendous success of *The Garden of Allah* (1904) and sustained by *Bella Donna* (1909) and *The Fruitful Vine* (1911). His vogue, however, passed with the war and the twenty-odd novels that he wrote between 1919 and 1942 commanded little attention. Ford Maddox Hueffer (who changed his last name to Ford) began as an historical romancer but turned for his later material to contemporary life. Early in his career he was Joseph Conrad's collaborator in *The Inheritors* and *Romance.* A meticulous stylist with French rather than English standards of fiction, he was a technician rather than a creator and served literature less by his own writings than by his introduction of new authors in the *English Review* and the *transatlantic Review* which he edited before and after the war. Leonard Merrick and Oliver Onions were debarred from great success simply by their failure to please the public. The delightful comedy of Merrick's books bordered disturbingly on tragedy in a way that disappointed equally those who wanted a "pleasant" and those who wanted a "strong" story. Onions was a vigorous writer with a wholly negative attitude; he showed his readers a despicable world in which he had nothing to offer but his anger. J. C. Snaith, E. F. Benson, and the eccentric and exuberant M. P. Shiel were without durable substance. The catalogue of unfulfilled promise may be completed with Eden Phillpotts who appeared in the later nineties as a regional novelist of Devon. He had undoubted talent but as his writing was the whole interest of his life he produced too much—more than a hundred novels besides plays and short stories.

The most curious story in Edwardian letters is that of William De Morgan, a retired manufacturer of art pottery who in 1906 astonished readers and critics by producing a remarkably successful first novel, *Joseph Vance*, at the age of sixty-seven. Had De Morgan discovered his talent sooner he would probably have held a high place among his contemporaries: as it was he established a solid reputation with half a dozen excellent, if somewhat old-fashioned, novels before he died of influenza in 1917.

The lighter novelists were led by William J. Locke, who captivated the public with the delicate gaiety of *The Morals of Marcus Ordeyne* (1905) and *The Beloved Vagabond* (1906). Archibald Marshall wrote quiet, humorous stories of the county families, the best being *The Eldest Son* (1911) and *The Honour of the Clintons* (1913); and "George A. Birmingham" farcical stories of Irish life. "Elizabeth" wrote with a more subdued humor her stories of life in Prussia, the fruits of a trying first marriage. "CN and AM Williamson" exploited the new interest in motoring in *The Lightning Conductor* (1902) and with a series of light, clever stories that were half touring guides, won a popularity that lasted until the novelty of the sport, as it was then considered, had worn away. Adventure seekers were entertained by E. Phillips Oppenheim's novels of international intrigue and secret diplomacy, or the exploits of Baroness Orczy's Sir Percy Blakeney *The Scarlet Pimpernel*).

An isolated event of great importance was the publication in 1903 of *The Way of All Flesh* a year after the death of its author. Written between 1872 and 1884 it was the work of the eccentric genius Samuel Butler (1835-1902), who authorized its publication on his death bed. Largely autobiographical, it is a bitter attack on old-fashioned piety and the narrow tyranny of the Victorian household. Its influence which became even greater after the war, when it appealed to the general spirit of revolt, can be traced in the work of Somerset Maugham and others.

In the field of the short story, though there was no one to compete with the now veteran Kipling, the Edwardian years developed a number of able writers. Most of the novelists mentioned produced one or more volumes in the genre, Wells, Galsworthy, Hewlett, and Locke being the more skillful. W. W. Jacobs could be counted on for an annual volume, collected from *The Strand Magazine*, of his tales of comic seafaring men or the incredible rustics who gathered at the Cauliflower Inn. Much more skillful and sophisticated, "Saki" recounted the social flippancies of irresponsible young men in a vein that P. G. Wodehouse was later to make more popular. Horace Annesley Vachel, of little account as a novelist, wrote some exceedingly clever and amusing stories, especially the three volumes about Quinney's antique shop, and Algernon Blackwood gave a new flavor to the occult. For a few years Richard Middleton contributed to magazines delicate, fantastic stories that after his tragic death filled a couple of volumes. One of these, *The Ghost Ship*, has a deserved reputation as a masterpiece of fantasy but has never received the credit due it as an early, subtle, and artistically successful experiment in the stream-of-consciousness. Another master of the fantastic, impossible to classify, is Arthur Machen whose tales of diabolism, long and short, are neither novels nor short stories. In spite of the remarkable skill with which he could evoke the horror and evil of an ancient pagan world he was little read and had only a transient popularity when his work was "discovered" in the nineteentwenties.

Edwardian fiction will be remembered chiefly for the splendid picture it preserves of England in the early twentieth century. It was intensely contemporaneous; at no time in the nineteenth century were so few good historical stories written. But if its writers were concerned with their own world, their attitude toward it was on the whole conservative. Of the major novelists only Galsworthy and Wells were actively critical of society. Bennett was keenly aware of social injustice but inclined to accept it with a shrug, and Galsworthy was an evangelist calling to repentance rather than a reformer. Wells alone went to the roots of social organization with constructive, if impractical, criticism. The attitude of novelists toward religion and politics, though not always complacent, had not changed noticeably since the eighties and nineties. The problems created by the changing position of women were discussed in many novels, such as *Ann Veronica* and *The Man of Property*, but the experience of Hardy and Moore had made writers shy of attempting any frank treatment of sex. The old prudishness died hard, and D. H. Lawrence, the first of the younger men to come out and fight it during the war, was severely punished by the suppression of *The Rainbow* and the refusal of all publishers to handle *Women in Love.*

Conservatism was as marked in the form as in the content of fiction. The Edwardians were much occupied with questions of technique but too well satisfied with the study of Flaubert, Turgeniev, and Henry James to make any experiments of their own. Bennett in the Clayhanger novels and Galsworthy in *The Forsyte Saga* made use of the trilogy to get the sustained effect of the old three-volume novel without its inconveniences, but there was no marked technical change until 1920.

The absence of women writers in these years is noticeable and at first surprising. After Mrs. Ward and Marie Corelli there were few new names except May Sinclair whose reputation was made by *The Divine Fire* (1904). There was presumably no lack of talent, but the best feminine minds were politically focused on the struggle for the vote and the movement for higher education that accompanied it. After the war, when these issues had been settled, women became as prominent as men in nearly all branches of literature.

Joseph Conrad

When Joseph Conrad (1857-1924) began to write English fiction he had already lived two lives as different from each other as both were from the new one on which he was entering. He was born near Kiev in the Ukraine and christened Teodor Josef Konrad Korzeniowski. In his early childhood he shared with his parents political exile in Vologda, the punishment for his father's nationalistic activities.

His mother died under the hardship; his father survived his release by one year. Left an orphan in 1869 at the age of twelve, Conrad was brought up by his maternal uncle. The

Bobrowskis, his mother's family, were landholders in the Ukraine, and expected him to follow the tradition of Polish gentlemen. To their consternation, at the age of fifteen, he announced his intention of becoming a merchant seaman.

Conrad's father had been a highly cultivated man, a poet and the translator of Shakespeare into Polish. He had introduced his son to English letters, and it was by the sea stories of Frederick Marryat and of Fenimore Cooper (so little regarded now) that Conrad's imagination was turned toward the sea. Promises, dissuasions, travel with a tutor could not divert him, nor would he consent to go to the Imperial Naval Academy at Pola and become an officer in the Austrian service. He would be a merchant seaman and in English ships. At length in desperation the family consigned him to friends in Marseilles who would take him in hand while he served his apprenticeship to a pilot of the port. Experience of hardship it was thought would cure him. Nothing of the sort. He learned his trade, while Marseilles of the 'seventies educated him in the world. His great moment came when one night in the pilot's boat he touched the side of a veritable English ship.

Conrad's second life began with his first deep-water voyage to the West Indies. Seasoned by two or three such he went to England and began his service in her ships. To understand the years that followed one should read *The Mirror of the Sea,* the most revelatory of all his books, defining, as he says "the terms of my relation to the sea." And more, for there in half a dozen significant statements one will find the keys to his art: "To see! To see!—this is the craving of the sailor, as of the rest of blind humanity." "Ships are all right; it's the men who are in 'em." To return, he passed for master in 1880, held command, and became a British subject in 1886. He had achieved what he set out to do. Then he was led into the adventure that put an end to his seafaring. He tells in *A Personal Record* how at the age of nine he put his finger on a blank space in the map of Africa and said, *"When I grow up I shall go there."* In 1889 he went, commanding a river steamer for a Belgian development company, and it was then that the first seven chapters of *Almayer's Folly* were written. The adventure ended in West Coast fever that sent him home a very sick man. After a stay ashore and a visit to Poland, he shipped again, this time as first mate of the *Torrens,* a crack passenger-carrying clipper in the Australian trade. Not long after his impaired health obliged him to go ashore for good, and the novel at which he had been working for five years was completed.

With the publication of *Almayer's Folly* in 1895 Conrad began his career as an English author. Galsworthy and Edward Garnett, who had recommended its publication, introduced him to a brilliant literary circle including Henry James, Stephen Crane, W. H. Hudson, CunninghameGraham, and Ford M. Hueffer his collaborator. Among these he won an almost immediate *succes d'estime,* but for years the public was dishearteningly indifferent to his work The way to popular success in the first decade of the century was through the magazine serial and Conrad's books, conceived in total effect, were wholly lacking in "serial quality." He was a laborious writer, each book causing him fresh agonies, and his eighteen years of struggle against poverty and obscurity were bitter. Only a Civil List pension and the help of his literary agent J. B. Pinker enabled him to weather the worst of them. Yet during these years he did nearly all of his enduring work. His wife, Jessie George Conrad, whom he married in 1896, has left an indiscreetly candid record of the stress of their domestic life in this trying time. When popular recognition came at length in 1913 it was for *Chance,* not one of his greatest books. Thereafter he enjoyed roughly a decade of literary celebrity, culminating in his visit to the United States in 1923. He died in the following year and was buried in the Catholic cemetery in Canterbury, in the county he loved and had made his home.

Conrad's stories are either novels or shorter pieces which he called "tales" since they are not technically short stories.

The difference is in the scale of events and characters. Of the former he thought *Nostromo* and *The Nigger of the "Narcissus"* his best; the first choice is sure, the second questionable. *The Heart of Darkness, Lord Jim,* and *The Rescue* stand high in the list. Of the tales, *Youth* and *Typhoon,* already mentioned, are among the best. Of the major Edwardian novelists he is the purest artist, the only one without any sort of propagandist axe to grind. "It had to be done," he said of *Nostromo.* He wrote under the artist's compulsion to express his vision "with the ineradicable hope—of ultimately, some day, at some moment, making myself understood."

Fiction: *Almayer's Folly* (1895), *An Outcast of the Islands* (1896), *The Nigger of the "Narcissus,"*, *Tales of Unrest* (1898), *Lord Jim* (1900), *The Inheritors, with F. M. Hueffer* (1901), *Typhoon* (1902), *Youth* (1902), *Romance, with F. M. Hueffer* (1903), *Typhoon and Other Stories* (1903), *Nostromo* (1904), *The Secret Agent* (1907), *A Set of Six* (1908), *Under Western Eyes* (1911), *'Twixt Land and Sea* (1912), *Chance* (1913), *Victory* (1915), *Within the Tides* (1916), *The Shadow Line* (1917), *The Arrow of Gold* (1919), *The Rescue* (1920), *The Rover* (1923), *Suspense (unfinished)* (1925), *Tales of Hearsay* (1925), *The Sisters* (1928), *The Complete Short Stories of Joseph Conrad* (1933).

Plays: *One Day More* (1919), *The Secret Agent* (1921), *Laughing Anne* (1923), *Three Plays* (1934). *Essays: The Mirror of the Sea* (1906), *Some Reminiscences, Notes on Life and Letters* (1921), *Notes on My Books* (1921), *Last Essays* (1926), *Conrad's Prefaces to His Works* (1937).

Letters: *Joseph Conrad's Letters to His Wife* (1927), *Conrad to a Friend:* 150 *Selected Letters from Joseph Conrad to Richard Curle* (1928), *also pub. as Letters of Joseph Conrad to Richard Curle* (1928), *Letters from Joseph Conrad,* 1895-1924 (1928), *Lettres françaises* (Paris, 1930), *Letters from Joseph Conrad to Marguerite Poradowska* (1940).

Herbert George Wells

The career of Herbert George Wells (1866-1946) may be divided conveniently into two periods, the first, to 1900, of escape from the narrow conditions of his childhood, the second, to his death, of search for a better world and a more rational society. To this search his work as a literary artist is incidental.

He was born in a cramped little house in Bromley, Kent, behind a crockery shop which his father, a gardener and cricketer, ran helplessly into bankruptcy. His mother, a former ladies' maid, worked hard to raise her children and, when the shop failed, went back into service as a housekeeper to support them. She was anxious to see her sons placed in respectable trades, and so at the age of fourteen, after a very sketchy schooling, Wells was sent "on trial" to a draper's in Windsor. This was the first of six starts in life that he has recorded. To follow him through them all, as pupil-teacher, chemist's assistant and again at a draper's, would be tedious, and for such details the reader is referred to *Experiment in Autobiography* (1934) of which they make the most interesting part.

Wells' literary career dates virtually from his second marriage; what he did before that was largely prentice work. *The Time Machine* appeared in 1895, *The Island of Dr. Moreau* in 1896, and *The Invisible Man* in 1897. These, which made his reputation, and other stories he wrote in this period exploit the "marvelous" aspects of science in fantasies—"violent visions" Chesterton called them—which have still a power over the popular imagination. *The Time Machine* is the first projection of the four dimensional continuum in fiction and *The Island of Dr. Moreau* a horrible dramatization of biological evolution. Down to 1905 Wells was known almost exclusively for work of this kind.

His second phase as a realistic novelist began in 1900 with *Love and Mr. Lewisham,* the story of a schoolmaster, containing some autobiographical matter. *Kipps* appeared in

1905 and *Ann Veronica* and *Tono Bungay* both in 1909-Wells' *annus mirabilis*. The last is unquestionably his masterpiece, a satiric contrast of two false ideals, that of the feudal aristocracy of Bladesover, and that of the modern business world in which Uncle Ponderevo achieves wealth by fraudulent advertising. Wells hated both of them; the first he knew intimately from Up Park where his mother had been housekeeper, the second only from general but shrewd observation. Between them they seemed to possess the world of that day. If modern society was to escape complete decivilization, it seemed to Wells that it must find other ideals to which the scientist and the educator could best point the way. More and more social ideas developed in dialogue usurped the place of character and action in his novels, to the detriment of their literary art. During World War I his sturdy unbelief yielded temporarily to the mysticism that affected many of the older generation and he wrote *Mr. Britling Sees It Through* (1916) and *The Soul of a Bishop* (1917). With *Joan and Peter* (1918) and *The Undying Fire* (1919) the second phase of his literary work ended.

Perhaps the most important act of Wells' youth was his reading of Plato *Republic*. It disclosed to him the possibility of a rational and ordered society that his scientific mind thoroughly approved. Confirmed in socialism by experience and further reading, he joined the Fabian Society and soon going beyond its rather academic policies began to plan a socialized world of his own. In 1900 he published in the *Fortnightly Review* the series of far-seeing articles on population and society which became *Anticipations*, and two years later a second series, *Mankind in the Making*. *A Modern Utopia* (1906) is his manifesto for the organization of the new world and is in effect a free adaptation to modern conditions of the leading ideas of Plato. It places the direction of the state in the hands of an elite order, the "Samurai," for which Wells later found parallels in the Russian Communist party and the Italian Fascists. Following its publication he tried to "capture" the Fabian Society, as a means of making its principles effective and, failing, resigned. Thereafter he thought and worked alone.

For some years Wells' propaganda for a planned society ran side by side with his literary work, but in time it absorbed the best part of his thought and effort. World War I, weakening whatever it did not overthrow of the old order, seemed to him a unique opportunity for a new beginning. The confusion of public and private thought during the peace negotiations brought home to him the necessity of educating an entire generation to new political concepts and he began his series of world surveys, *The Outline of History* (1920), *The Science of Life*, with Julian Huxley and G. P. Wells (1929), and *The Work, Wealth and Happiness of Mankind* (1932). The indifference of England's first Labor Government (1923) disappointed but did not discourage him. He now had a world-wide audience and the popularity of his later books revived interest in his earlier ones. But as the world marched toward another world war, and neither his "educative" nor his political works produced any appreciable effect Wells. became increasingly despondent. *The Anatomy of Frustration: A Modern Synthesis* (1936), *The Fate of Man* (1939) and *The New World Order* (1940) mark the decline of his effort and influence.

Whether the world gained when Wells sacrificed his undoubtedly great powers as a novelist to his preoccupation with the world-state each reader may decide for himself. His *Experiment in Autobiography* makes it perfectly clear that for Wells nothing else was possible. The novel as an art form failed to satisfy him: he needed a more elastic and more dramatic vehicle for his ideas. His fiction developed, as he says, more and more toward the dialogue and therefore always farther from the symbolism through which alone the novel can convey ideas. It was inevitable that his scientific mind with its passion for completeness and precision should ultimately prefer direct exposition. But though it was more satisfactory to Wells, his work of this sort has shown no clear superiority to an equal amount of fiction of the quality of *Tono Bungay*.

Autobiography: *An Experiment in Autobiography* (1934).

Fiction: *The Time Machine* (1895), *The Wonderful Visit* (1895), *The Stolen Bacillus* (1896), *The Island of Doctor Moreau* (1896), *The Wheels of Chance* (1896), *The Red Room* (1896), *The Invisible Man* (1897), *Thirty Strange Stories* (1897), *The Plattner Story* (1897), *The War of the Worlds* (1898), *When the Sleeper Wakes* (1899), *A Cure For Love* (1899), *Tales of Space and Time* (1899), *The Vacant Country* (1899), *Love and Mr. Lewisham* (1899), *The First Men in theMoon Moon* (1901), *The Sea Lady* (1902), *Twelve Stories and a Dream* (1903), *The Food of the Gods* (1904), *Kipps* (1905), *A Modern Utopia* (1905), *In the Days of the Comet* (1906), *The War in the Air* (1908), *Ann Veronica* (1909), *Tono Bungay* (1909), *The History of Mr. Polly* (1909), *The New Machiavelli* (1911), *The Country of the Blind* (1911), *Marriage* (1912), *The Passionate Friends* (1913), *The World Set Free* (1914), *The Wife of Sir Isaac Harman* (1914), *Bealby* (1915), *The Research Magnificent* (1915), *Mr. Britling Sees It Through* (1916), *The Soul of a Bishop* (1916), *Joan and Peter* (1917), *The Undying Fire* (1919), *The Secret Places of the Heart* (1922), *Men Like Gods* (1923), *The Dream* (1924), *Christina Alberta's Father* (1925), *The Adventures of Tommy* (1925), *The World of William Clissold* (1926), *Meanwhile* (1927), *Mr. Blettsworthy on Rampole Island* (1928), *The King Who Was a King* (1929), *The Autocracy of Mr. Parham* (1930), *The Bulpington of Blup* (1933), *The Shape of Things To Come* (1933), *The Man Who Could Work Miracles* (1936), *The Croquet Player* (1936), *Brynhild* (1937), *The Camford Visitation* (1937), *Star Begotten* (1937), *The Brothers* (1938), *Apropos of Dolores* (1938), *The Dictator* (1939). *The Holy Terror* (1939), *Babes in the Darkling Wood* (1940), *All Aboard For Ararat* (1940), *You Can't Be Too Careful* (1941).

Nonfiction: *Select Conversations With an Uncle* (1895), *Certain Personal Matters* (1898), *The Discovery of the*

Future (1902), *Mankind in the Making* (1903), *New Worlds For Old* (1908), *First and Last Things* (1908), *The Great State* (1912), *An Englishman Looks at the World, God, the Invisible King* (1917), *The Outline of History* (1920), *The Salvaging of Civilization* (1921), *Socialism and the Scientific Motive* (1923), *After Democracy* (1929), *The Way to World Peace* (1930), *The Work, Wealth and Happiness of Mankind* (1931), *The Science of Life* (1931), *The Anatomy of Frustration* (1936), *World Brain* (1938), *The Enlarged and Revised Outline of History* (1940), *The New World Order* (1940), *The Common Sense of War and Peace* (1940), *The Conquest of Time* (1942), *Mind at the End of Its Tether* (1946).

Arnold Bennett

Arnold Bennett (1867-1931) , a pushing Philistine and a sensitive artist, a puritan and a sybarite, is very hard to judge fairly. Though he is the most straightforward of writers and though he has written of himself more candidly than any of his contemporaries, both the man and his work are curiously elusive, almost impossible to comprehend in a statement that will adequately present at once their surprising strength and equally surprising weakness.

He came to London in 1888 at the age of twenty-one (he was Enoch Arnold Bennett then) to try his luck, but principally to escape his father's domination and his native town of Hanley, where he had passed his youth in the ugly, puritanical atmosphere of the Staffordshire potteries. He had behind him an average schooling, some knowledge of the law, gained in his father's office, and a taste of journalism as a contributor to a local paper. His self-confidence was unbounded.

Bennett's first twelve years in London (1888-1900) were a period of apprenticeship and discovery of his own powers. He began as cost clerk to a law firm at twenty-five shillings a week, but though he did his work well, he was irresistibly drawn toward letters. In 1891 he went to live in Chelsea among artists, and under the influence of his new friends began to work at free lance journalism, though without much success. In 1893 he won a competition in Tit Bits and in the same year became, not, he says, by merit but by influence, assistant editor of *Woman*, a "smart" weekly. Two years later his story *A Letter Home* was published in *The Yellow Book* (July, 1895). When his chief retired shortly after, Bennett succeeded him and held the job for four years (1896-1900). During his connection with the paper Bennett not only learned the business of journalism, as he did everything else quickly and thoroughly, but found his feet as a writer. His first novel, *A Man from the North*, was published by Lane in 1898; he sold a number of serials to newspaper syndicates, and comedies to theatrical producers; he became dramatic critic to the *Academy* and principal reader to a publishing house. At thirty-three, satisfied that he could do well in any profitable branch of literature, he retired from journalism and from London, settling in Bedfordshire to follow his true vocation as a novelist.

In the years between this hegira and World War I, Bennett produced most of his best and a great deal of his worst fiction. *Anna of the Five Towns, Sacred and Profane Love, The Old Wives' Tale, Clayhanger, The Card,* and *Hilda Lessways*, established him unshakeably.

These, although the action often takes place in London or abroad, are regional stories of the Five Towns of Staffordshire. The characters are Bennett's own people, rebels in one way or another against the drab atmosphere that oppressed his youth. He writes of them with a shrewd, humorous understanding that gave him the reputation of being able to make the dullest people interesting. They are by no means all equally good—*Clayhanger*, containing a large element of autobiography, is the best—but taken all together, they constitute an impressive achievement in naturalistic fiction.

At the same time—just as poets write detective stories to pay their way—he was turning out light fiction of an entirely different sort. The *Grand Babylon Hotel, The Gates of Wrath, The Loot of Cities, The City of Pleasure,* and others are thrillers, set in an atmosphere of sham splendor and weighed down with all the claptrap of melodrama—frank pot-boilers. From them he made an excellent income, an important matter to a man who always frankly regarded literature as a business, his journal showing that he received £1200 for 375,000 words in 1907 and £16,000 for 160,000 words by 1912.

During these years Bedfordshire failed to hold Bennett, as all things did once the novelty had worn off. France drew him more and more. In 1903 he began to live in Paris: four years later he married there and made Fontainebleau his home until 1912, when he took a country house in Essex. During the First World War he was active on many civilian committees and was appointed by Lord Beaverbrook director of British propaganda in France. In 1916 he published *These Twain,* completing the Clayhanger trilogy (*Clayhanger, Hilda Lessways*), and two years later *The Pretty Lady,* the pathetic story of a French prostitute in London during the war.

In the years between the war and his death Bennett had ceased to write about the Five Towns. His later novels, *Lillian, Mr. Prohack, Riceyman Steps, Lord Raingo, Imperial Palace* deal mostly with London and reflect Bennett's enlarged experience, compensating in scope and variety for the intimate knowledge that distinguished his earlier work. *Riceyman Steps,* the grim tragedy of a miserly bookseller, and *Imperial Palace,* the prose epic of a great hotel, are easily the best. The latter is especially characteristic, embodying as it does Bennett's lifelong interest in superlative catering and efficient organization. Aside from these two, there is nothing really distinguished among his later books and on the whole they sustained rather than increased the reputation he had made by 1912.

Though he will be remembered chiefly as a novelist, Bennett was as versatile as he was prolific. His bibliography includes thirty-seven novels, seven volumes of short stories, fourteen volumes of essays and travels, ten of his popular "philosophies" (*The Human Machine, How to Live on Twenty-Four Hours a Day*, etc.) seventeen plays, to say nothing of his autobiographical writing (*T he Truth About an Author, Journals*) and a mass of uncollected contributions to the press. In none of these was he a failure, though his plays are far below the level of his fiction. He was at his best as a critic, at his worst as an essayist because outside of literature he had few general ideas, only an intense interest in specific things. As "Jacob Tonson" in the *New Age* (1908-11) he made a reputation that gave him wide popular authority. His standard was high, though he was willing to recognize the public taste, he was honest, his perception, if uneven was acute, and his style vigorous, clear and often amusing. At the last he shared with Gosse, the critic, the power to assure the popular acceptance of a new book or author.

"I began as a journalist," Bennett wrote in *The Savour of Life* (1928), "and I have never ceased to be a journalist." And further—"I write for money. I write for as much money as I can get." This commercial attitude toward the business of authorship he insisted upon throughout his life. It was not a pose: it was part of a thoroughly sincere materialism, an absorbing interest in things, a desire to own them, to know about them. In his novels plot and character are in constant danger of being lost in details of milieu, especially of ways of earning a living. His people "get on" or are desperately trying to, and how they do it is as important to him as to them. He held that "the evidence of the superficies is valuable" and his works are pre-eminently a document of the superficies of the Edwardian world. If the artist in him had not been of real magnitude he might have been no more than a writer of first rate "features."

Artistically Bennett was formed abroad. Until he was mature his knowledge of the English classics was astonishingly imperfect; many of them he never esteemed. He felt at home in France, and Gallic culture and thought came easily to him. Flaubert, the Goncourts, Zola, and Dostoievsky were his literary models. He acquired the French passion for form and discipline of style. As with George Moore, the acquisition of a foreign culture totally unconnected with his native tradition, left a part of him, the cocky provincial, isolated and unmodified and thus often betrayed him into appalling lapses of style and taste. He despised English puritanism for its artistic timidity, yet whenever he attempted a Gallic truth of naturalism his early puritanism made him recoil from his own audacities, leaving them ineffectual and sometimes silly. France refined to fastidiousness his natural love of excellence, but his English provincialism too often interpreted it in terms of shops, trains, and hotels. He never resolved this conflict.

Throughout life Bennett had the superb self-confidence of genius. The young man of thirty-three who wrote a book about his career was certain of his success. He succeeded in the world beyond question: in art his complete success is not so clear. He will probably be considered third among the major Edwardian novelists.

Fiction: *A Man from the north* (1898), *the grand babylon hotel* (1902). *Anna of the five towns* (1902), *leonora* (1903), *the gates of wrath* (1903), *a great man* (1904); *teresa of watling street* (1904), *the loot of cities* (1905), *sacred and profane love* (1905), *re-published as the book of carlotta* (1911), *tales of the five towns* (1905), *whom god hath joined* (1906), *hugo* (1906), *the grim smile of the five towns* (1907), *the city of pleasure* (1907), *the ghost* (1907), *the old wives' tale* (1908), *buried alive* (1908), *the glimpse* (1909), *clayhanger* (1910), *helen with the high hand* (1910), *the card* (1911), *hilda lessways* (1911), *the matador of the five towns* (1912), *the regent [the old adam]* (1913), *the price of love* (1914), *these twain* (1915), *the lion's share* (1916), *the pretty lady* (1918), *the roll call* (1918), *lillian* (1922), *mr. Prohack* (1922), *riceyman steps* (1923), *elsie and the child* (1924), *lord raingo* (1924), *the woman who stole everything* (1927), *accident* (1928), *the strange vanguard [the vanguard]* (1928), *imperial palace* (1930).

Plays: *Cupid and common sense* (1908), *what the public wants* (1910), *the honeymoon* (1911), *the great adventure* (1913), *the title* (1918), *sacred and profane love* (1919), *judith* (1919), *body and soul* (1921), *the love match* (1922), *don juan de marana* (1923), *the bright island* (1924).

Miscellaneous: *The truth about an author* (1903), *things that interested me* (1906), *the reasonable life* (1907), *the human machine* (1908), *how to live on twenty-four hours a day* (1908), *literary taste* (1909), *those united states* (1912), *paris nights* (1913), *from the log of the velsa* (1914), *the author's craft* (1914), *books and persons* (1917), *self and self-management* (1918), *things that Have Interested Me* (1921, *Second Series* 1923, *Third Series* 1926), *The Savour of Life* (1928), *The Journals of Arnold Bennett* (1932-33).

Georve Moore

Georve Moore (1852- 1933) was the eldest son of George Henry Moore, M.P., of Moore Hall, County Mayo. The Moores were an old family in the tradition of Anglo-Irish squires and it was a disappointment to his parents when the heir failed to develop the character needed to carry on that tradition. A "slow boy" at Oscott, the English school to which he was sent, he showed none of the qualities of the soldier or the country gentleman to compensate for his lack of scholarship. Consequently he drifted into adolescence with a feeling of inferiority, of being an ugly duckling for whom there was no place in the family's scheme of things. His father left him largely to himself to pick up a knowledge of the world from the tenantry and the grooms of the racing stable. He read indiscriminately and blundered into the discovery of Shelley, whose spell remained upon him for life.

In 1869, when Moore was seventeen, the family moved to London to be near the House of Commons. It was there, through the influence of a cousin, that Moore first became interested in art and for a while took lessons at the South Kensington Museum school. He continued to be an avid reader of the poetry to which Shelley had led him, though his statement that he had read most of the English poets before he was twenty-one is probably inaccurate. In 1870 his father died and three years later at his majority he became master of the heavily mortgaged estate of 12,500 acres that gave him an income of about £500 a year. On this he went to Paris to study art. Three years in the ateliers convinced him that he could never be a painter and he turned, rather feebly and affectedly at first, to literature. Though his work of these days is negligible—two plays and two volumes of immature and derivative verse—Paris gave him his vision of the world of culture and the acquaintance of artists and writers, especially Manet and Zola. Admiration of Balzac followed. The café Nouvelle Athènes in the Place Pigalle was his not wholly adequate substitute for the formal education he never had.

When the Irish Land League troubles of 1879 cut off his income from the estate, he returned to London to write seriously for a living, taking chambers in the Temple. After a period of art criticism and reviewing, he published his first novel, *A Modern Lover,* in 1883. In 1894 he published *Esther Waters,* an unsparingly realistic story of a betrayed servant girl. By this time he was the author of eight novels, none of them except the last remarkable, all in the tradition of French naturalism. *Esther Waters* is a work of considerable power, but the fact that it shared the moral censure of Hardy's last novels had much to do with making the reputation of the book and its author. *Celibates,* a volume of short stories and *Evelyn Innes,* a novel inferior to *Esther Waters,* complete his fiction of this period.

In London Moore had seen much of W. B. Yeats, who in 1899 carried him off to Dublin to help in the literary revival going forward there. Moore was not reluctant, his French culture made him contemptuous of English art, and he hated the brash jingoism of the Boer War period. He was full of enthusiasm for the Celtic Revival, but before long he found Ireland bigoted and unsympathetic. He renounced

Catholicism and called himself a Protestant. After 1906 his discontent grew steadily and in 1911 he left Ireland for good. In one view this time was unproductive; he published *The Untilled Field,* a volume of short stories, in 1903, *TheLake* Lake, a novel, in 1905, *Reminiscences of the Impressionist Painters* and *Memoirs of My Dead Life* in 1906, and nothing further until he went to England. But Ireland gave him abundant material, and in the sterile years, 1906-1911, he conceived or began much that appeared later.

Upon his return to London, Moore took his well-known house in Ebury Street, where he spent the rest of his days. Here he produced the first fruits of his Irish sojourn, the trilogy *Hail and Farewell* (Ave, 1911, *Salve,* 1912, *Vale,* 1914). This Shandean mixture of inaccurate autobiography, malicious gossip, and prejudiced criticism is, in spite of a hundred faults of taste and style, a work of unmistakable genius. So too *Avowals* (1919) and *Conversations in Ebury Street* (1924), books of much the same sort. His novels of this period show a completely new manner of treating historic romance with antique simplicity. *The Brook Kerith* (1916) and *Heloise and Abelard* (1921), which Moore called the only prose epics in English, are his finest work. The deceptive naturalness of their manner effectively conceals the heavy labors of research and the discipline of a new style that went to their making. After *Ulick and Soracha* (1926) he wrote nothing of any note.

Moore's plays of which he wrote eight, from the early *Worldliness* (1874?) to the amusing Shakespearean burlesque *The Making of an Immortal* (1937), add little if anything to his reputation: he himself had a poor opinion of some of them. Their theatrical history is unimportant.

It has been said of Moore that he "conducted his education in public"; certainly his books, and it is part of their interest, show more than any other major writer's his gropings toward artistic maturity. Many of his faults remained undisciplined to the end, but it is remarkable that he should have formed upon his unadmirable character, pretentious, untrustworthy, and somewhat vulgar, an artist of great variety and subtlety of expression and, though inconstantly, of power and conscientiousness. All but his worst lapses are redeemed by a passionate love of beauty in which few English writers have exceeded him.

Fiction: *A Modern Lover* (1883), *A Mummer's Wife* (1885), *A Drama in Muslin* (1886), *A Mere Accident* (1887), *Spring Days* (1888), *Mike Fletcher* (1889), *Vain Fortune* (1892), *Esther Waters* (1894), *Celibates* (1895), *Evelyn Innes* (1898), *Sister Teresa* (1901), *The Untilled Field* (1903), *The Lake* (1905), *Muslin, revision of A Drama in Muslin* (1915), *The Brook Kerith* (1916), *Lewis Seymour and Some Women, based on A Modern Lover* (1917), *A Story Teller's Holiday* (1918), *Héloise and Abelard* (1921), *Fragments from Héloise and Abelard, additions and corrections* (1921), *In Single Strictness* (1922), *Ulick and Soracha* (1926), *Peronnick the Fool* (1926), *Celibate Lives, revision of In Single Strictness* (1927), *Aphrodite in Aulis* (1930), *The Talking Pine* (1930), *A Flood* (1930).

Plays: *Worldliness* (1874), *Martin Luther, with Bernard Lopez* (1879), *The Strike at Arlingford* (1893), *The Bending of the Bough* (1900), *The Apostle* (1911), *Esther Waters* (1913), *Elizabeth Cooper* (1913), *The Coming of Gabrielle* (1920), *The Making of an Immortal* (1927), *The Passing of the Essenes* (1930).

Miscellaneous: *Flowers of Passion* (1878), *Pagan Poems* (1881), *Literature at Nurse* (1885), *Parnell and His Island* (1887), *Confessions of a Young Man* (1888), *Impressions and Opinions* (1891), *Modern Painting* (1893), *The Royal Academy, 1895* (1895), *Reminiscences of the Impressionist Painters* (1906), *Memoirs of My Dead Life* (1906), *Hail and Farewell* (191114), *Avowals* (1919), *Conversations in Ebury Street* (1924), *Pure Poetry: An Anthology,* (1924), *The Pastoral Loves of Daphnis and Chloe* (1924,) *A Communication to My Friends* (1933).

Letters: *Letters from George Moore to Ed. Dujardin, 1886-1922* (1929), *Letters of George Moore, with an Introduction by John Eglinton* (1942).

Arthur Conan Doyle

As the creator of Sherlock Holmes, Arthur Conan Doyle (1859 -1930) occupies a unique position in modern letters. To the reader of modern detective fiction the famous stories do not seem, in spite of the praise of devotees, supremely clever in either plot or atmosphere, nor Holmes himself remarkable except for his encyclopedic knowledge. That is because Doyle took the detective story where Wilkie Collins had left it and brought it almost at once to its high modern development. Thus Sherlock Holmes as the archetype of almost all fictional detectives since his day has become a legend, the most famous character in English letters, known even to the illiterate and preserved by the screen and radio into another age.

Doyle was born in Edinburgh, the son of an unsuccessful civil servant and grandson of the famous Irish cartoonist, John Doyle. As the family were pious Catholics Doyle was educated in Jesuit schools in England and Austria. In 1876 he entered the medical school at the University of Edinburgh and five years later began the practice of medicine. After going to sea as surgeon, first in a whaler and then in a West African passenger liner, he established an office and awaited a practice. It was the failure of the latter to support him that drove him to writing.

The character of Holmes was built largely upon recollections of Joseph Bell, a lecturer in anatomy at Edinburgh. Holmes made his first appearance in 1887 in a full-length novel, *A Study in Scarlet,* with a background of London and early Utah. Three years later appeared *The Sign of the Four.* Both of these were revenge plots in which the story behind the crime shared the interest with the process of detection. But it was not until the adventures began to appear as short stories in the *Strand Magazine* that the great popularity of Holmes began. Thereafter Doyle stuck with one exception to the episodic story which threw all the emphasis on the achievements of Holmes. The exception was the best, and probably the most popular, of all the series, *The Hound of the Baskervilles* (1902), a novel that combined the full excitement of detection with an atmosphere of authentically "gothick" terror. The Holmes cycle proper ended with *His Last Bow* (1917); *The Case Book of SherlockHolmes* Holmes (1927) was a not completely successful attempt to revive it.

But though Sherlock Holmes made his fortune, it was as an historical romancer that Doyle wished to be known. In 1888 he wrote *Micah Clarke*, a really fine story of Monmouth's rebellion, and two years later *The White Company*, his far better known picture of the days of Edward III. *Rodney Stone* dealt with the sporting world of the Regency, the "Gerard" books with Napoleon's campaigns, and *Sir Nigel* (1906) again with the Hundred Years' War. These show a real gift of narration and an ability to create absorbing plot and atmosphere but not character. The best of them, *The White Company*, owes a good deal to Reade *The Cloister and the Hearth*. They are stories of exciting action, singularly weak in "romantic" interest or entirely without it. Inevitably, they have become schoolboy reading, the better reading of the better schoolboy, like the novels of Marrayat, and like those capable of being enjoyed again in middle age—but they are fatally immature. He must be put among the great yarn spinners, to whom, regrettably, literary appraisals can never do justice in proportion to the pleasure they give us.

In 1912 he began to weave tales of adventure in a new vein about the leonine figure of Professor Challenger and in 1915 wrote his only detective story outside the Holmes cycle, *The Valley of Fear*, based on the history of the "Molly Maguires," a gang who terrorized the coal regions of Pennsylvania. In all Conan Doyle wrote some fifty volumes of fiction. With literary success Doyle abandoned medicine for good. He soon attained affluence and public recognition. In 1902 he was knighted and appointed Deputy-Lieutenant of Surrey—but for political rather than literary services. He was twice married, in 1885 and in 1907.

The death of his son during World War I was a turning point in Doyle's life. He had left the Catholic church many years before, and now the desire to communicate with the dead led him, with many of his generation, to spiritualism. Thereafter, with Sir Oliver Lodge, he devoted himself to psychical research and to propaganda for his belief. What he then wrote, however interesting, was of no importance as literature, and in any case the quality of his work had fallen off steadily since about 1910.

Autobiography: *Memories and Adventures* (1924).

Fiction: *A Study in Scarlet* (1887), *Micah Clarke* (1889), *The Sign of the Four* (1890), *The White Company* (1891), *The Adventures of Sherlock Holmes* (1892), *The Great Shadow* (1893), *The Memoires of Sherlock Holmes* (1894), *Round the Red Lamp* (1894), *The Stark Munro Letters* (1895), *Rodney Stone* (1896), *The Exploits of Brigadier Gerard* (1896), *Uncle Bernac* (1897), *The Hound of the Baskervilles* (1902), *The Adventures of Gerard* (1903), *The Return of Sherlock Holmes* (1905), *Sir Nigel* (1906), *The Last Galley* (1911), *The Lost World* (1912), *The Valley of Fear* (1914), *His Last Bow* (1917), *The Great Keinplatz Experiment* (1919), *The Last of the Legions* (1922), *The Black Doctor* (1925), *The Case Book of Sherlock Holmes* (1927), *The Maracot Deep* (1929).

Hector Hugh Munro

"Saki." (Hector Hugh Munro, 1870 -1916) was born at Akyab, Burma, where his father was inspector-general of police. "*The Munro clan,*" writes E. H. Munro, his sister, "has always been composed of fighters and writers. Our grandfather was a colonel in the Indian Army. My mother's mother . . . .belonged to the Macnab clan. So Hector was Celtic on both sides of his family." At the age of two he was brought home to England with his elder brother and sister, and left in the care of two maiden aunts near Barnstaple,

North Devon. The aunts, to judge from Miss Munro's account of them, were singularly unamiable women whose government of their charges was a spiteful tyranny. Unhappiness is often the lot of Anglo-Indian children, and Hector Munro endured it stoically, but it left a deep impression on him as his work shows. He attended school at Exmouth and Bedford until he was seventeen, and then for two years was taught by his father with whom he travelled widely on the continent. In 1893 Munro left England to join his father's service, the Burma Military Police, in which his elder brother had preceded him. A year of Burma broke his health completely and he returned to Devon to recover.

Those who know only the Saki of the stories are often unaware that Munro was a journalist first of all. In 1896, having recovered from his Burmese experience, he went to London where be began by writing satires for the *Westminster Gazette*. In 1902 he became foreign correspondent for the *Morning Post* and for the next six years represented it in the Balkans, in Warsaw, in St. Petersburg (whence he reported the Red Sunday of 1905), and in Paris. In 1908, after his father's death, he settled in London, writing for several journals, publishing his only novel, *The Unbearable Bassington* (1912), and the Saki stories. He was still known chiefly as a political writer and satirist.

Although he was forty-four when war in 1914 broke out, Munro enlisted early in the 22d Royal Fusiliers, refused a commission, and went out to France as a corporal. He was from all testimony an excellent soldier. He was killed by a sniper at Beaumont-Hamel in November, 1916.

The stories for which Munro is gratefully remembered were collected in a series of volumes beginning with *Reginald* (1904) and ending with *The Square Egg and Other Sketches* (1924). Most of them recount with remarkable swiftness and economy the adventures of those insouciant young men Reginald and Clovis. Readers will recognize them as the literary ancestors of Bertie Wooster, but as often with the ancestors of aristocratic nincompoops superior in character and attainments to their notorious descendant. They are "nuts," but highly intelligent "nuts," purposeful and consistent in their devastating raids upon stupidity and convention, suave and subtle in their methods. It is not hard to trace them to Saki's boyhood and to the child's desire for revenge upon the adult world. All that is complacent, tiresome, or pretentious in maturity is fair game for them, and the child in the reader enters delightedly into a game that gives its instinctive derision of grown-up ways the fullest satisfaction.

The world of Reginald and Clovis shows the lighter side of Saki but he was not all of one mood. "Both aunts," says Miss Munro, "were guilty of mental cruelty: we often longed for revenge with an intensity I suspect we inherited from our Highland ancestry." The revenge that Saki took in "The Lumber Room" is merely amusing and might have belonged to the childhood of Clovis, but in "*Srendi Vashtar*" there is a rather horrible, if understandable, cruelty. In several other stories, such as "*The Music on The Hill*" and "*The Wolves of Cernogratz*" the sombre side of the Celtic imagination is very effectively at work. "*Esme*" is a perfect fusion of the macabre and the comic. In these as in his lighter stories Saki is a master of swift effect, creating a situation in two or three sentences and touching even his climaxes so lightly that only the alert will appreciate them at once. It is this delicacy and sureness of touch, rather than his impish humor, that gives his work its durability.

Though the sketches collected in *The Square Egg* were written from the Western Front, the tales of Saki belong to the prewar years of the century and often require a knowledge of that lost, untroubled time for their full relish. Nevertheless the omnibus edition of them published in the United States in 1930 ran through ten printings in thirteen years. Whatever may be topical in Saki, there is enough of the perennial human comedy to assure him a high place among the writers of the short story.

Stories and sketches: *Reginald* (1904), *Reginald in Russia* (1910), *The Chronicles of Clovis* (1912), *Beasts and Super Beasts* (1914), *The Toys of Peace and Other Papers* (1919), *The Square Egg and Other Sketches* (1924), *The Complete Short Stories of Saki* (1930).

Novel: *The Unbearable Bassington* (1912).

William Wymark Jacobs

One of the most popular short story writers before the First World War was William Wymark Jacobs (1863 -1943), whose yarns cleverly illustrated by Will Owen were for years a regular feature of the *Strand Magazine*. He was born in Wapping (H. M. Tomlinson's "shipping parish") where his father managed the South Devon Wharf. From school he entered the Post Office as a Civil Service clerk, remaining there until he had turned a taste for writing into professional success. In 1899 with three books published, he resigned and for the next twenty years held his public with a steady flow of amusing but monotonously similar stories.

Arnold Bennett found Jacobs lacking in the curiosity that broadens and matures the mind. It is true; his last books are exactly like his first; his rare fertility in the invention of incident seldom rose above the schoolboyish hoax or practical joke set forth with all the obviousness of a cartoon. The fun, though, was undeniably funny of its kind and he could achieve shrewd touches of characterization though never sustained character. In tales of horror, of which he wrote a few, he had a small mastery. "The Monkey's Paw" is a classic in its field, often reprinted. But generally he is a supreme comic-strip artist in prose, repeating endlessly the ludicrous blunders and infantile revenges of impossible sailors and rustics.

Fiction: *Many Cargoes* (1896), *The Skipper's Wooing* (1897), *More Cargoes* (1898), *A Master of Craft* (1900), *Light Freights* (1901), *The Lady of the Barge* (1902), *At Sunwich Port* (1902), *Odd Craft* (1903), *Dialstone Lane* (1904), *Captains All* (1905), *Short Cruises* (1907), *Salthaven* (1908), *Sailors' Knots* (1909), *Ship's Company* (1911), *Night Watches* (1914), *The Castaway* (1917), *Deep Waters* (1919), *Sea Whispers* (1926), *Snug Harbor* (1931).

6
Chapter

Fiction in Late Twentieth Century

INTRODUCTION

The peace brought into prominence several novelists whose early work before the war had been overshadowed by the established Edwardian writers. Frank Swinnerton made his mark in 1917 with *Nocturne,* a unique little work whose perfection he never approached again. His studies of middleclass London were carefully realistic but unimaginative, and after a few years his readers found them monotonous. If Swinnerton was not sufficiently versatile, Compton Mackenzie, a fine writer at his best, energetic and provocative, was too much so. By being unpredictable he alienated the large class of critics and readers who attach themselves to an author whose character and ideas they think they know. J. D. Beresford had solid unspectacular merit: Stephen McKenna wrote brilliantly but rather superficially of smart political society. The dismal collapse of Sir Hugh Walpole's reputation before his death made it clear that he owed it more to his social talents and skilful journalism than to his literary merit. He was far too prolific and swamped a few good novels like *The Cathedral* (1922) in a mass of inferior work. William McFee began vigorously in the tradition of

Conrad with *Aliens* (1914) and *Casuals of the Sea* (1916) and wrote some admirable novels until he left the sea and settled in the United States in 1923, after which his work became verbose and mannered.

In contrast to these men whose reputations, high in the twenties, dwindled steadily in the next decade is Somerset Maugham. After twenty years of steady effort he was first considered seriously in 1915 when *Of Human Bondage* revealed a new depth and scope in his work. Never as good as the best of the others at their best, he rose for the next thirty years in popularity, if not in critical estimation, to attain one of the most remarkable reputations made by a writer who was a great craftsman but not a great artist. Belated recognition of another order came to E. M. Forster with the publication of *A Passage to India* in 1924. He alone of those named has held a place among the first-rate novelists, though he has written no further novels for more than twenty years. His perceptive social criticism, his genuinely liberal philosophy, and the authenticity and clear realization of his characters show him to be a genius who in his earlier work was a generation ahead of his time.

It was inevitable that severe criticism of the old social and moral standards should be the dominant note of the newer fiction and in this the leader was D. H. Lawrence. He had begun his protest before the war, but the suppression by authority of *The Rainbow* (1915) and *Women in Love* (1920) had postponed the impact of his work to a more receptive time. Disgusted with idealism and intellectualism, Lawrence believed that he had found in "the dark wisdom of the blood" the key to a more natural and more fully expressive life. His paganism and the mystical value he attached to primitive sexuality effectively concealed his fundamental puritanism and created a widespread cult among a generation that was violently antipuritanical. It was only when the Fascist tendencies of his later novels became suspect that he lost credit as the prophet of a new morality. A decade after his early death in 1930 he was more correctly appreciated as a remarkable but very imperfect artist. A far more dangerous, because genuinely pagan, attack upon accepted morals was Norman Douglas *South Wind* (1917). Learned, mature, witty, and urbane, it was the antithesis of the violence and seriousness of Lawrence.

A younger man than either of these, Aldous Huxley belonged wholly to the postwar literary movement. *Crome Yellow* (1921) was the first of a series of novels that under the brilliance of their satire were detached and pitiless clinical studies of a dislocated society. By the end of the twenties disgust and then despair succeeded to the detachment until at last Huxley turned to mysticism as a means of social regeneration, and the mantle of satire descended to Evelyn Waugh. Less subtle and penetrating than Huxley's, Waugh's novels are still exquisitely witty satires on the amoral, insolvent smart people of the thirties. Rose Macaulay, highly praised in 1920 for *Potterism,* had all the qualifications of an excellent social satirist except strong convictions. Without these her gifts were dissipated in urbane derision, enjoyable but insignificant.

Complementary to the objectivism of the satirists was the new subjectivism of another group. As early as 1915 Dorothy M. Richardson had quietly begun the series of novels collectively called Pilgrimage, of which five had appeared by 1920 when they began to attract general attention. Her impressionistic technique was not wholly new; variants of it had been used by Sterne, by Eduard Dujardin, and by others, but it was now spoken of as the "stream-of-consciousness" and its development became the most important technical advance of modern fiction. Miss Richardson carried the sensations and perceptions of a single character through a dozen novels. Virginia Woolf applied the method more subtly in a variety of new patterns, prolonging a single consciousness unbroken through several generations, or exhausting the sensational content of successive moments of being. May Sinclair, once widely known as the author of *The Divine Fire* (1904), also belongs in her later writing to this school. The farthest development of the stream-of-consciousness to the present is, of course, in Joyce's *Ulysses* (1922) and Finnegan *Wake* (1939), the latter requiring a new handling of language to express simultaneous consciousness at different levels. Closely related to these are such experiments with time as are found in Rumer Godden *Take Three Tenses* (1945) and the dream sequences and dream symbolism of Mervin Peake *Titus Groan* (1946). The work of most novelists since 1925 shows the occasional influence of this technique. The whole group are indebted to Proust, to William James, to Freud and Jung. Going beyond the practical and intuitive knowledge of psychology on which novelists have always relied, they have availed themselves of the modern science and have tried to translate its discoveries into literary terms.

Regional fiction after the war was more abundant than ever. Francis Brett Young and Mary Webb wrote of the West Midlands; Phyllis Bentley and Storm Jameson of Yorkshire. R. H. Mottram explored the rich past of his native city of Norwich. Sheila Kaye-Smith continued the tradition of Hardy in her studies of country life in Sussex. Scotland was represented by Neill Gunn, A. J. Cronin, and George Blake; Wales by Richard Llewellyn and (unsympathetically) by Caradoc Evans. They produced, on the whole, a body of very good work with some outstanding books, such as Mary Webb's *Precious Bane* (1924), Sheila Kaye-Smith *Joanna Godden* (1921), and Richard Llewellyn *How Green Was My Valley* (1939).

The closely related type, the family chronicle novel, was represented—aside of course from Galsworthy long-a-making *Forsyte Saga* (1922)—by such books as G. B. Stern *The Matriarch* (1924) and its successors, by Clemence Dane *Broome Stages* (1931) and Victoria Sackville-West *Family History* (1932).

Historical fiction remained weak, the twenties having little to show beyond the romances of "*E. Barrington*" (Mrs. L. Adams Beck). In 1934 Robert Graves, the poet, appeared in a new role with *I, Claudius,* a scholarly classical novel. This was followed by others of the same sort, then by two good stories of the American Revolution, a new version of the voyage of the *Argo,* and the rather disappointing *King Jesus* (1946). He is now England's best historical novelist. On a somewhat more popular level C. S. Forester has written stirring military and naval stories, chiefly of the Napoleonic wars, the best known being the Captain Horatio Hornblower series. There have also been isolated works like F. Tennyson Jesse's excellent *Lacquer Lady* (1929).

In 1918 appeared the first of the war novels *The Return of the Soldier* by Rebecca West, a study of a shell-shocked veteran. For fifteen years they appeared steadily, forming at best a fairly large group, most of them centering in realistic accounts of battle experience, with few touches of the lighter side of war to relieve their tragedy and bitter disillusionment. Probably the best was R. H. Mottram *Spanish Farm trilogy* (1924); C. E. Montague *Rough Justice* (1926), Richard Aldington *The Death of a Hero* (1929) and C. S. Forester's *The General* (1936) are noteworthy in this group.

Violence and crime have been ingredients of popular fiction from its beginnings and in the discord of the postwar years they regained the prominence they had in the ballads and lost after the Elizabethan dramatists. Though in 1930 Priestley seemed about to revive the jolly popular novel with a strong flavor of Dickens and though the perennial supply of saccharine romances has never failed, the most vigorous popular writing of the past quarter-century has gone into tales of secret service and detection. During the war John Buchan stepped suddenly into popularity with The *ThirtyNine Steps* (1915) and *Greenmantle* (1916), and until his death in 1940 continued to write thrillers of international intrigue and espionage, mostly of high quality. Nearly as good were the similar tales of *"Francis Beeding,"* collaborations by two members of the League of Nations Secretariat. Since 1930 Graham Greene has raised the estimation of this sort of work by giving a new importance to its psychological aspects. In the detective field, though a great deal of trash has been written, the work of Dorothy Sayres, Margery Allingham, Agatha Christie, Freeman Wills Crofts, and R. A. J. Walling is generally of reliable goodness. The field has been occasionally invaded by such writers as A. A. Milne, Father Ronald Knox, the poet C. Day Lewis (under the pseudonym Nicholas Blake), the economist G. D. H. Cole and his wife, C. M. Cole.

As reading for escape the detective story has completely replaced the romance of far away and has relegated other rivals to unimportance. In its frankly artificial world the reader finds a keen excitement free of serious moral connotations that no other sort of fiction can provide. Daphne Du Maurier has had considerable success with the old-fashioned terrors of the Gothic school but the appeal of the terrible and fantastic seems to have waned. Particularly curious in view of the widespread belief in spiritualism after the war, is the decline of interest in the supernatural. Indicative of the new direction that fantasy has taken is Richard Hughes' *A High Wind in Jamaica* (in the American edition The *Innocent Voyage*), really a rather grim study of the imperviousness of innocence in a world of violence. A different direction, reminiscent of Rider Haggard, is represented by the pseudo-mystical escapism of James Hilton *Lost Horizon.*

In five years, between 1919 and 1925, the technique of the short story was radically changed by the work of Katherine Mansfield. Her method, employing suggestions rather than statements and replacing the well-contrived incident with a subtly created atmosphere, has influenced nearly all writers in the field, and has rendered the traditional type of short story hopelessly old fashioned. In spite of the decline of the literary periodicals that have always been its principal vehicle, the short story because of this refreshment of its technique has more than held its own in recent years. Among the best writers since 1920 have been Elizabeth Bowen, Virginia Woolf, Monday or Tuesday (1921), Rosamund Lehmann , *The Gypsy's Baby* (1946), E. M. Forster,

The Eternal Moment (1921), C. E. Montague, *Fiery Particles* (1923), and Osbert Sitwell, *Open The Door* (1941). Of these only Miss Bowen is known chiefly for her work in this field, in which she is perhaps second only to Miss Mansfield. D. H. Lawrence and Aldous Huxley were less successful in their short stories than in their novels. Somerset Maugham's attractive blend of Kipling and Conrad has given his stories, like his novels, a sustained popularity. The fantasies of A. E. Coppard kept alive by their poetic freshness a type that generally declined after the war. In 1916 Thomas Burke recalled attention to the East End with his *Limehouse Nights*.

A significant feature of this period is that it has not produced any of those "great novelists" that have hitherto appeared in every generation since Richardson. Genius has not been wanting but in the wide diffusion of talent no single author has achieved the old pre-eminence among many who are thoroughly good. Not only has the general level of fiction risen but the temper of the period has been averse to making national institutions of its authors or to encouraging monumental collected works. Even the recognition accorded such writers as Lawrence, Huxley, Joyce, and Virginia Woolf, while it has given them a high position has given them a different sort of position from the solid emplacements of the leading Edwardians. To the many of varying degrees of talent and competence a short review can do no sort of justice—even in several cases the bare justice of mention—nor pause for such ephemeral reputations as those of Ronald Firbank and Michael Arlen. The assignment of authors to schools and groups, always a somewhat arbitrary business, has become, owing to the multiplicity of new patterns—structural, thematic, and stylistic—in the novel, more highly artificial than ever. Nothing, therefore, has been attempted here beyond the indication of characteristic movements and tendencies.

From these one generalisation may be made: that the changes in the character of fiction advocated and begun by Meredith have been almost wholly realized in our time.

Meredith, himself an indifferent story teller, regretted the dominance of narrative in the novel, which he felt could become mature only by becoming a vehicle for ideas. This we have seen. Since 1920 there has been a general and sharp decline in story-telling and plot throughout fiction: in many of the best novels these elements are negligible. At the same time, not merely through discussion and analysis, but by a new use of symbolism borrowed from poetry, music, and painting, a higher degree of significance has been achieved than ever before. If, say, *Clayhanger* and *Nostromo* are compared with *Mrs. Dalloway* and *The Ballad and The Source,* there can be no doubt that the latter make a greater demand upon the intellect and proceed from a wholly different conception of the function of the novel. They are immeasurably inferior as stories. Which are the better is a pointless question: the difference is not specific but generic. Unfortunately since about 1935 the intellectual tendency in fiction has become involved with the propagandist tendency in all the arts so that many novels, especially toward the left, are avowed vehicles of "ideologies." Those who believe that this is merely a transient fashion may turn for comfort to the beginning of the last century when Charles Lamb was reproved for his political indifference and Walter Scott was accused by Hazlitt of writing to bolster up a decaying society.

Somerset Maugham

(William) Somerset Maugham spent his early childhood in Paris, where he was born. His mother died when he was eight years old, his father, who was solicitor to the British Embassy, two years later. An orphan of ten, Maugham was taken into the household of a clerical uncle at Whistable on the coast of Kent. England was virtually a foreign country to the child and as he grew older he found the atmosphere of narrow social and religious orthodoxy in which he was reared unbearable. King's School, Canterbury, which he entered at thirteen, meant little to him one way or the other, and he used his health—he had inherited tubercular weakness from his mother—as an excuse to escape from it to private tutors in Hyeres and later in Heidelberg.

Maugham continuing writing nightly whilst at the same time studying for his degree in medicine, and in 1897 he presented his second book for consideration. (The first had been a biography of Meyerbeer written by the 16 year old Maugham in Heidelberg). Liza of Lambeth, a tale of working-class adultery and its consequences, drew its details from Maugham's experiences as a medical student doing mid-wifery work in the slums of London, (Lambeth being then a slum district of London), and its over-all subject from the school of social-realist "slum-writers" such as George Gissing and Arthur Morrison. The book proved popular with both reviewers and the public, and the first print-run sold out in a matter of weeks. This was enough to convince Maugham to drop medicine (he qualified as a doctor but never practiced) and embark on his sixty-five year career as a writer.

The writer's life allowed Maugham to travel and live in places such as Spain and Capri for the next decade, but his next ten works never came close to rivalling the success of *Lisa*. This changed dramatically in 1907 with the phenomenal success of his play *Lady Frederick*; by the next year he had four plays running simultaneously in London, and Punch published a cartoon of Shakespeare biting his fingernails nervously as he looked at the billboards.

By 1914 Maugham was famous, with 10 plays produced and 10 published novels. Too old to enlist when World War I broke out, Maugham served in France as a member of the British Red Cross's so-called *Literary Ambulance Drivers*, a group of at some 23 well-known writers including Ernest Hemingway, John Dos Passos, and E.E. Cummings. During this time he met Frederick Gerald Haxton, a young San Franciscan who became his companion and lover until Haxton's death in 1944. (Haxton appears as Tony Paxton in Maugham's 1917 play, *Our Betters*). Throughout this period

Maugham continued to write; indeed, he proof-read Of Human Bondage at a location near Dunkirk during a lull in his ambulance duties.

Of Human Bondage (1915) was described at the time by critics as "one of the most important novels of the twentieth century.". The book appeared to be closely autobiographical, (Maugham's stammer is transformed into Philip Carey's club foot, the vicar of Whitestable becomes the vicar of Blackstable, and Phillip Carey is a doctor) although Maugham himself insisted it was more invention than fact. Nevertheless, the close relationship between fictional and non-fictional became Maugham's trademark, despite the legal requirement to state that "the characters in this or that publication are entirely imaginary".

Maugham was clearly not exclusively homosexual: his affair with the then-married Gwendoline Maud Syrie Barnardo, a daughter of orphanage founder Thomas John Barnardo and wife of American-born English pharmaceutical magnate Henry Wellcome produced a daughter later officially named Elizabeth 'Liza' Mary Maugham (1915-1998); Syrie's husband Henry Wellcome then sued for divorce, naming Maugham as co-respondent. In May of 1916, following the *decree nisi*, Syrie and Maugham were married. Syrie became a noted interior decorator who popularized the all-white room in the 1920s. In 1922 he dedicated his short story collection *On a Chinese Screen* to her. They divorced in 1927/1928 after a tempestuous marriage complicated by Maugham's frequent travels abroad and his relationship with Haxton.

Maugham returned to England from his ambulance unit duties to promote *Of Human Bondage* but once that was finalised, he became eager to assist the war effort once more. Unable to return to his ambulance unit, Syrie arranged for him to be introduced to a high ranking intelligence officer known only as "R", and in September 1915 he began work in Switzerland, secretly gathering and passing on intelligence while posing as himself - that is, as a writer.

In 1916, Maugham travelled to the Pacific to research his novel *The Moon and Sixpence,* based on the life of Paul Gauguin. This was the first of those journeys through the late-Imperial world of the 1920s and 1930s which were to establish Maugham forever in the popular imagination as the chronicler of the last days of colonialism in India, Southeast Asia, China and the Pacific, although the books on which this reputation rests represent only a fraction of his output.

In June, 1917 he was asked by Sir William Wiseman, chief of the British Secret Intelligence Service (later named MI6) to undertake a special mission in Russia to keep the Mensheviks in power and Russia in the war by countering German pacifist propoganda. Two and a half months later the Bolsheviks took control. The job was probably always impossible, but Willie subsequently claimed that if he had been able to arrive 6 months earlier, he might have succeeded. Never losing the opportunity to turn real life into a story, his spying experiences became a collection of short stories about a gentlemanly, sophisticated, aloof spy, *Ashenden,* (1928), a volume which Ian Fleming cited as an influence on his character of James Bond.

Maugham's last years were marred by several quasi-scandals which can probably be set down to a progressive loss of judgement as he grew older. The worst of these, and one which cost him many friends, was a bitter attack on the deceased Syrie in his 1962 volume of memoirs, *Looking Back.* In his last years Willie adopted Searle as his son in order to ensure that he would inherit his estate, a move hotly contested by his daughter Liza and her husband, and which exposed Maugham to much public ridicule.

Fiction: *Liza of Lambeth* (1897), *The Making of a Saint* (1898), *Orientations* (1899), *The Hero* (1901), *Mrs. Craddock* (1902), *The Merry-go-round* (1904), *The Bishop's Apron* (1906), *The Explorer* (1907), *The Magician* (1908), *Of Human Bondage* (1915), *The Moon and Sixpence* (1919), *The Trembling of a Leaf, also pub. as Rain and Other Stories* (1921), *The Painted Veil* (1925),

The Casuarina Tree (1926), *Reprinted as The Letter* (1929), *Ashenden* (1928), *Cakes and Ale* (1930), *Six Stories Written in the First Person Singular* (1931), *The Narrow Corner* (1932), *Ah King* (1933), *Altogether,* (1934), *Don Fernando* (1935), *Cosmopolitans* (1936), *Theatre* (1937), *Creatures of Circumstance* (1937), *Princess September and the Nightingale* (1939), *Christmas Holiday* (1939), *The Mixture as Before* (1940), *Up at the Villa* (1941), *The Horn Before the Dawn* (1942), *The Unconquered* (1944), *The Razor's Edge* (1944), *Then and Now* (1946), *Catalina* (1948).

Plays: *A Man of Honour* (1903), *Penelope* (1907), *The Explorer* (1909), *Mrs. Dot* (1912), *Lady Frederick* (1912), *Jack Straw* (1912), *The Tenth Man* (1913), *Landed Gentry* (1913), *The Land of Promise* (1913), *The Unknown* (1920), *The Circle* (1921), *East of Suez* (1922), *Caesar's Wife* (1922), *Home and Beauty* (1923), *Our Betters* (1923), *The Unattainable* (1923), *Loaves and Fishes* (1924), *The Letter* (1925), *The Constant Wife* (1926), *The Sacred Flame* (1928), *The Bread Winner* (1930), *Plays* (1931), *For Services Rendered* (1932), *Sheppey* (1933).

Miscellaneous: *The Gentleman in the Parlor* (1930), *The Summing Up* (1938).

ALDOUS (LEONARD) HUXLEY

Aldous Huxley (1894-1963), English novelist and critic, best known for his dystopian novel *Brave New World*(1931). Besides novels he published travel books, histories, poems, plays, and essays on philosophy, arts, sociology, religion and morals.

Aldous Huxley was born in Godalming, Surrey on July 26, 1894, into a well-to-do upper-middle-class family. His father, Leonard Huxley, was a biographer, editor, and poet. He first studied at Eton College, Berkshire (1908-13). When Huxley was fourteen his mother died. At the age of 16 Huxley suffered an attack of keratitis punctata and became for a period of about 18 months totally blind. By using special glasses and one eye recovered sufficiently he was able to read and he also learned Braille. Despite a condition of near-blindness, Huxley continued his studies at Balliol College, Oxford (1913-15), receiving his B.A. in English in 1916. Unable to pursue his chosen career as a scientist - or fight in World War on the front - Huxley turned to writing. His first collection of poetry appeared in 1916 and two more volumes followed by 1920.

Huxley's first novel, *Crome Yellow* (1921), a witty criticism of society, appeared in 1921. Huxley's style, a combination of brilliant dialogue, cynicism, and social criticism, made him one of the most fashionable literary figures of the decade. In eight years he published a dozen books, among them *Point Counter Point* (1928) and *Do What You Will* (1929)

During the 1920s Huxley formed a close friendship with D.H. Lawrence with whom he traveled in Italy and France. For most of the 1920s Huxley lived in Italy. In the 1930s he moved to Sanary, near Toulon, where he wrote *Brave New World,* a dark vision of a highly technological society of the future. In the1930s Huxley was deeply concerned with the Peace Pledge Union. He moved in 1937 with the guru-figure Gerald Heard to the United States, believing that the Californian climate would help his eyesight, a constant burden. After this turning point in his life, Huxley abandoned pure fictional writing and chose the essay as the vehicle for expressing his ideas.

Brave New World Revised appeared in 1958. Huxley's other later works include *The Devils Of Loudon* (1952), depicting mass-hysteria and exorcism in the 17th-century France. *Island* (1962) was an utopian novel and a return to the territory of Brave New World, in which a journalist shipwrecks on Pala, the fabled island, and discovers there a kind and happy people. But the earthly paradise is not immune to the harsh realities of oil policy. In 1963 appeared *Literature And Science,* a collection of essays.

In 1954 Huxley published an influential study of consciousness expansion through mescaline, *The Doors Of*

Perception and became later a guru among Californian hippies. He also started to use LSD and showed interest in Hindu philosophy. In 1961 Huxley suffered a severe loss when his house and his papers were totally destroyed in a bush-fire. Huxley died in Los Angeles on November 22, 1963.

Fiction: *Limbo* (1920), *Crome Yellow* (1922), *Mortal Coils* (1922), *Antic Hay* (1923), *Little Mexican and Other Stories* (1924), *Those Barren Leaves* (1925), *Two or Three Graces* (1926), *Point Counter Point* (1928), *Brief Candles* (1930), *Brave New World* (1932), *Eyeless in Gaza* (1936), *After Many a Summer Dies the Swan* (1939), *Time Must Have a Stop* (1944), *Ape and Essence* (1948).

Miscellaneous: *On the Margin* (1923), *Along the Road* (1925), *Essays New and Old* (1926). *Jesting Pilate* (1926), *Proper Studies* (1927), *Do What You Will* (1929), *Holy Face and Other Essays* (1929), *Music at Night* (1931), *Texts and Pretexts* (1932), *Beyond the Mexique Bay* (1934), *The Olive Tree* (1936), *Ends and Means* (1937), *Grey Eminence* (1941), *The Perennial Philosophy* (1945), *Science, Liberty and Peace* (1946).

Rose Macaulay

Rose Macaulay was born, probably toward the end of the eighties, in Cambridge, where her father was a university lecturer in English literature. Accustomed to an intellectual environment from childhood and educated largely abroad, she grew naturally into a "good European," sophisticated and intelligent. Before she had entered Newnham College, Oxford, she had written her first novel, *Abbot's Verney* which was published in 1906. During the next fourteen years she wrote five more without becoming very well known, but in 1920 *Potterism* brought her sudden reputation. Its cold scorn of the second rate and its pitiless exposure of the inadequacies of the postwar generation made it one of the most widely discussed books of the year. For the next ten years everything she wrote was well received and she was considered second only to Aldous Huxley among contemporary satirists. Then, like many authors highly esteemed in the twenties, she suffered a decline of popularity. Her wit belonged wholly to that decade of irresponsible mockery, and as the thirties became more serious, she could not adjust herself to the new feeling of the times. What had seemed so clever when *Told By An Idiot* (1923) and *Crewe Train* (1926) first appeared, no longer appealed, and dispraise, as always, retroactive in effect, did serious injustice to her earlier reputation. What she wrote in the twenties is as good as ever, and that is very good. But it is also true that she had little of new importance to say.

In her pacifist novels, Macaulay displays a variety of opinions concerning war and peace and exposes their shortcomings by making her characters counterattack one another. She seems to believe that the reader can grasp the truth, which she defines as the 'thing seen,' concerning war and peace in the midst of diverse voices represented by various characters. However, whether the reader comprehends the truth is uncertain. By presenting such diversity and complexity, Macaulay's novels successfully demonstrate that all divisions—of age, sex, religion, ideology, nation—are foolish. They also subtly emphasize the writer's belief that all human race should make an effort to advance humanity. Despite all the diverse approaches to peace, including the use of force, she has suggested that the entire human race would be against war if all of us only focused on civilized humanity. She has never believed that human race would be so civilized that it might be free from war. As a writer and a pacifist, Macaulay simply has tried to contribute to improving human decency by writing novels which present some 'fragments of truth' about war and peace.

Abbot's Verney (1906); *The Furnace* (1907); *The Valley Captives* (1911); *The Lee Shore* (1912); *The Making of a Bigot* (1914); *What Not* (1919); *Potterism* (1920); *Dangerous Ages* (1921); *Mystery at Geneva* (1922); *Told By An Idiot* (1923); *Orphan Island* (1924); *Crewe Train* (1926); *Daisy and Daphne* (1928); *Staying With Relations*

(1930); *The Shadow Flies* (1932); *Going Abroad* (1934); *I Would Be Private* (1937); *And No Man's Wit* (1940); *They Went to Portugal* (1946).

Virginia Woolf/sh

Virginia Woolf (1882-1941) was the daughter of Leslie Stephen by his second wife, Julia Duckworth. (Harriet Thackeray was Stephen's first wife; Mrs. Woolf was not, therefore, as has been stated, Thackeray's granddaughter). Leslie Stephen, a former Cambridge don, became well known as essayist and editor of *The Cornhill Magazine* and later of *The Dictionary of National Biography*. His house was a center of literary associations and his daughter's life must have been much like that of Katherine Hilbery in her novel *Night and Day*. Hardy, Stevenson, Ruskin, and Meredith were visitors to the household; James Russell Lowell was her godfather. A delicate child, she was educated at home, largely self-educated in her father's library, especially complete in its collection of eighteenth-century authors. Holidays were spent in Cornwall. Her intellectual environment was of the highest quality, but her youth, without experience of school or travel, was outwardly uneventful. About the time of her father's death in 1904 she began re-viewing for *The Times Literary Supplement* and two years later wrote her first novel, which remained for some years unpublished.

In 1912 she married Leonard Woolf, a former colonial civil servant who had resigned to devote himself to history and journalism. After her marriage she reworked the manuscript of her novel, *The Voyage Out*. It was published in 1915 but because of the war attracted less attention than it deserved. The following year Mrs. Woolf suffered a mental breakdown, and upon her recovery she and her husband started the Hogarth Press, at first a hobby for which they did all the printing themselves, but before long a fullfledged publishing enterprise which brought to notice such writers as Katherine Mansfield, T. S. Eliot, and E. M. Forster. In 1919 she published her second novel, *Night and Day*, a long, laborious work and a comparative failure. A volume of short stories, *Monday or Tuesday* (1921), showed a marked increase of power. This was followed by three distinguished novels, *Jacob's Room* (1922), *Mrs. Dalloway* (1925), and *To the Lighthouse* (1927). These placed Mrs. Woolf unquestionably among the best of modern novelists.

In 1928 appeared the most unusual of Mrs. Woolf's books, *Orlando*. Called a biography and dedicated to her friend Victoria Sackville-West, it traces an unbroken individual consciousness through all the generations of ancestors who contributed to the making of Miss Sackville-West's poem *The Land*. The life of Orlando, a boy in the reign of Queen Elizabeth who becomes a woman at Constantinople at the end of the seventeenth century and is still a young woman in modern England, is a literary pageant of three centuries, developing its theme unostentatiously in episodes of great vigor and beauty. *Orlando* was followed by *The Waves* (1931) and *The Years* (1937). In addition to her novels she published two volumes of literary essays, *The Common Reader* (1925) and *The Second Common Reader* (1932), and two volumes, *A Room of One's Own* (1929) and *Three Guineas* (1938), in advocacy of women's rights. In 1941 experiencing a recurrence of the symptoms of her earlier breakdown, and fearing permanent madness, she drowned herself. A further volume of essays, *The Death of the Moth*, containing some of her best work, was published in 1942.

Since *The Voyage Out*, which was largely traditional in its technique, Mrs. Woolf has been identified with the experimental school of psychological novelists. Perhaps because of her limited experience she preferred to treat the life of the mind rather than that of the body. Hardly to be called a follower of Joyce and Proust, she has explored the modes of consciousness, especially the "moment of being." Her way of developing its significance can best be studied in her essays *The Mark on The Wall* and *The Death of the Moth*. The impact of experience on her characters may be compressed within a day as in *Mrs. Dalloway* or extended over a lifetime as in *The Waves*. The essential "moments of being" are carried upon as light a structure of narrative as possible. Moreover Mrs. Woolf believes that the full implications of a character are to be found only in their extension into other characters. These may be as, again, in *Mrs. Dalloway* all the persons surrounding the central character at a given time or, as in *Orlando*, a series of' progenitors whose qualities are focussed in the last of the line. Her novels are studies rather than stories.

The world of Mrs. Woolf's novels is a very narrow one, in many ways like that of Jane Austen except that it is metropolitan instead of provincial. She restricts herself almost entirely to the English scene and to the intellectual middle class that she knew. She takes her people largely for granted and passes few moral judgments. Like Jane Austen she knows only two unforgivable sins, stupidity and vulgarity. The resemblance is not accidental; both minds were formed by the literature of the eighteenth century and saw their own impassioned times in the light of that more reasonable and realistic age.

The eighteenth-century quality of Mrs. Woolf's mind becomes even more salient when one turns to her literary criticism. The two *Common Reader* volumes and *The Death of the Moth* show her to have been, almost uniquely among her contemporaries, a critic without a "system." She read a book to extract its essential quality and passed judgment on what she found. She could therefore take apparently incompatible positions and make contradictory statements. But under this superficial inconsistency one soon discovers a sound sense, a firm grasp of the uncodified rules of good taste, and an unshakable belief in the supremacy of the intellect. Her view, expressed in *A Room of One's Own*, that economic independence and leisure are necessary for women (men already have them) if they are to make the best of their minds is certainly an eighteenth-century view rather than a modern one. However ruthlessly in her fiction and experimental essays she may have discarded traditional apparatus, her fundamental views are all traditional and her exploration of consciousness is derived from Sterne rather than from Freud.

In her essays Mrs. Woolf wrote firm, lucid prose, beautifully suited to the conveyance of critical ideas. In her subjective experiments and increasingly in her novels her style was elaborate, delicately, sometimes too self-consciously wrought. Sometimes the reader's attention is fixed upon some minute object—a snail on the wall, the cold feet of insects, a dying moth—that serves to focus a moment of experience, at others a succession of symbols make a kaleidoscopic pattern. It is a technique that sometimes involves her in the common fault of English prose stylists, that of trespassing upon the ground of poetry. But she was trying to express difficult things in a new way, and her style shows the energy of an original creative mind.

Mrs. Woolf's influence on her contemporaries was intense rather than broad. Her house was the center of a coterie, the Bloomsbury group—Lytton Strachey, the Bells, Roger Fry, and the authors published by the Hogarth Press. They were a distinguished but rather exclusive and selfcentered circle. Mrs. Woolf did not, like Strachey, found a popular school of writing, nor did she leave great promise of work undone. Indeed it seems as if when she ended her life she had said about all she had to say. But she had done a great deal in applying the methods of the Imagists to the novel and in developing the technique of the stream-ofconsciousness. She will be praised by discriminating critics and will occupy an important place in the historical development of English fiction.

Novels: *The Voyage Out* (1915), *Night and Day* (1919), *Jacob's Room* (1922), *Mrs. Dalloway* (1925), *To the Lighthouse* (1927), *Orlando* (1928), *The Waves* (1931), *The Years* (1937), *Between the Acts* (1941).

Short stories: *Two Stories, with Leonard Woolf* (1917), *Kew Gardens* (1919), *The Mark on the Wall* (1919), *Monday or Tuesday* (1921).

Miscellaneous: *Mr. Bennett and Mrs. Brown* (1924), *The Common Reader* (1925). *A Room of One's Own* (1929), *On Being Ill* (1930), *Beau Brummell* (1930), *Street Haunting* (1930), *The Common Reader: Second Series*, (1932), *A Letter to a Young Poet* (1932), *Flush: A Biography* (1933), *Walter Sichert: A Conversation* (1934), *Three Guineas* (1938), *Roger Fry: A Biography* (1940), *The Death of the Moth* (1942), *The Leaning Tower* (1947), *The Moment* (1947).

James (Augustine Aloysius) Joyce

James (Augustine Aloysius) Joyce (1882-1941) was born to middle class parents of declining fortunes in a suburb of Dublin. His father, John Stanislas Joyce, an easy-going, convivial man, lost first his capital and then a post in municipal politics, letting his family sink to the sordid lowwater mark of shabby gentility. The one exception to his general neglect of their affairs was the education of his eldest son. At the age of six James was placed in Clongowes Wood College where he stayed for three years (18881891); later he attended Belvedere College (1894-1897) and University College, Dublin (1898-1902). All these were Jesuit schools, and there is no better education, within its limits, than that given by the Order. Joyce received from them, besides his A.B., a remarkably thorough grounding in letters, philosophy, and languages, to which he was rapidly adding a wider culture of his own acquiring.

In 1902 Dublin offered excellent prospects to young Joyce. His character and abilities had impressed his teachers from his early school days, assuring his career as a Jesuit scholar if he chose to join the order. He once considered it, encouraged by his mother's piety, but he distrusted the priests, who had, he felt, betrayed Parnell and would always sacrifice the interests of the people to those of the Church. Alternatively his abilities could not fail of distinction in the Irish literary revival then in full swung, but to Joyce the narrow emphasis upon its national character seemed a betrayal of culture to political ends. He wanted to develop his genius, of which he felt sure, free of priests and politicians, and to him that did not seem possible at home.

In the fall of 1902 Joyce went to Paris to study medicine, but was too poor to pay his tuition and for six months lived grimly on the edge of starvation. In the spring he was called home by his mother's last illness and spent the next year in various "digs" around Dublin—including the Martello tower of *Ulysses*—supporting himself by teaching. After his marriage in the fall of 1904 to Norah Barnacle he went abroad for the second time.

Familiar with several modern languages, Joyce obtained through an agency a post with the Berlitz School in Zurich. Arriving there he found the agency was a fraud and that he had no job. The Berlitz people, however, placed him in Trieste where he lived for the next ten years and where his children were born. Up to this time Joyce had earned nothing by literature. As a young collegian he had put forth a critique of Ibsen and a pamphlet attacking the national theater: his early verse, *Chamber Music* (1907), had been published but brought him nothing, and *Dubliners* (written 1904-5), offensive to Irish patriotism and too strong a brew for English taste, could not find a publisher. He was working out a new technique in a spiritual record of his youth, *A Portrait of the Artist as a Young Man,* the outgrowth of an earlier and abandoned manuscript called *Stephen Hero* (posthumously published, 1944). In the meantime he kept his family on his Berlitz salary of £80 a year, meagerly supplemented by private effort.

In 1914 the First World War drove Joyce from Trieste, then an Austrian city, back to Zurich, where work as correspondent in a bank and a small grant from the English government continued him in poverty. Ezra Pound, who was to be a loyal and helpful friend to Joyce, serialized *Portrait of the Artist in The Egoist,* the organ of the AngloAmerican literary exiles in Paris, and the book was published in New York in 1916.

After the war Joyce returned to Trieste for a year and then removed to Paris, which was his home for his remaining twenty years. Here in 1921 he completed *Ulysses,* which overlapping *Portrait of the Artist,* had been in the making since he first conceived it as an episode for *Dubliners.* The first edition was published in Paris, 1922, by "Shakespeare and Co." (Sylvia Beach) and was followed by a prolonged and disheartening struggle to legalize its circulation in England and the United States, in both of which it was banned. The first "legal" American edition appeared in 1933, following a favorable decision in a U. S. District Court. In 1927 Joyce published *Pomes Penyeach,* his second volume of verse, and in the magazine *transition* a curious prose experiment *Haveth Childers Everywhere,* the first of several instalments of *Work in Progress,* which when completed became *Finnegan's Wake* (1939). Once again war drove Joyce to Switzerland, in 1940. He was still poor, worried over family troubles, and ill. Following an operation he died in Zurich in 1941.

Joyce's life was a disheartening struggle sustained with the utmost courage. He was a teacher and writer, dependent upon his eyes; yet these gave him constant pain and anxiety. In spite of repeated operations he was for long periods nearly blind, and during his latter years always wrote with difficulty. Like D. H. Lawrence he had to fight bitter public hostility. His first three important books were published only after heartbreaking and ruinous delays, and when *Finnegan's Wake* at last appeared without hindrance the public was contemptuous or apathetic. By mortally offending his fellow Irishmen and the Catholic Church he had cut himself off completely from home. Only a strong character and a just estimate of his own genius could have sustained him.

Joyce is the terrible *homo unius libri;* his verse and single play aside, all that he wrote is virtually a single book unfolding from *Stephen Hero* to *Finnegan's Wake* with the organic wholeness and inevitability of a strong, slow-growing plant. *Stephen Hero* tentatively and *Portrait of the Artist as a Young Man* consummately present youth's quest of integrity.

Stephen Daedalus (Joyce) come to manhood, examines the forces that have shaped him ftom infancy-family, community, church—and considers the claims of each to his loyalty. In pain his character is born: he frees himself of them all and stands alone, self-realized. His hero brought to birth, Joyce in *Dubliners* explores his environment, the historic, vulgar Dublin he loved and despised. In *Ulysses* he brings them together again in a new relation. Stephen (no longer Joyce but the protomartyr) goes about his affairs in Dublin on 16 June, 1904: elsewhere in the city Leopold Bloom, advertising solicitor, goes about his. Eventually their paths join, each being the complement of the other in the father and son relationship of the spirit. Between them in the course of the day and in the microcosm of the city they have surveyed human life from birth to death. Each is the eternal wanderer in the maze of experience, repeating the endless martyrdom, each, being temporal, is incomplete and seeking his complementary link (UlyssesTelemachus) in the chain of being. *Ulysses* traces the streamof-consciousness in the individual's waking life, touching only at points the world of dreams. *Finnegan's Wake* is the dream of life in which the whole race is involved. In the dream of a single night the martyrdom is repeated again and again, the last words of the book linking to the first to make it an endlessly recurring cycle. With its characters of multiple identity, appearing now as one person, now another, yet always themselves, and its subtle idiom in which a word or phrase may have a like multiplicity of meaning, it is the expression of the many in one and the hardest work of fiction in any language to read and understand. It completes the synthesis of Joyce's epic of man from the unfolding of the individual to the cosmic history of the race.

Not since Milton has an English writer brought so much scholarship to a work of imagination as Joyce, or made such demands upon his reader. Theology, philosophy, psychology, history, a dozen languages, and the classics of as many literatures form the background for the appreciation of

Ulysses and *Finnegan's Wake*. It was incomprehension from incapacity or malevolence that caused most of the moral denunciation of the former. In these books Joyce shows unsparingly the coarseness of physical life just as Swift did, but they are in no sense pornographic. And the reader who does not bring his whole mind and education to bear at every moment in penetrating the circumstance to get at the meaning will have wasted his time. It may be noted here, parenthetically, that the reader should not rely implicitly on the "keys" to these books: each interpreter emphasizes the elements that interest him, makes his mistakes, and leaves many things untouched.

Finally Joyce is one of the great modern masters of English style. The gradually unfolding maturity of expression in the *Portrait of the Artist* as Stephen grows and develops, the historical evolution of the Holles Street chapter of *Ulysses*, the voices that break out in *Finnegan's Wake* as from some cosmic radio, show his perfect control of word and cadence. He achieved at length the most original idiom of his time for the expression of the deeper levels of the subconscious and the extra-temporal elements in human nature and experience. It is the antithesis of the subjectivism of Gertrude Stein, as objective as a mathematical demonstration, and uncouth and outrageous as it may at first appear, it will prove on consideration curiously traditional. Joyce had a cosmopolitanism of intellect rare since the best minds of the seventeenth and eighteenth centuries, and he used all his resources. It will be hard to estimate his contribution to the resources of the language until a successor of equal gifts appears.

Fiction: *Dubliners* (1914), *A Portrait of the Artist as a Young Man* (1916), *Ulysses* (1922), *Finnegan's Wake* (1939).

Play: *Exiles* (1918).

J. B. Priestley

John Boynton Priestley was born in Bradford in 1894. On the outbreak of the First World War Priestley immediately joined the British Army. He was sent to France and in September 1915 took part in the Battle of Loos. After being wounded in 1917 Priestley sent back to England for six months. Soon after returning to the Western Front he endured a German gas attack. Treated at Rouen he was classified by the Medical Board as unfit for active service and was transferred to the Entertainers Section of the British Army.

When Priestley left the army he became a student at Trinity Hall, Cambridge. At university Priestley he gained valuable experience by writing for the *Cambridge Review*. After completing a degree in Modern History and Political Science, Priestley found work as theatre reviewer with the *Daily News*. He also contributed articles to the *Spectator*, the *Challenge* and *Nineteenth Century*. Priestly also began writing books and his early critical writings such as *The English Comic Characters* (1925), *The English Novel* (1927), *English Humour* (1928) established his reputation as an important commentator on literature.

Priestley also wrote popular novels such as *The Good Companions* (1929), *Angel Pavement* (1930) and over fifty plays; the most notable being *Dangerous Corner* (1932), *Time and the Conways* (1937), *When We Are Married* (1938) and *An Inspector Calls* (1947).

In the 1930s Priestley became increasing concerned about social problems. This is reflected in *English Journey* (1934), an account of his travels through England.

During the Second World War Priestley became the presenter of Postscripts, a BBC Radio radio programme that followed the nine o'clock news on Sunday evenings. Starting on 5th June 1940, Priestley built up such a following that after a few months it was estimated that around 40 per cent of the adult population in Britain was listening to the programme.

Some members of the Conservative Party complained about Priestley expressing left-wing views on his radio programme. As a result Priestley made his last talk on 20th

October 1940. These were later published in book form as *Britain Speaks* (1940).

Priestley and a group of friends now established the 1941 Committee. One of its members, Tom Hopkinson, later claimed that the motive force was the belief that if the Second World War was to be won "a much more coordinated effort would be needed, with stricter planning of the economy and greater use of scientific know-how, particularly in the field of war production."

Priestley became the chairman of the committee and other members included Edward G. Hulton, Kingsley Martin, Richard Acland, Michael Foot, Peter Thorneycroft, Thomas Balogh, Richie Calder, Tom Winteringham, Vernon Bartlett, Violet Bonham Carter, Konni Zilliacus, Victor Gollancz, Storm Jameson and David Low.

In December 1941 the committee published a report that called for public control of the railways, mines and docks and a national wages policy. A further report in May 1942 argued for works councils and the publication of "post-war plans for the provision of full and free education, employment and a civilized standard of living for everyone."

On 26th July 1941 Priestley, Richard Acland and other members of the 1941 Committee established the socialist Common Wealth Party. The party advocated the three principles of Common Ownership, Vital Democracy and Morality in Politics. The party favoured public ownership of land and Acland gave away his Devon family estate of 19,000 acres (8,097 hectares) to the National Trust.

Priestley was chairman of the new party but after a dispute with Acland he resigned on 28th September. The C went on to win by-elections against Conservatives at Eddisbury, Skipton and Chelmsford. However, in the 1945 General Election only one of its twenty-three candidates was successful - at Chelmsford, where there was no Labour contestant. The Common Wealth Party was dissolved in 1945 and most members joined the Labour Party.

Some members of the Labour Party disapproved of the electoral truce between the main political parties during the Second World War and in 1942 Priestley and Richard Acland formed the socialist Common Wealth Party. The party advocated the three principles of Common Ownership, Vital Democracy and Morality in Politics. The party favoured public ownership of land and Acland gave away his Devon family estate of 19,000 acres (8,097 hectares) to the National Trust.

The party won by-elections against Conservatives at Eddisbury, Skipton and Chelmsford. However, in the 1945 General Election only one of its twenty-three candidates was successful - at Chelmsford, where there was no Labour contestant. The Common Wealth Party was dissolved in 1945 and most members joined the Labour Party.

After the war Priestley continued to wrote on politics and literature. He wrote an article for the *New Statesman* entitled *Russia, the Atom and the West,* where he attacked the decision by Aneurin Bevan to abandon his policy of unilateral nuclear disarmament (2nd November, 1957). The article resulted in a large number of people writing letters to the journal supporting Priestley's views. Kingsley Martin, the editor of the *New Statesman,* organised a meeting of people inspired by Priestley and as result they formed the Campaign for Nuclear Disarmament (CND). Early members of this group included Priestley, Bertrand Russell, Fenner Brockway, Victor Gollancz, Canon John Collins and Michael Foot .

In his later years Priestley wrote two volumes of autobiography: *Margin Released* (1962) and *Instead of the Trees* (1977). John Boynton Priestley died on 14th August, 1984.

Fiction: *Adam in Moonshine* (1927), *Benighted* (1927), *The Good Companions* (1929), *Angel Pavement* (1930), *The Town Major of Miraucourt* (1930), *Faraway* (1932), *Albert Goes Through* (1933), *Wonder Hero* (1933), *I'll Tell You Everything, with Gerald Bullitt* (1933), *Four-in-Hand* (1934), *They Walk in the City* (1936), *The*

Doomsday Men (1938), *Let the People Sing* (1939), *Blackout in Gretley* (1942), *Daylight on Saturday* (1943), *Three Men in New Suits* (1945), *Bright Day* (1946), *Jenny Villiers* (1947).

Plays: *Dangerous Corner* (1932), *The Roundabout* (1933) *Laburnum Grove* (1934), *Eden End* (1934), *Cornelius* (1935), *Duet in Floodlight* (1935), *Bees on the Boat Deck* (1936), *Time and the Conways* (1937), *Mystery at Greenfingers* (1937), *People at Sea* (1937), *I Have Been Here Before* (1938), *When We are Married* (1938), *Johnson Over Jordan* (1939), *Four. Plays [Music at Night, The Long Mirror, They Came to a City, Desert Highway]* (1944), *How Are They At Home?* (1945), *An Inspector Calls* (1947).

Miscellaneous: *George Meredith* (1926), *Thomas Love Peacock* (1927), *English Journey* (1934), *Midnight on the Desert* (1937), *Rain Upon Godshill* (1939), *Russian Journey* (1946), *The Arts Under Socialism* (1947).

Arthur Joyce Cary

English novelist Joyce Cary developed a trilogy form in which each volume is narrated by one of three protagonists. He used this form in two trilogies that include his most well-known works.

Arthur Joyce Lunel Cary was born on Dec. 7, 1888, in Londonderry, Ireland (now Northern Ireland), to an old Anglo-Irish family. At age 16 he studied painting in Edinburgh and later moved to Paris. From 1909 to 1912 he was at Trinity College, Oxford, where he studied law. Having joined the civil service in 1914 in what was then the British colony of Nigeria, he served in the Nigeria Regiment during World War I. He was wounded while fighting in the Cameroons and returned to civil duty in Nigeria in 1917 as a district officer. West Africa became the locale of his early novels.

Resolved to become a writer, Cary returned to England and settled in Oxford in 1920. Although that year he published ten short stories in the *Saturday Evening Post*, an American magazine, he decided he knew too little about philosophy, ethics, and history to continue writing in good conscience. Study occupied the next several years, and it was only in 1932 that his first novel, *Aissa Saved*, appeared. The story of an African girl converted to Christianity but still retaining pagan elements in her faith, it was followed by three more African novels—*An American Visitor* (1933), *The African Witch* (1936), and *Mister Johnson* (1939)—and a novel about the decline of the British Empire, *Castle Corner* (1938). Childhood was the theme of his next two novels: that of a cockney wartime evacuee in *Charley Is My Darling* (1940) and his own in *A House of Children* (1941).

Cary's first trilogy begins with the first-person narration of a woman, Sara Monday, in *Herself Surprised* (1941) and follows with that of two men in her life, the lawyer Tom Wilcher in *To Be a Pilgrim* (1942) and the artist Gulley Jimson in *The Horse's Mouth* (1944), Cary's best-known novel. Jimson is a social rebel and visionary artist whose humorous philosophy and devilish adventures in *The Horse's Mouth* helped make him one of the best-known characters in 20th-century fiction.

Similarly, Cary's other trilogy is seen from the vantage of a politician's wife in *A Prisoner of Grace* (1952), the politician himself in *Except the Lord* (1953), and the wife's second husband in *Not Honour More* (1955). Cary planned a third trilogy on religion but was afflicted with muscular atrophy and knew he could not live to complete it. Hence he treated the theme in a single novel, *The Captive and the Free*, which was published in 1959 after his death. Cary died in Oxford on March 29, 1957. His short stories were collected in *Spring Song* (1960).

Novels: *Aissa Saved* (1932), *The American Visitor* (1933), *The African Witch* (1936), *Castle Corner* (1938), *Mister Johnson* (1939), *Charley Is My Darling* (1940), *The House of Children* (1941), *Herself Surprised* (1941), *To Be a Pilgrim* (1942), *The Horse's Mouth* (1944), *The Moonlight* (1946), *A Fearful Joy* (1950).

George Orwell

George Orwell (1903-1950) was born Eric Arthur Blair in 1903 in Motihari, Bengal, India. His father, Richard Walmesley Blair was a civil servant for the British government. In 1904 Orwell moved with his mother and sister to England where he remained until 1922. He began to write at an early age, and was even published in college periodicals, but he did not enjoy school. Orwell wrote about his unfavorable prep-school experiences in the essay *Such Such were the Joys* (1968).

Orwell failed to win a university scholarship and without the opportunity to continue his education he went to Bruma and served in the administration of the Indian Imperial Police from 1922 to 1927 when he resigned in part due to his growing dislike of British imperialism, a dislike he vocalized in his essays *Shooting an Elephant* (1950), and *A Hanging* (1931).

Starting in 1930 Orwell became a regular contributor to the New Adelphi, and in 1933 he assumed the name "George Orwell" by which he would become famous. For his first novel he used his recent experience with poverty as inspiration and wrote *Down and Out in Paris and London* (1933). While teaching in a private school he published his second major work, *Burmese Days* (1934). Two years later Orwell married Eileen O'Shaugnessy. Orwell wrote a book on Spain, *Homage to Catalonia*, which was published in 1938.

During the second World War Orwell served as a sergeant in the Home Guard and also worked as a journalist for the BBC, Observer and Tribune, where he was literary editor from 1943 to 1945. It was toward the end of the war that he wrote *Animal Farm*, and when it was over he moved to Scotland.

It was *Animal Farm* that made finally Orwell prosperous. His other world wide success was *Nineteen Eighty-Four*, which Orwell said was written "to alter other people's idea of the kind of society they should strive after." Sadly Orwell never lived to see how successful it would become.

Fiction: *Burmese Days* (1934), *A Clergyman's Daughter* (1935), *Keep the Aspidistra Flying* (1936), *Coming Up For Air* (1939), *Nineteen Eighty Four* (1949).

Miscellaneous: *Down and Out in Paris and London* (1933), *The Road to Wigan Pier* (1937), *Homage to Catalonia* (1938), *Inside the Whale* (1940), *The Lion and the Unicorn* (1941), *Animal Farm* (1945), *Dickens, Dali and Others* (1946), *The Death of an Elephant* (1950).

Graham Greene

Greene was born in Berkhamsted, Hertfordshire, the fourth of six children - his younger brother Hugh was later to become the Director-General of the BBC, and older brother Raymond was an eminent doctor and mountaineer. Their parents, Charles Henry Greene and Marion nee Raymond, were first cousins and members of a large and influential family which included the owners of the Greene King brewery, and various bankers and businessmen. Charles Greene was "second master" at Berkhamsted School, where the headmaster was Dr Thomas Fry (who was married to another cousin of Charles).In 1910, Charles Greene succeeded Dr Fry as headmaster of the school, and Graham attended the school as a pupil. Bullied and profoundly unhappy as a boarder, Greene made several attempts at suicide (some of them purportedly by playing Russian roulette - though Michael Shelden's biography of Greene persuasively discredits the truth of these incidents), and in 1921 at the age of seventeen he underwent six months of psychoanalysis in London to deal with depression. After this he returned to the school as a day boy, living with his family. Schoolfriends included Claud Cockburn and Peter Quennell.He went to Balliol College, Oxford, and his first work (a volume of poetry) was published in 1925, while he was an undergraduate, but it was not widely praised.

After graduation, Greene took up a career in journalism, firstly in Nottingham (a city which recurs in his novels as an epitome of mean provincial life), and then as a subeditor on

The Times. While in Nottingham he started a correspondence with Vivien Dayrell-Browning, a Roman Catholic who had written to correct him on a point of Catholic doctrine. Greene converted to the faith in 1926, and the couple were married the following year. They had two children, Lucy (born 1933) and Francis (born 1936). In 1948 Greene left Vivien for Catherine Walston, but they remained married.

Greene's first published novel was *The Man Within* in 1929, and its reception emboldened him to give up his job at *The Times* and work full-time as a novelist. However, the following two books were not successful (Greene disowned them in later life), and his first real success was *Stamboul Train* in 1932 – as with several of his subsequent books, this was also adapted as a film (*Orient Express*, 1934).

His income from novels was supplemented by freelance journalism, including book and film reviews for *The Spectator*, and co-editing the magazine *Night and Day*, which closed down in 1937 shortly after Greene's review of the film *Wee Willie Winkie*, starring a nine-year-old Shirley Temple, caused the magazine to lose a libel case. Greene's review claimed that Temple displayed "a certain adroit coquetry which appealed to middle-aged men", and is now seen as one of the first criticisms of the sexualisation of young children by the entertainment industry.

His fiction was originally divided into two genres: thrillers or mystery/suspense books, such as *Brighton Rock*, that he himself cast as "entertainments" but which often included a notable philosophical edge, and literary works such as *The Power and the Glory*, on which his reputation was thought to be based.

As his career lengthened, however, Greene and his readers both found the "entertainments" to be of nearly as high a value as the literary efforts, and Greene's later efforts such as *The Human Factor*, *The Comedians*, *Our Man in Havana* and *The Quiet American* combine these modes into works of remarkable insight and compression.

Greene's novels are written in a contemporary, realistic style, often featuring characters troubled by self-doubt and living in seedy or rootless circumstances. The doubts were often of a religious nature, echoing the author's ambiguous attitude to Catholicism (by the end of his life he seems to have lost his faith, but still considered himself a Catholic). He converted at a young age in order to marry his first love, whom he cheated on many times. The man would have two or three serious affairs at a time and a few casual flings. He was not the type of man to desert his religion but he struggled with it as his characters often do.

Unlike other "Catholic writers" such as Evelyn Waugh and Anthony Burgess, Greene's politics were essentially left-leaning, though some biographers believe politics mattered little to him. In his later years he was a strong critic of what he saw as American imperialism, and he supported the Cuban leader Fidel Castro, whom he had met.

Fiction: *The Man Within* (1929), *The Name of Action* (1930), *Rumor At Nightfall* (1931), *Stamboul Train* (1932), *It's a Battlefield* (1934), *The Bear Fell Free* (1935), *The Basement Room* (1936), *A Gun For Sale* (1936), *Brighton Rock* (1938), *The Confidential Agent* (1939), *The Power and the Glory* (1939), *The Ministry of Fear* (1943), *The Heart of the Matter* (1948), *Nineteen Stories* (1949).

Miscellaneous: *England Made Me* (1935), *Journey Without Maps* (1936), *The Lawless Roads* (1939), *British Dramatists* (1942).

Henry Green

Henry Green was the nom de plume of Henry Yorke, who was born just over a hundred years ago, and died in 1973. He was an aristocrat, with an aristocrat's rich confidence; he felt no need to explain himself to his readers, either on or off the page. Off the page, he preferred to be photographed from behind - there is a famous Cecil Beaton photograph, with a Magritte-like surrealism, of the dark glossy back of Green's head - and for many years successfully delayed the publication of his books in America or in paperback. On the page he removed those vulgar spoors of presence whereby authors communicate themselves to readers: he never internalizes his characters' thoughts, hardly ever explains a character's motive, and avoids the authorial adverb, which so often helpfully flags a character's emotion to readers ("She said, grandiloquently"). He can be a difficult writer, is a scrambler of syntax, and in many ways is the last English Modernist novelist: his best-known novel, Loving, was published in 1945, after which English literary Modernism essentially expired. Green is a novelist of ideas, but one without the marked moral or political partisanship of some of his contemporaries. A strong influence of Kafka in the symbolism that is the heart of his work places him among the moderns, but his robust sense of comedy comes straight from the eighteenthcentury tradition of the English novel. *Party Going* (1938) is a clever social satire on the middle class, a conversation piece reminiscent of T. L. Peacock and Aldous Huxley, but with a new note of austere symbolism that removes it from the derivative. *Caught* (1943) is a much grimmer tale reflecting Green's wartime experience in the Auxiliary Fire Service. *Loving* (1945), his finest work to date, again satirizes, under the thin disguise of a servants' hall comedy, the modern dilemma of the middle class. In satiric power and characterization it shows a great advance over *Party Going*. The confusion of the idealist after the war is the theme of *Back* (1946), and the bureaucratic state of the near future that of *Concluding* (1948).

The most impressive satiric novelist since the appearance of Huxley in the early twenties, Green, if less brilliantly witty than Huxley, has a richer humor and a greater power to create effective characters. His best have a life of their own beyond the qualities and ideas they serve to express, just as his novels while blended of satire and allegory are, with the exception of *Party Going*, good stories in their own right. His strongly individual style, though it has many roots in the past, is not conventionally traditional but thoroughly modern, an excellent medium to express the grim and foolish years in which he has written.

Novels: *Blindness* (1926), *Living* (1931), *Party Going* (1938), *Caught* (1943), *Loving* (1945), *Back* (1946), *Concluding* (1948), *Nothing* (1950).

Reminescences: *Pack My Bag* (1939).

Alfred Edgar Coppard

Alfred Edgar Coppard was born of working class parents at Folkestone in Kent. He attended school at Brighton until he was nine, when he was withdrawn because of poor health. He had no further formal education. Soon after, he was apprenticed to a tailor in Whitechapel, for whom he worked thirteen hours a day. From then on he worked steadily at anything he found to do: at various times he was an office boy, a messenger, a professional sprinter, and a clerk. He outgrew the sickliness of his childhood and made up for his lack of schooling by voracious reading. At length he qualified himself as an accountant, and in 1905, at the age of twenty-seven, he married. Two years later a position with an engineering firm took him to Oxford, where for the first time he found himself in an intellectual society.

Oxford stimulated a literary impulse latent in Coppard and about 1911 he began, half seriously, writing "poems and tales." After a while he made friends in a circle of literary undergraduates which included Aldous Huxley, L. A. G. Strong, and Richard Hughes. Occasionally W. B. Yeats attended the informal meetings at which they read and discussed books. The example of these younger men who were beginning to publish set Coppard to writing in earnest, and from 1916 onward his stories and verses appeared from time to time in magazines. By the end of the First World War, during which he worked in a munitions factory, he decided to give up clerical work for authorship. The first two years were discouraging; by the beginning of 1921 he was destitute and only an unexpected check from an American magazine saved his career. A few months later the Golden

Cockerel Press began its publications with the issue of his first volume, *Adam and Eve and Pinch Me*. From that time on his success, though never spectacular, has been steady, his seventeen volumes of short stories being the most distinguished work in that genre during the fifteen years after the death of Katherine Mansfield.

Though a self-educated working man, Coppard is in no sense a proletarian writer. His tales are often about working people and are grim with immediate knowledge of the harder aspects of life, but they are without bitterness or class consciousness. He is too objective an artist to be a propagandist, and his fantastic humor mitigates his deep and constant sense of the tragedy of most lives. The pervading emotion of his work is a sort of wry pity for those who are defeated through some tragic misapprehension of a situation or of the actions of their fellows.

Coppard is a thorough traditionalist. His model in narrative is the folk tale—and, reviewing his work, one would add the ballad. To analysis and the creation of atmosphere he prefers the revelation of character in action, and his tales generally march with military directness to their main events. He wants his reader to feel that he is being "talked to, not written at." His prose style, like that of his verse, strongly influenced by the seventeenth century, has the ease and grace of complete competence. Method and style together give to most of his tales an effect of austere poetry. In fact it is in the tales rather than in his verse, though that is often good, that one recognizes the essential poet in Coppard.

He turned like Katherine Mansfield away from the contrived short story of the French school, but by a different path, bringing back something of the old simplicity of narrative. His work is like fresh air in a time when the short story is increasingly influenced by the probings and intricate symbolisms of Kafka.

Short stories: *Adam and Eve and Pinch Me* (1921), *Clorinda Walks in Heaven* (1922), *The Black Dog* (1923),

Fishmonger's Fiddle (1925), *The Field of Mustard* (1926), *Count Stefan* (1928), *Silver Circus* (1928), *The Man From Kilsheelan* (1930), *The Hundredth Story of A. E. Coppard* (1931), *Nixey's Harlequin* (1931), *Cheefoo* (1932), *Crotty Shinkwin* (1932), *Dunky Fitlow* (1933), *Ring the Bells of Heaven* (1933), *Emergency Exit* (1934), *Nine-penny Flute penny Flute* (1937), *Tapster's Tapestry* (1938), *You Never Know, Do You?* (1939). *VERSE: Hips and Haws* (1922), *Pelagea* (1926), *Yokohama Garland* (*Philadelphia,* 1926), *Collected Poems* (1928). *Cherry Ripe* (1935).

Katherine Mansfield

Katherine Mansfield was the pen name of Kathleen Mansfield Beauchamp, daughter of Sir Harold Beauchamp, a banker and business man of Wellington, New Zealand. In the nineties her father was not so wealthy and prominent as he afterward became, and her childhood was somewhat like that of Kezia Burnell, the little girl who appears in several of her stories. She attended a local school in the suburban village to which her family had moved and later Wellington Girls College, where her stories, which she had been writing since the age of eight or nine, were published in the school magazine. At fifteen she was sent to complete her education at Queen's College, an old-fashioned finishing school in London. In 1906, school over, she went back to the family in New Zealand and spent the next two years in a fight to get away from it again. It was then that she adopted her pen name to sign her contributions to *The Native Companion.* At length her father reluctantly allowed her £100 a year on which to live in London.

Her early years in London were hard and discouraging. Her health was delicate and her allowance inadequate. She found no encouragement in her work. In 1909, at twentyone, she married, but left her husband almost immediately. In a desperate interval that followed she took a lover and was delivered of his still-born child at an obscure resort in Bavaria. Here she gathered the materials for her first literary success, a series of sketches of German bourgeois types which she contributed to *The New Age*. The next year these were published as her first volume, *In a German Pension* (1911). Later Katherine Mansfield was ashamed of these stories, and during the war would not allow them to be republished. They are caricatures, it is true, without the subtlety and sureness of her later work; they ridicule unkindly but not unjustly the weaknesses of the German character. But they are thoroughly good work.

In 1911 began the long and close relation with John Middleton Murry that, after her writing, was the most important thing in Katherine Mansfield's life. When they met he was a young journalist, poorer than she, trying to edit a literary magazine called *Rhythm*, to which she had offered a story, *The Woman in the Store*. Work for the magazine drew them together and she rented Murry a room in her flat. Before long they were living together, but it was not until 1918 that her husband would obtain a divorce so that they might marry. Though they were completely devoted to each other, their life together was always harassed by want of money, by her increasing ill-health, by separations, and by constant moving about. Katherine Mansfield had a restless spirit and even in love could not always accept the life of laborious poverty their circumstances enforced. They were completely happy only for a few months in 1915-16 when they took a small villa at Bandol in the south of France. Here she did some of her best work.

The spiritual pressure of the war and the death of a brother at the front turned Katherine Mansfield's mind back to her childhood as an escape from sorrow. Out of this came *Prelude*, written at Bandol, and later *The Garden Party*, drawn directly from memories of her home at Karori. But she could not escape for long: her restlessness and tubercular weakness increased and in 1918 she returned, alone, to France. *Je ne parle pas français* expresses her despairing mood at this time.

Recognition as an artist did not come to Katherine Mansfield until after the war, tragically too late. *Prelude* was published by Leonard and Virginia Woolf at the Hogarth

Press in 1918, *Je nè parle pas français* appeared in 1919, and *Bliss* in 1920. She was married to Murry and was helping him by reviewing for the Athenaeum, of which he was now editor. But her tuberculosis had reached an advanced stage and it was too late to find the abiding peace for which they both had struggled desperately. She tried to achieve a calm of the spirit to compensate for her broken life. In October of 1922 she went to take the psychophysical therapy of the Gudjieff Institute near Fontainebleau. She died there January 9, 1923.

Katherine Mansfield was small and dark in person, aloof and reserved in manner. She had great warmth of sympathy and affection: as she wrote to Murry, "All I write or ever, ever will write will be the fruit of our love—." But there was something in her that she could not give to others, that insisted on separateness with a fierce independence, and she had the gift of sarcasm that sometimes belongs to quiet, clear-seeing women. She was wholly an artist, a good musician as well as a writer, a brilliant but not wholly integrated personality. Sustained happiness would probably have been impossible for her.

The work of Katherine Mansfield marks a critical change in the technique of the English short story. Conventionally a story was built upon a well-contrived incident, or a facet of a character. For this she substituted a technique in which the implications of a story are more important than its statement, in which the "atmosphere" evokes a revealing central mood, as in the familiar essay. This may be attributed partly to the influence of Chekhov, whom she greatly admired, but more to her own nature, writers being generally better explained by what they are than by what they read. She wrote less from observation than from understanding, and this was drawn from that withheld, secluded part of her character to which things and people appeared inseparable from the mood in which they were known. To her ability to create a scene or a moment in its totality of experience, she adds remarkable clarity of perception, a keen irony, and an unfailing instinct for simplicity of means that give her unpretentious stories their curious charm and power.

After her death Katherine Mansfield's journals, letters, poems, and book reviews were collected and published by Murry, as well as a selection of her stories. Her last volume, *Something Childish* (called *The Little Girl* in the American edition), appeared in 1924.

Short stories: *in a German Pension* (1911), *Prelude* (1918), *Je ne parle pas français* (1919), *Bliss and Other Stories* (1920), *The Garden Party* (1922), *The Doves' Nest* (1923), *The Little Girl and Other Stories* (1924), *Something Childish* (1924), *The Aloe* (1930), *The Short Stories of Katherine Mansfield* (1937).

Herbert Ernest Bates

Born in a Northamptonshire village of country-bred parents, Herbert Ernest Bates has become one of the most sensitive portrayers of English rural life in his generation. After local schooling a few years' experience of business routine proved unbearably irksome and hastened his escape into the freer life his writing allowed him. He had been writing for six years when his first novel, *The Two Sisters*, was published in 1926. He was just twenty-one. Five years later he married and since then has lived in Kent close to the life he writes about. He served the Second World War in the RAF.

Like Katherine Mansfield, Bates was strongly influenced by Chekhov, and his stories, like hers, depend for their effect upon atmosphere and emotion rather than contrived incident. Less of a literary Brahmin than she, he misses something of her delicate sensitivity, but his greater robustness is suitable to his material. He writes of those aspects and moments of country life that have a poetic significance at best half comprehended by the actors in them, generally simple people of average character and capacity. He has an ability to express the poignancy of the "lyrical moment" that has made him conspicuously successful in the short story. In his novels, of which he has written ten, he is not always successful in sustaining his created mood.

One of the most thoroughly English writers of the present both in his choice and his treatment of material, Bates was little read in the United States until the serialization of his novel *Spella Ho* in the Atlantic Monthly in 1938. Since then the amusing stories of *My Uncle Silas* (1939) and his romance of the war, *Fair Stood the Wind for France* (1944), have increased his popularity, but some of his books are still hard to obtain.

Short stories: *The Seekers* (1926), *The Spring Song* (1927), *Seven Tales and Alexander* (1929), *The Tree* (1930), *Mrs. Esmond's Life* (1931), *A German Idyll* (1932), *The Black Boxer* (1932), *The Woman Who Had Imagination* (1934), *Cut and Come Again* (1935), *Something Short and Sweet* (1937), *The Flying Goat* (1939), *My Uncle Silas* (1939), *Country Tales* (1940), *The Beauty of the Dead* (1940), *The Cruise of the Breadwinner* (1946).

Under pseudonym "Flying Officer X: The Greatest People in the World (1942), *How Sleep the Brave* (1943), *Something in the Air* (1944).

Novels: *The Two Sisters* (1926), *Catherine Foster* (1929), *Charlotte's Row* (1931), *The Fallow Land* (1932), *The Poacher* (1935), *A House of Women* (1936), *Spella Ho* (1938), *The Bride Comes to Evensford* (1943), *Fair Stood the Wind for France* (1944), *The Purple Plain* (1947).

7

Chapter

Prose

INTRODUCTION

In Victorian hands the essay had become almost exclusively formal and didactic. Between Leigh Hunt and Stevenson only Thackeray and Alexander Smith kept alive the tradition of the familiar essay. But when in the eighties and nineties a lighter type of literary periodical began to supplant the ponderous reviews there was a brisk revival of the informal essay in all its varieties: familiar, satiric, apprecitive, and picturesque. The field of the essay then became once more, as it had been in the seventeenth century, a literary Everyman's Land which all might, and did invade at will. Thus the twentieth century, rich in general prose writers, has comparatively few essayists in the strict sense of that classification, and has seen a general relaxation of the formal distinctions of the various types of the essay.

Essay writing in the eighteen-nineties was marked by the estheticism and preciousness of style that permeated the entire "Decadence" and that were derived chiefly from Pater *Renaissance*. The arts of pagan Greece or neopagan Italy interpreted with exquisite discernment inspired a great deal of work that was polished and charming but too fragile for survival. Above the general level of beautiful triviality rose Oscar Wilde *Intentions* (1891), Maurice Hewlett's *Earthwork Out of Tuscany* (1895), the early essays of W. B. Yeats, and those of Lionel Johnson, collected in *Post Liminium* (1912). Above all rose Max Beerbohm, a young Oxonian brilliantly impudent in *The Yellow Book*, affecting to be *passé* in 1895, and delicately reminding the public at intervals for the next thirty years that he was the most accomplished familiar essayist of the twentieth century. His latest volume *Mainly on the Air* (1946) shows that in his radio talks before and during the Second World War there was no failure of the gifts that have delighted two generations.

Among works of less popular appeal than Beerbohm's but enjoyed by the bookish of two generations were the fastidious essays of Alice Meynell, often too precious in style, the delicate eighteen-century studies of Austin Dobson, and the scholarly ironic judgments of Augustine Birrell.

Between 1900 and 1930 the regular appearance of certain essayists in weekly periodicals brought something like a renewal of the popularity the light journalistic essay had enjoyed in the eighteenth century. G. K. Chesterton in *The Illustrated London News*, E. V. Lucas and A. A. Milne in *Punch*, Robert Lynd in *The New Statesman*, and Edmund Gosse in *The Times Literary Supplement* were the most talented of a group, each of which had a regular following of readers. Their contributions, of varying degrees of popularity, the challenging paradoxes of Chesterton, the pleasant connoisseurship of Lucas, the literary causeries of Gosse-appealed to all sorts of tastes.

Chesterton and Hilaire Belloc were foremost among the Edwardian writers of general prose. A curious pair, the one sturdily English, the other as sturdily Gallic, they were united by their religious and political views. Between them they covered a wide range of biography, criticism, controversy, and familiar commentary with a trenchancy that won the public by its very defiance of public sentiment and prejudice. At the opposite pole was the moody, donnish sentimentalism of A. C. Benson's self-revelation which were much admired until the war shattered the gentle academic world in which he mused. By that time the more vigorous academic mind of Dean Inge had begun to impress the public with the outspoken criticism of modern life and society that was later to make him famous as "The Gloomy Dean."

Robert Cunninghame-Graham and W. H. Hudson were less popular but stood higher in critical estimation. The characters of both had been formed in the spacious pampas of the Argentine that stamped them forever aliens in modern commercial England. Cunninghame-Graham contemned with aristocratic scorn a world emptied of all graciousness; Hudson ignored it and went freely among unspoiled natural things.

H. M. Tomlinson published *The Sea and the Jungle* in 1912, but recognition of it as one of the great works of English travel was delayed for some years. Though nothing that he wrote afterward quite equalled it in quality, his vigorous thought and rich individual style have secured him the foremost place among the essayists of his generation. The reputation as stylists of the brothers John Cowper Powys and Llewellyn Powys, once high, has declined somewhat, and while Llewellyn's work especially is often excellent in both matter and art it does not approach the force and originality of Tomlinson's.

A great many notable essays, of course, were written throughout the period by authors better known in other fields. Among the novelists Galsworthy, Aldous Huxley, D. H. Lawrence, Virginia Woolf, E. M. Forster, and William McFee stand out; among the poets, Masefield and Edmund Blunden.

In the early twenties the writing of biography was revolutionized by the work of Lytton Strachey. In *Eminent Victorians* (1918) and *Queen Victoria* (1921) Strachey, abandoning the biographer's traditional reserve and reverence, gleefully played skittles with hallowed reputations. Often blemished by prejudice and caricature, his work was salutary and spectacularly effective in humanizing and popularizing biography. His influence can be seen in the work of Phillip Guedalla, Gamaliel Bradford, André Maurois, Emil Ludwig and others who have created a public appetite for biography second only to that for fiction. Charles Whibley, a master of the short biography, known for his contributions to the *Dictionary of National Biography* as well as for his general essays, is chiefly interesting as the last of the essayists to express uncompromising Toryism. Winston Churchill's *Marlborough* is a major biography in the traditional style.

In 1907 appeared an anonymous autobiography *Father and Son* that treated with admirable candor and restraint the spiritual struggle of its author's youth. When later it was honored by the French Academy it proved to be the work of Edmund Gosse. In its kind it has been equalled only by Joyce *Portrait of the Artist as a Young Man*. These are, as literature, the best self-studies that the period has produced. In memoirs, war books aside, the best work has been done by Osbert Sitwell and Siegfried Sassoon.

Among the critics at the beginning of the century the romantic Arthur Symons stands out for his breadth of interest and reasoned esthetic consistency. He is best known for his treatments of the Romantic Movement in England and the Symbolist Movement in France. In scholarly criticism, Professor W. P. Ker of London University occupied a high place as an authority on mediaeval literature. Sir Edmund Gosse and Professor George Saintsbury were bookmen rather than critics, widely read scholarly gossips of literature valuable for their service in bringing authors to readers. Also a bookman and essayist, Holbrook Jackson showed himself a capable critic in his studies of Shaw and William Morris, as well as a bibliophile capable of communicating his enthusiasms in books and reading. On the whole, however, Edwardian criticism, aside from book reviewing, which was excellently done, was not remarkable. The pure esthetic doctrine had proved inadequate, but no new principle had been defined or old one restored.

In the twenties there appeared a number of vigorous young critics stimulated rather than inspired by the American, T. S. Eliot. Of these John Middleton Murry and Herbert Read have attained the most widely recognized authority. Both are humanists with romantic leanings, Murry excelling in biographical interpretation, Read having, like Symons, a wide scope of artistic knowledge and sympathy. The distinguishing features of the newer criticism are a more sensitive social consciousness and an increasing use of the aid of psychology in critical analysis. It has brought little change in fundamental esthetic principles but rather a larger understanding of them that promotes the appreciation of new works of unorthodox form.

The rapid growth of interest in psychology during the years between the wars gave momentum to an increasing stream of full-length lives and biographical essays in which the authors were primarily concerned with the inner forces in man's nature which shape personality and achievement. The American Gamaliel Bradford went so far as to call his studies of personality "psychographs" in order to differentiate his essays from the factual records of events which had been the biographers' traditional approach. In such portrait studies as Bonamy Dobree *Essays in Biography* (1925), F. L. Lucas "Dorothy Osborne" in *Studies French and English* (1934), Virginia Woolf "Miss Ormerod" in *The Common Reader* (1925), and Harold Nicholson "Hindenburg" in *The Yale Review* (Summer, 1931), there are evidences of the psychological approach. Full-length biography was influenced as well, as for example in the several sustained studies of Byron by Peter Quennell. Although many biographers held to the traditional manner, including Winston Churchill in his substantial *Marlborough* (1933-38), the trend of the times was toward the manner of the fiction writers, a manner supported if not originated by Strachey in such passages as the death-bed scene in *Queen Victoria* (1921) and by the influence of the French André Maurois in *Ariel* (1923). The tendency to adopt the methods of the novelist became so prevalent that in 1934

Hugh Walpole expressed the hope that "there will not be too many biographies so gayly imaginative that there is nothing to differentiate them from fiction." Walpole's hope has in some measure been realized: the biographies which appeared in the late thirties and forties show something of a reaction. Although the two schools of biographical writing continue to flourish—the well documented traditional life and the fictionized narrative which often adopts a psychoanalytical approach, the best of the more recent biographies show a fusion of the two, with relatively few of the extremes which were prevalent in the mid-twenties.

Since 1930 there has been a general decline of essaywriting thoughout the English speaking world, as the temper of the time has discouraged the habit of leisurely cultivated reading that the essay requires. Though many of the older essayists have kept on writing, few new ones have appeared. The most spectacular of these is C. S. Lewis, an Oxford don known through his critical writings for some years before he became immensely popular during the Second World War as a Christian apologist. Cyril Connolly, editor of *Horizon,* who writes under the pseudonym of "Palinurus," and George Orwell attracted attention as essayists during the forties, but in general the scarcity of good new work in this field is discouraging. In the past the essay has often been most vigorously written immediately after great wars: the work of Addison and Steele followed the victories of Marlborough, that of Lamb, Hazlitt and Hunt followed Waterloo. There was an abundance of good essays after the First World War, but as yet there is no such prospect after the Second.

Joseph Hilaire Belloc

(Joseph) Hilaire (Pierre) Belloc was born on the family estate near Fontainebleau. His father, Louis Swanton Belloc was an advocate. His mother, Bessie Parkes Belloc, was a young English woman of strong and independent character, a descendant of Joseph Priestly and a pioneer of women's rights. Belloc, though educated in England, was brought up a French citizen. He was schooled at the Oratory School, Edgbaston (near Birmingham), where he came under the influence of Newman. From the Oratory he went to Balliol, reading history and taking a First in his subject as well as winning the Brachenbrey Scholarship. In 1892 he interrupted his education to perform his obligatory service in the French army as a driver in the 3rd Battery, 6th Field Artillery. Belloc had a peculiar pride in the military history of France; four of his ancestors were generals in the armies of Napoleon, and though he had only the ordinary experiences of a recruit, his year of service made a lasting impression on him.

After leaving Oxford in 1895, Belloc made a trip to the United States, where he married Elodie Hogan of Napa Valley, California. They returned to England and have made their permanent home at King's Land, Sussex.

In 1903 Belloc became a British subject by naturalization, and from 1906 to 1910 represented South Salford in Parliament. Except for the part he played with Cecil Chesterton (G. K. C.'s brother) in exposing the "Marconi Scandal" in 1912 after he had left the House of Commons, his political career was undistinguished. Repudiating the major parties of his day as merely different groups of the same aristocratic political machine, Belloc developed a political theory based on the personal responsibility of monarchy coupled with democratic institutions. He bitterly hates the control of politics throughout the world by international financiers, and it is from this that his strong but not violent antiSemitism arises.

Belloc's most ambitious writings are historical. After completing Lingard's unfinished History of England in 1915, he wrote his own in four volumes between 1925 and 1931. More generally read are his historical biographies. All of these develop the thesis that European culture is a single whole, essentially Latin and essentially Christian, derived from the Roman Empire and preserved by the Catholic Church. European destiny he finds in the lives of men such as

Richelieu, Milton, James II, and Napoleon, who have affected the growth or decline of this culture. Though not esteemed for accuracy by some historians, these books are capably and vigorously written, and are good correctives to uncritical acceptance of conventional views.

With an historian's sense of time and a soldier's eye for terrain, Belloc is an admirable writer of books of travel and survey. Such books are often picturesque and trivial, but in Belloc's the description and personal adventure are mixed with a deep feeling for the earth and the tragedy and glory of the men who have lived on it. *The Path to Rome* is his best; *Towns of Destiny* and *Esto Perpetua* are good.

As an essayist he is in many of his moods too dogmatic to be pleasing, but when he can lose himself for a moment in his subject the result is absolutely first rate. *The Mowing of a Field* has become, deservedly, a minor classic and there are half a dozen others of comparable quality. The essays of *Hills and the Sea* are among the best in this century, and through a couple of dozen later volumes to *The Silence of the Sea,* his latest before the war, there is enough to keep a fastidious reader satisfied. The selection made from them by Father Dineen, while not perfect, will serve as a good introduction. There are, regrettably, few critical essays among them, for, though Belloc has generally refrained from literary criticism, in his *Milton* and elsewhere through his work there is evidence of great competence in this field.

In satire and verse he is far less successful. He is too heavy-handed for the first, belaboring the obvious to weariness, and insufficiently subtle in his responses for the second. With a few exceptions—his *Tarentella* has made a delightful concert piece—his poems are high-keyed and rhetorical and are not in the ballad style that makes these faults forgivable. When unrestrained robustness is in order, as in his classic vituperation against the don, they cease to be faults at all, but Belloc seems never to have recognized his limitations in verse.

Belloc's sociopolitical works are not especially pertinent to this survey except *The Contrast*, which in its analysis of British and American institutions points to some significant differences generally neglected on both sides of the Atlantic.

In spite of his versatility and appeal to readers of many different interests Belloc has not been a widely popular author. He is opinionated and iterative, forcing his views upon the reader in and out of season. But if these irritating qualities are put in their proper place of unimportance, the reader will be impressed by a mind as tough and vigorous as any of our day and a style that is genuinely classical in its clarity. Belloc has variety and substance, and the strength that comes of controlled emotion. The excellence of his style is the firm Latin beauty of monumental carving.

History and biography: *Danton* (1899), *Robespierre* (1901), *The Eyewitness* (1908), *Marie Antoinette* (1909), *The French Revolution* (1911), *High Lights of the French Revolution* (1915), *The Last Days of the French Monarchy* (1916), *The House of Commons and Monarchy* (1920), *A Shorter History of England* (1924), *The Campaign of* 1812 *and the Retreat from Moscow* (1924), *Miniatures of French History* (1925), *A History of England, 4 v.* (1925-41), *Oliver Cromwell* (1927), *James the Second* (1928), *How the Reformation Happened* (1928), *Joan of Arc* (1929), *Richelieu* (1930), *Wolsey* (1930), *Cranmer* (1931), *Six British Battles* (1931), *Napoleon* (1932), *Charles the First, King of England* (1933), *William the Conqueror* (1933), *The Tactics and Strategy of the Great Duke of Marlborough* (1933), *Cromwell* (1934), *Milton* (1935), *The Battleground* (1936), *Characters of the Reformation* (1936), *The Crusade* (1937), *Monarchy: A Study of Louis XIV* (1938), *The Great Heresies* (1938), *The Last Rally: A Story of Charles II* (1940), *Elizabethan Commentary* (1942).

Essays: *Hills and the Sea* (1906), *On Nothing* (1908), *On Something* (1910), *On Everything, On Anything* (1910), *First and Last* (1911). *This that and the Other* (1912), *At the Sign of the Lion* (1916). *On* (1923), *Short*

Talks With the Dead (1926), *A Conversation With an Angel* (1928), *Survivals and New Arrivals* (1929), *Essays of a Catholic Layman in England* (1931), *A Conversation With a Cat* (1931), *The Silence of the Sea* (1941).

Miscellaneous: *The Path to Rome* (1902), *Avril* (1904), *Esto Perpetua* (1906), *The Historic Thames* (1907), *The Pyrenees* (1909), *The River of London* (1912), *The Servile State* (1912), *Europe and the Faith* (1920), *The Contrast* (1923), *The Cruise of the Nona* (1925), *The Catholic Church and History* (1926), *An Essay on the Nature of Contemporary England* (1937), *On the Place of Gilbert Chesterton in English Letters* (1940), *The Catholic and the War* (1940).

Verses: *Verses and Sonnets* (1896), *Verses* (1910), *Sonnets and Verse* (1923).

Edward Verall Lucas

Edward Verall Lucas (1868-1938) was born at Eltham in Kent, but grew up in Brighton. His family were solid, middle-class Quakers. He attended various schools until he was sixteen, when his father stopped his education and apprenticed him to a bookseller. In 1889, his apprenticeship completed, Lucas joined the staff of the *Sussex Daily News*, and two years later left home for London, where the kindness of his uncle enabled him to attend University College. In 1893 he joined the *London Globe* and published his first prose work, *Bernard Barton and His Friends*, a pleasant but unimportant book.

For the next twenty years he worked hard at whatever came to hand, anthologies, essays, light novels, publishers' reading and editorial work. He joined the editorial staff of *Punch* in 1904. During the First World War he wrote propaganda satires and served the Red Cross on the Italian Front. In all this period he was remarkably productive and by 919 he was prosperous and sufficiently popular to make a lecture tour around the world.

Lucas lived in London and in Sussex. He was a sociable but reserved man with many acquaintances and few intimate friends. He was an enthusiastic cricketer and an intelligent amateur of art. Early in life he had withdrawn from the Society of Friends and thereafter maintained a saddened agnosticism. In 1925 he became chairman of the publishing house of Methuen and Co.; in 1932 he was made Companion of Honour and later LL.D. of St. Andrews. He died June 26, 1938.

From his boyhood reading of the *Essays of Elia* Lucas was interested in Charles Lamb. In 1887 he wrote some verses on *Old China*. The Bernard Barton book increased his interest in Lamb and his circle. Later a publisher commissioned him to do a book on Lamb and the Lloyds. For Methuen he wrote an introduction to the *Essays of Elia* and in 1900 prepared a new pocket edition with a new biography. His *Life of Lamb* (1905) has blemishes but is the best and fullest work on the subject. It was reissued in 1935 and was followed by the *Letters of Charles and Mary Lamb* in 1936. At the *Shrine of St. Charles* (1934), stray papers on Charles Lamb, is a charming book. These constitute his most important work.

Lucas is most widely popular through his familiar essays, issued in some thirty volumes from 1901 to 1934. These have sometimes been compared with the *Essays of Elia*, but the reader will not find in them the delicate grace of Lamb nor his depth of feeling. Urbanity and wit are their chief merits and they have a limpid charm that justifies their reputation. As a cicerone of pictures and cities Lucas is admirable. In the first group his books on Vermeer are the best, in the second those on London. For the rest his novels, satires, and miscellaneous works are of no great merit.

His autobiography, *Reading, Writing and Remembering*, is merely, as he said of it, "a selection intended to entertain." Real understanding of his background may be gained from *The Old Contemporaries* (1935). More may be gathered from *E. V. Lucas: A Portrait*, by Audrey Lucas (1939).

Essays: *The Friendly Town* (1905), *Fireside and Sunshine* (1906), *Character and Comedy* (1907), *One Day and Another* (1909), *Old Lamps for New* (1911), *A Little of Everything* (1912), *Loiterer's Harvest* (1913), *Harvest Home* (1913), *Landmarks* (1914), *Cloud and Silver* (1926), *A Boswell of Baghdad* (1917), *'Twixt Eagleand Dove and Dove* (1918), *The Phantom Journal* (1919), *Mixed Vintages* (1919), *Adventures and Enthusiasms* (1920), *Specially Selected* (1920), *Urbanities* (1921), *Giving and Receiving* (1922), *You Know What People Are* (1922), *Luck of the Year* (1923), *Encounters and Diversions* (1924), *Events and Embroideries* (1926), *A Fronded Isle* (1927), *A Rover I Would Be* (1928), *Out of a Clear Sky* (1928), *Turning Things Over* (1929), *Travellers Luck* (1930), *Down the Sky* (1930), *If Dogs Could Write* (1930), *French Leaves* (1931), *Visibility Good* (1931), *". . . and such small deer"* (1931), *Lemon Verbena* (1932), *At the Sign of the Dove* (1932), *Saunterer's Rewards* (1933), *English Leaves* (1933), *At the Shrine of St. Charles* (1934), *Pleasure Trove* (1935), *Only the Other Day* (1936), *All of a Piece* (1937), *Adventures and Misgivings* (1938).

Miscellaneous: *Bernard Barton and His Friends* (1893). *The Life of Charles Lamb* (1905), *A Wanderer in Holland* (1905), *A Wanderer in London* (1906), *A Wanderer in Paris* (1909), *A Wanderer in Florence* (1912), *London Lavender* (1912), *The British School* (1913), *Roving East and Roving West* (1921), *Vermeer of Delft* (1922), *A Wanderer Among Pictures* (1924), *A Wanderer in Venice* (1924), *John Constable* (1924), *Introducing London* (1925), *London* (1926), *A Wanderer in Rome* (1926).

Robert Lynd

Robert Lynd (1879-1949) was born and raised in his father's manse in Belfast. As the son of a Presbyterian minister in Ulster he was taught by his childhood associates to be a good, that is an intolerant, Orangeman. But there was a breadth of sympathy in his character and an affection for his country that made him by the time he was mature a serious

Nationalist. It may have been this that led him when he had taken his M. A. at Queen's College, Belfast, in 1899 to leave Ulster for England. He has told almost nothing of his early days there—he appears to have worked for a while in the Midlands—but he soon became a journalist in London and has followed this career successfully ever since. One gathers from his books that he was married, was rejected for service in World War I, had a wide spectator interest in sports, and was a discriminating reader.

Mr. Lynd's books fall into three groups. First there are four volumes intended to promote a better understanding of Ireland. *Ireland: A Nation* (1919) is a sympathetic and realistic presentation of Ireland's case for political and social autonomy. The others are local-color and travel sketches. His essay *"If the Germans Had Conquered England,"* drawing, in the midst of the war and the Irish troubles, a parallel between Ireland under the English and England under the Germans, was a courageous and illuminating piece of work. He avoided the common excesses of the convert and was that rare person, an Irishman who could write about Ireland with restraint. His patriotism did not absorb his critical sense.

"The good critic," writes Mr. Lynd, "communicates his delight in genius." His business, in other words, is synthesis rather than analysis, the recreation for his reader of the best he has found in a work of art. Mr. Lynd's criticism was sometimes brilliant, always sound, and pleasantly free from the preciosity of some of the moderns. He took the reading of books for granted and was interpretative rather than informative. His own reading was wide and his sympathy failed only toward illiberal authors.

Above all Mr. Lynd was a familiar essayist. For a generation readers enjoyed his work in the *New Statesman* over the signature "Y.Y."—a childhood nickname. They have been issued in a series of volumes whose titles—*The Blue Lion, The Peal of Bells, The Orange Tree, The Green Man, The Cockleshell*—carry a genial echo of tavern signs. Their range of subject and mood is wide, but all are marked by an unobstrusive, whimsical humor pointing an eminently sane philosophy and an unfailing enjoyment of all sorts of human activity and character. He had the rare gift of self-revelation without egotism, and of making fun without dispraise. Of all contemporary familiar essayists Mr. Lynd is nearest to Lamb. This does not imply equality with Elia, but it puts him in very good company. Like all journalistic essayists who have had to furnish their weekly essays year after year, Mr. Lynd did some inferior work, but his general level is high, and among his best *"The Herring Fleet"* is unexcelled in its kind. An admirable selection of these essays, "Y.Y." (1933), has been made by Eileen Squire.

He was well known in England as the literary editor of the London *News Chronicle*, as an editorial writer for the *New Statesman and Nation*, and as a contributor to *John O'London's Weekly*. His wife, Sylvia Lynd, is known as a poet and novelist.

Essays: *Irish and English Portraits and Impressions* (1908), *The Book of This and That* (1915), *If the Germans Conquered England* (1917), *The Pleasures of Ignorance* (1921), *Solomon In All His Glory* (1922), *The Sporting Life* (1922), *The Blue Lion* (1923), *Selected Essays* (1923), *The Peal of Bells* (1924), *The Money Box* (1925), *The Little Angel* (1926), *The Orange Tree* (1926), *The Goldfish* (1927), *The Green Man* (1928), *It's a Fine World* (1930), *Rain, Rain, Go to Spain* (1931), *The Cockleshell* (1933), *"Y Y"* (1933), *Both Sides of the Road* (1934), *I Tremble To Think* (1936), *In Defence of Pink* (1937), *Searchlights and Nightingales* (1939), *Life's Little Oddities* (1941), *Essays on Life and Literature* (1951).

Criticism and sketches: *Home Life in Ireland* (1909), *Rambles in Ireland* (1912), *Ireland, a Nation* (1919), *Old and New Masters* (1919), *The Art of Letters* (1920), *The Passion of Labour* (1920), *Books and Authors* (1922), *Dr. Johnson and Company* (1927).

William Henry Hudson

"A traveller in little things," a phrase he liked and used as a title for a book, very aptly characterises William Henry Hudson (1841- 1922) . He was all his life a traveler, a migrant without fixed habitat. Though he liked to call himself "an Exeter man," his grandfather had been an emigrant from England to Massachusetts. His father was from Marblehead, his mother a Kimball from Maine. His parents migrated from New England to the Argentine pampas west of Buenos Aires and there Hudson was born. He was a solitary child, as later in spite of wife and friends he was a solitary man, and drew his early education more from the open country around his father's store near Quilnes than from the itinerant tutors who from time to time stayed for a while to give the Hudson children a little schooling. In *Far Away and Long Ago* he has left a delightful record of this childhood.

Of Hudson's youth and early manhood little is known definitely. He visited Patagonia and perhaps other parts of South America. His father died in 1868 and two years later Hudson came to England, but for a long time remained obscure. His almost superstitious reluctance to recall unpleasant things made him always reticent about these years. He married in poverty and after a succession of dismal lodgings, managed a down-at-heels apartment house, moving from flat to flat as they fell vacant. He did not become a British subject until 1900.

Hudson's writing began in 1885 with *The Purple Land That England Lost*, a romance of Uruguay, but for some time it went unrecognized. By the time he received a Civil List pension in 1901 he had nine books to his credit, including *A Naturalist in La Plata, Idle Days in Patagonia,* and *Nature in Downland*. And it was not until the success of the American edition of *Green Mansions* in 1915 that his earnings became adequate. Long recognized as a master of prose by his fellow writers, he received little public appreciation in England and almost none in America until toward the close of his life.

"My flesh and the soil are one, and the heat in my blood and in the sunshine are one, and the winds and the tempests and my passions are one," wrote Hudson. "I feel the 'strangeness' only with regard to my fellow men, especially in towns, where they exist in conditions unnatural to me but congenial to them." He was pre-eminently a field naturalist with a lifelong knowledge of plants and animals and birds, especially of birds keenly observed and interpreted by temperamental sympathy. He could comprehend anything in nature and had a quick instinctive friendship for peasants and children and such, who, like himself, lived simply and quietly in touch with natural things. The pageantry of life had little appeal for him: he had seen the beaten army of Rosas streaming across the pampas, and had cared for it less than for the ombu trees or the rising of a heron from a lake.

It is about little things that he writes best, things to be found in the homes of villages, in the talk of children and shepherds, in watching a deer at the edge of a wood. He found them over years, cycling or afoot through the byways of England, storing his exact, vivid memory with what others passed by. And at the last the little things gave him a wonderful understanding of the great things. When he died he had all but finished *A Hind in Richmond Park*. The book is an exploration backward through the senses and instincts of animals to the mind of primitive man and the origins of the artistic impulse. It is impressive not only for its encyclopedic nature lore but for the vistas it opens into remote, dim regions of the human mind.

Though he is known chiefly as an ornithologist, and birds fill the greater part of his work, there is hardly an aspect of nature and rural life in the south of England or on the South American plains that he has not treated in faithful detail in his volumes of essays, sketches, and stories written over thirty years. The general reading public, however, has cared most for what are really less characteristic works, his two South American romances, *The Purple Land* and *Green Mansions*. By the time he died the latter had achieved the rank of "classic," and Epstein's much abused sculpture of Rima adorns the bird sanctuary in Hyde Park dedicated to his memory in 1925. Few more haunting stories have been written than this of the bird woman, Rima, found and loved by a European in the Venezuelan jungle and lost to him by the malice of hostile savages. Not a woman but something unutterably beautiful seems to have perished when the flames sweep Rima's forest, where she should have lived forever, passionately loved but never possessed, a symbol of eternal desire.

Something, it is true, must be withdrawn from Hudson's credit as an inventive artist since Carlos Baker has shown that the story in general and in detail is closely copied from Lady Morgan's all but forgotten novel *The Missionary*. But if this study leaves Hudson convicted of something very like plagiarism, it does not touch the power of the treatment, wholly lacking in Lady Morgan. *Green Mansions* is a story, said Galsworthy, "which immortalizes, I think, as passionate a love of all beautiful things as ever was in the heart of man."

Much of the charm of all Hudson's work is due to the intensity of his feeling and the quietness of his style that Conrad compared to the growth of grass. He is not an easy author to quote, for his goodness is diffused throughout the whole and does its surprising work unperceived. He was like that himself, a tall, intense, quiet man, deliberate, certain of what he was to do and doing it simply. Though he had a large circle of friends—Conrad, Cunninghame Graham, Galsworthy, Edward Garnett, and Belloc among others—he always moved apart in an element of his own. Even after he had escaped from poverty and was famous he lived unfashionably in a shabby part of London.

The spirit of independence that Huson brought from the pampas had nothing of the fierceness of Cunninghame Graham's; he neither denounced nor satirized the alien culture of cities in which he was obliged to live. Instinctively as an animal would, he kept himself apart from it and avoided it when he could. There was not a grain of the political man in him; if human polity disgusted him it was a fact of nature like the polity of a rabbit warren. He turned from it to find the eternal interest of simple things.

Essays and nature studies: *Argentine Ornithology, with P. L. Sclater* (1888-89), *The Naturalist in La Plata* (1892), *Idle Days in Patagonia* (1893), *Birds in a Village* (1893), *British Birds* (1895), *Birds in London* (1898), *Nature in Downland* (1900), *Birds and Man* (1901), *Hampshire Days* (1903), *The Land's End* (1908), *Afoot in England* (1909), *A Shepherd's Life* (1910), *Adventures Among Birds* (1913), *Far Away and Long Ago* (1918), *Birds in Town and Village* (1919), *The Book of a Naturalist* (1919), *Birds of La Plata* (1920), *A Traveller in Little Things* (1921), *A Hind in Richmond Park* (1922), *Men, Books and Birds* (1923).

Fiction: *The Purple Land That England Lost* (1885), *A Crystal Age* (1887), *Fan, as Henry Harford* (1892), *El Ombu* (1902), *reissued as South American Sketches* (1909), *and again with two additions as Tales of the Pampas* (1916), *Green Mansions* (1904), *A Little Boy Lost* (1905), *Dead Man's Plack* (1920), *Ralph Herne* (1923).

Robert Bontine Cunninghame Graham

Robert Bontine Cunninghame Graham (1852-1936) was born in London. His immediate ancestry, aristocratic but not illustrious, was three-quarters Scotch, one-quarter Spanish. His early training he had from his maternal grandmother, who formed him in the school of Spanish gentlemen. Later he was sent to Harrow, but unhappy and ill-suited to the life of an English school, he left when he was sixteen. For the next sixteen years he lived a life of adventure in South America, Mexico, and Texas, ranching, living with gauchos on the pampas, teaching fencing. He became a splendid horseman. In 1879 he married a Chilean, Gabriela de la Balmondiere.

Five years later, at the age of thirty-two, he inherited the debt-encumbered family property at Gartmore and returned to Scotland to farm the estate and clear the debt. In

1886 a chivalrous championship of the working man and a hatred of modern commercialism led him into politics and he was elected to Parliament as Liberal member for Lanark. In the House he consistently supported "labour" measures. In the Bloody Sunday riots in Trafalgar Square, that climaxed the dockers' strike of 1887, he led a charge of strikers against the police. He was arrested and sentenced to two months in jail. Thereafter he found himself without influence in Parliament and withdrew from politics in 1892.

Though he had written articles for newspapers (his first published work appeared in the *San Antonio Times*), Cunninghame Graham's career as a writer did not begin until he was forty-three, when he published *Notes on the District of Menteith*. The next year, in collaboration with his wife, he produced a volume of short stories, *Father Archangel of Scotland*. This was followed at intervals until 1932 by fifteen volumes of "tales and sketches." In form they are like the similar work of Galsworthy, sometimes approaching the short story, sometimes the essay; in material they draw upon a cosmopolitan experience as varied and rich as Kipling's. A knifing on the pampas, a starving beggar in London, provide him occasion to pour contempt on the vulgarity, brutality, and impotence of the modern sophisticated world.

A second group of Cunninghame Graham's works deals with the history of South America and the lives and exploits of the Conquistadores. There his Spanish blood and his adventurous youth enabled him to understand and to interpret sympathetically. *The Conquest of New Granada* is a really splendid book.

Two books of travel complete his works. *Mogreb-el-Acksa* (Morocco of the West) is the account of a trip undertaken in 1898 to reach Tarudant, a city then forbidden to Europeans. *Cartagena and the Banks of the Sinu* describes aspects of Colombia observed during the First World War when the author was buying remounts there for the British service.

Cunninghame Graham was a Spanish hidalgo of the fifteenth century strayed into the twentieth. He saw the world through the eyes of a free man who carries his honor through a world open to his fortune. The degradation of the individual in regimented societies dominated by money provoked his scorn. In such a world success is vulgar, only defeat is honorable. In his style he is afraid neither of the sentiment that is the complement of Scottish dourness nor of the high rhetoric of Spanish prose. But his prevailing tone when writing of the modern world is one of fierce aristocratic contempt. These qualities have won the appreciation of the few he esteemed but have denied him any wide popularity.

Sketches and stories: *Father Archangel of Scotland, with Mrs. Cunninghame-Graham* (1896), *Aurora La Cujini* (1898), *Thirteen Stories* (1900), *Success* (1902), *Progress* (1905), *His People* (1906), *Faith* (1909), *Hope* (1910), *Charity* (1912), *A Hatchment* (1913), *Scottish Stories* (1914), *Brought Forward* (1916), *The Dream of the Magi* (1923), *Inveni Portum, Joseph Conrad* (1924), *Redeemed* (1927), *Writ in Sand* (1932), *Mirages* (1936).

Biography: *Hernando do Soto* (1903), *Bernal Diaz del Castillo* (1915), *A Brazilian Mystic* (1920), *Doughty Deeds* (1925), *Pedro de Valdivia* (1926), *José Antonio Paez* (1929), *Portrait of a Dictator* (1933).

History and travel: *Notes on the District of Mentieth* (1895), *Mogreb El Acksa* (1898), *The Ipané* (1899), *A Vanished Arcadia* (1901), *Cartagena and the Banks of the Sinu* (1921), *The Conquest of New Granada* (1922), *The Conquest of the River Plate* (1924), *The Horses of the Conquest* (1930).

Charles Montague Doughty

Though Charles Montague Doughty (1843-1926) lived the greater part of his life and wrote his most important book in the nineteenth century, he is by accident of delayed recognition as well as by a late developing poetic gift virtually a writer of our own times.

He came of "county" families on both sides, his father being the Rev. C. M. Doughty of Theberton Hall, Suffolk, squire and parson in one, his mother a Beaumont of the East Riding of Yorkshire. Both of them died while Doughty was still a little boy and he was brought up by an uncle and an aunt.

Intensely patriotic from boyhood, Doughty determined to enter the navy and was heartbroken when he was rejected for a speech defect. At eighteen he entered Cambridge, devoting himself principally to geology. His first published work (1866) was a monograph on the glaciers of Norway. Upon taking his degree in the same year he transferred his interest from geology to literature and spent the next four years in intensive reading.

In 1871 Doughty began his travels, going first to Holland and progressing easily by way of France, Italy, Spain, and Greece to Palestine and Egypt, studying as he went. This occupied him until 1875. He then wanted to visit and report upon the monuments of Medain Salih in the Arabian desert and, his family being no longer wealthy, tried to secure the backing of the Royal Geographical Society for an expedition. Failing in this he set out in 1876 privately in the character of a Syrian physician. He went with the Haj (the Mohammedan pilgrim caravan) to Medain Salih and then, leaving it, spent eighteen months wandering with Bedouins in the desert. He was in poor health, he underwent great hardships, and his life was in constant danger from Arab fanaticism, but he reached Jidda and thence India safely and returned to England in 1879.

This remarkable adventure produced one of the most remarkable of modern books, *Travels in Arabia Deserta.* Published, after many delays and disappointments, by the Cambridge University Press in 1888, it remained almost unknown to the general public until the glamor of T. E. Lawrence's desert campaign created a wide interest in Arabian adventures. New editions in England and the United States were immediately popular and the work was belatedly recognized as a great English classic.

Arabia Deserta is not a light book to read either for the matter or the manner. It tells of wanderings in remote places and among obscure tribes and often the reader is fairly bewildered in a maze of uncouth names. The mind avid of action will grow impatient at the deliberate chronicling of campfires, wild Arab characters, and mean cruelties, though the cumulative effect is impressive. Moreover Doughty believed that good English began with Chaucer and ended with the Elizabethans, and in this belief created a style unique in modern letters. It is direct, dignified, and quaintly archaic, but not easy. But the whole book is like its subject; it holds one by its very austerities and leaves him with a sense of great experience.

Doughty's later years were almost placid. He married, settled in the country, travelled genteelly on the continent, and, living entirely apart from the contemporary world, devoted himself to writing ambitious poems. These, hitherto, neglected except by a few admirers, will probably never be as widely read as *Arabia Desertu*, for they are far more difficult without great compensating beauty. The *Dawn inBritain* Britain (1906) recounts the Celtic resistance to Rome from the campaign of Brennus to the conquest of Britain. It fills four volumes of the most crabbed verse in English. *Adam Cast Forth* followed in 1908; then two patriotic poems, *The Cliffs* (1909) and *The Clouds* (1912), and an allegory, *The Titans* (1916). His last poem was another allegory, *Mansoul: or the Riddle of the World* (1920, revised 1923). World War I brought Doughty to the brink of poverty but his distress was relieved by a small Civil List pension until a bequest and the returns from his great work gave him a competence again. He died in 1926.

Travel: *On the Jostedal Brae Glaciers* (1866), *Documents epigraphiques recuellis dans le nord de l'Arabie* (1884), *Travels in Arabia Deserta* (1888), *Wanderings in Arabia, excerpts from Arabia Deserta* (1908).

Poetry: *Under Arms* (1900), *The Dawn in Britain* (1906), *Adam Cast Forth* (1908), *The Cliffs* (1909), *The Clouds*

(1912), *The Titans* (1916), *Mansoul* (1920), *Mansoul, revised* (1923).

Thomas Edward Lawrence

Thomas Edward Lawrence (1888-1935) was one of the most fascinating and baffling characters of this century. He was born at Tremadoc, Wales, second son of Thomas Lawrence. During his early childhood the family moved about the British Isles and France, but in 1896 settled in Oxford for the education of the boys. For eleven years Lawrence attended the Oxford High School, at the end passing high (thirteenth) among the Firsts in the Oxford Local Examination.

In a household that encouraged plain living and high thinking, Lawrence was conspicuously Spartan, caring little for comfort and showing fortitude under pain. His daring led him into risky adventures. With a boy's activity he combined an interest in local archeology that before he left school grew into a mature interest in Norman military architecture. He spent his holidays of 1906 and 1907 cycling in France and studying castles, and later while in college extended his study to Syria.

From 1907 to 1910 he was an undergraduate in Jesus College, Oxford, pursuing history, but getting less from the university curriculum than from those independent studies that he embodied in his first work, *Crusader Castles*, written in the winter of 1909-10.

Between graduation and the war Lawrence worked as an archeological assistant to D. G. Hogarth at the Carchemish dig, which yielded such valuable knowledge of the Hittites, and for a while with Flinders Petrie in Egypt. Early in 1914 he went with C. L. Woolley on an expedition to Sinai which was a thinlyveiled British reconnaissance. Before he had completed his report of this survey (*The Wilderness of Zin*) the war had broken out and he was called to the War Office. By the end of 1914 he was attached to Intelligence at Cairo, where he quickly demonstrated his amazing abilities and his incapability of military discipline.

After nearly two years his superiors were glad to release him to work with Storrs in raising the Arab tribes to rebellion. It was this operation, probably the last picturesque campaign in modern war, that made Lawrence one of the most famous men of his generation. He returned from the East to find that Lowell Thomas had made "Lawrence of Arabia" almost a legend. After his work at the Peace Conference, in the interests of the Arabs, he could not take up his life where he had left it.

A poor man after all his achievements, he accepted a fellowship that All Souls College, Oxford, offered him so that he might work on his projected book about the Arabian campaign. But he was not to be let alone. In the spring of 1921 he was called to the Colonial Office by Winston Churchill, and gave valuable aid in settling some of the lamentable trouble the war had left in the Near East. A career was open to him but he declined it as he had declined honors for his war service, and once more he tried to live privately.

Lawrence was bitter. Britain and France had broken their pledges to the Arabs, and he felt that he was placed in an intolerably false position. To escape the world and his own identity he turned to the army as in another age he would have turned to a monastery. As Aircraftman Ross he enlisted in the RAF late in 1922, but was discharged after a few months when his identity was discovered. In March, 1923, he enlisted again, this time in the Royal Tank Corps, under the name of Shaw, which he later legally assumed by deed poll. In 1925 he obtained a transfer back to the RAF and remained in it for ten years, including a year's service in India.

Upon leaving the service in 1935 he went to a cottage at Clouds Hill, Dorset, which he had bought during his days in the Tanks. Here he had solitude and a choice library of books and records. But he had a passion for speed that he indulged by furious motor-cycling. In May 1935 he died shortly after the crack-up of his latest machine.

Seven Pillars of Wisdom was begun at the Peace Conference and continued until the end of the year, when the completed manuscript—the whole except two books—was lost in the Reading railway station. Lawrence's amazing memory enabled him to reproduce it correctly with all its multiple detail in some 400,000 words. This text was then reworked into literary form, and of it eight copies were printed by the *Oxford Times*. In 1926 the first edition, a reduction to 280,000 words, was published by subscription and an abridgment of about half that length, was made public in the following year under the title *Revolt in the Desert*. The public edition of *Seven Pillars* appeared after Lawrence's death in 1935.

In 1932 Lawrence, in need of funds, translated Homer *Odyssey* into approximately contemporary prose, an interesting but not altogether successful piece of work. At about the same time he was writing *The Mint*, a realistic narrative of his RAF experiences, which was not to be published until 1950. It has not been published, but the MS may be consulted in the Library of Congress. His miscellaneous writings with a selection of his war photographs were published in *Oriental Assembly* (1940). Since then *Crusader Castles* and *Secret Despatchers from Arabia* have been published in England in a limited edition.

There have been other modern Englishmen, such as Colonel Leachman and Glubb Pasha, whose military exploits among the Arabs have been nearly as amazing as Lawrence's, but they have been limited by their profession. England has had greater soldiers than Lawrence, but none who could fight a campaign and write about it with equal competence. *Seven Pillars*, like *Arabia Deserta*, is an inimitable work of modern prose, but unlike it, is easily readable. One cannot forget the beautifully fought battle of Tafileh, or the army of Feisal on the march with the tribesmen chanting antiphonally from wing to wing any more than one can forget Doughy's picture of the column of the Haj winding into the desert from Damascus. To begin to appreciate the fascinating and elusive character of Lawrence, however, it is necessary to read further. Two books are especially recommended, The *Letters of T. E. Lawrence* and *T. E. Lawrence By His Friends.*

Seven Pillars of Wisdom, (1926), Revolt in the Desert (1927), The Odyssey of Homer, translation (1932), Crusader Castles (1936), The Diary of T. E. Lawrence, MCMXI (1937), The Letters of T. E. Lawrence, (1938).

Henry Major Tomlinson

Henry Major Tomlinson was born in Poplar when that parish in the East End of London was inhabited by unpretentious people like his own—families of shipmasters, engineers, and others connected with the sea. His youth saw the passing of the sailing ship, on which the prosperity of Poplar was founded, and with it the color of an era and the simple standards of life to which he had been bred. That life had no superfluity; it was natural that he should go to work at twelve in a shipping office. His nineteen years of clerkship were a drudgery, connected tenuously with the ships he had come to love, but none the less drudgery from which he worked hard to escape. A steady reader from boyhood of Emerson, Melville, and Thoreau, he had apprenticed himself to letters and at length, after years of writing for exercise, had his contributions accepted by a London paper.

In 1904, at the age of thirty-one, he left shipping for journalism, joining the staff of the *Morning Leader*, with which he remained, except for one short interruption, until the middle of the First World War.

In 1912 Tomlinson made a voyage in a freighter across the Atlantic and two thousand miles inland up the Amazon and its tributary the Madeira to the head of navigation at the San Antonio Falls in the heart of Brazil. An unusual voyage, it produced an unusual book, The *Sea and the Jungle*, now a classic, some think the greatest, of modern travel literature. Published in the autumn of 1912, however, the book failed to attract attention in the troubled days that preceded the war and was remaindered at half a crown a copy.

When the war broke out, Tomlinson was sent to France as correspondent by the *Morning Leader*. Later he became official correspondent at British Headquarters, but there he proved too outspoken and truthful for the command and in 1917 he was back in London. He became literary editor of the Athenaeum, continuing under Middleton Murry's editorship until the periodical was sold in 1923.

Tomlinson's work as correspondent had attracted wide attention and had made his literary reputation. *The Sea and the Jungle* was "discovered" by critics and its quality recognized. In 1918 Tomlinson issued some war sketches with earlier journalistic work in *Old Junk*, and three years later his colorful essays on the "dockland" of his early love, *London River*. His position among modern prose writers was now assured and after leaving the *Athenaeum* he re mained a free lance, devoting himself entirely to his books. These appeared steadily but without sign of haste: another book of travel *Tide Marks* (1924) and three volumes of essays, *Waiting for Daylight* (1922), *Gifts of Fortune* (1926), *Out of Soundings* (1931). Besides these there was *Under the Red Ensign* (*The Foreshore of England* in the American edition), a survey of the shipping depression in 1926, and shorter works, his lecture *Between the Lines* (1928) and *Norman Douglas* (1931). After *South to Cadiz* (1934) Tomlinson's work shows signs of fatigue: the shadow of approaching war, which he saw more clearly than many of his contemporaries, lies over *Mars His Idiot* (1935); and *The Wind is Rising* (1941) and even *The Turn of the Tide* (1946), though their vivid reporting of another war often recalls his grim pictures of Flanders, have not emerged from it.

Meanwhile Tomlinson had appeared as a novelist with *Gallions Reach* in 1927. This and its half dozen successors have all been well received but have added little to his reputation, his genius being reflective and reminiscent rather than creative. His novels are thoughtful, but the narrative is often sluggish and few of the characters come to life or remain in the reader's memory.

There is a sense in which Tomlinson can be said to have a very narrow range; certain fundamental ideas and even the images and phrases that express them reappear frequently in his writing. Nearly all that he was to say, early or late, can be found in his origins. Poplar gave him his standards of plain living and high thinking, his independent attitude, his love of ships, his hatred of war, and his suspicion of the too rapid growth of the modern world. What his native place began was confirmed by the formative authors of his youth —Melville, Thoreau, and Whitman. He remains among these few first things, whether commenting on war or favorite books or surveying the world from China to Peru—but in no case do they restrict his mental horizon. When one considers the symbolism of the essays in his most mature volume, Out of Soundings, one feels that what he has to say is neither small nor narrow. Mankind has lost its way ("The Changeling") because mechanism has replaced human values in the modern world ("Beauty and The Beast") from which wisdom has departed ("A Brown Owl"). Our culture is derelict on a lee shore but something may be salvaged ("The Wreck") by an arduous strengthening of the spirit that will raise us to a higher plane of perception ("Gilolo"). He prefers to speak by symbols and parables and to the literal and imperceptive his meaning is not always clear.

To express his sense of the impermanence of the material world Tomlinson has developed a highly individual style and imagery. An essay will begin as simply as the best journalism and before we know it the prose will have passed imperceptibly into a stately largo in which phrase after phrase, image after image demolishes the solid world about us. Light fills space in solid cubes and wedges or blends land and clouds, sea and sky into a single continuum, the present dissolves before the past; everywhere matter attenuates until we find ourselves in a world of pure perception. It approaches poetry as nearly as writing can without ceasing to be authentic prose, and yet at all times it remains natural, with those colloquial rhythms that have always linked the best essay writing with the best talk. Tomlinson's excellence as a prose stylist is generally admitted; his right to be considered among the great English essayists rests on a broader basis.

Essays and travel: *The Sea and the Jungle* (1912), *Old Junk* (1918), *London River* (1921), *Waiting For Daylight* (1922). *Tide Marks* (1924), *Gifts of Fortune* (1926), *Under the Red Ensign* (1927), *A Brown Owl* (1928), *Illusion: 1915* (1928), *Thomas Hardy* (1929), *Côte d'Or* (1929), *Between the Lines* (1930), *Out of Soundings* (1931), *NormanDouglas Douglas* (1931), *South to Cadiz* (1934), *Below London Bridge* (1934), *The Wind Is Rising* (1941), *The Turn of the Tide* (1946), *The Face of the Earth* (1950).

Novels: *Gallions Reach* (1927), *All Our Yesterdays* (1930), *The Snows of Helicon* (1933), *Mars His Idiot* (1935), *All Hands!, Am. ed. Pipe All Hands!* (1937), *The Day Before* (1939), *Morning Light* (1946).

Lytton Strachey

Of the recent biographers none is of more historical significance and of more literary worth than (Giles) Lytton Strachey (1880-1932) . Although his Lives—both the fulllength pieces *Queen Victoria* (1921) and *Elizabeth and Essex* (1928) and the biographical essays in *Eminent Victorians* (1918), *Books and Characters* (1922), and *Portraits in Miniature* (1931)—show a pronounced inclination toward revealing the weak rather than the strong elements in human nature, they did much to bring biography away from the cold, factual records with their prevailing tone of eulogy to a readable, well-integrated interpretation of personality; and they showed an unmistakable brilliance of style. In his Preface to *Eminent Victorians*, he stated:-

The art of biography seems to have fallen upon evil times in England. We have had, it is true, a few masterpieces, but we have never had, like the French, a great biographical

tradition. . . . With us, the most delicate and humane of all the branches of the art of writing has been relegated to the journeyman of letters; we do not reflect that it is perhaps as difficult to write a good life as to live one. Those two fat volumes, with which it is our custom to commemorate the dead—who does not know them, with their ill-digested masses of material, their slipshod style, their tone of tedious panegyric, their lamentable lack of selection, of detachment of design? They are as familiar as the *cortege* of the undertaker, and wear the same air of slow, funereal barbarism. . . . The studies in this book are indebted, in more ways than one, to such works—works which certainly deserve the name of Standard Biographies. For they have provided me not only with much indispensable information, but with something even more precious—an example. How many lessons are to be learned from them! But it is hardly necessary to particularize. To preserve, for instance, a becoming brevity—a brevity which excludes everything that is redundant, and nothing that is significant—that, surely, is the first duty of the biographer. The second, no less surely, is to maintain his own freedom of spirit. It is not his business to be complimentary, it is his business to lay bare the facts of the case as he understands them. That is what I aimed at in this book-to lay bare the facts of some cases as I understand them, dispassionately, impartially and without ulterior intentions. . .

Giles Lytton Strachey was born in London in 1880, the son of Sir Richard and Lady Jane Strachey. He was educated by tutors before entering Trinity College, Cambridge,where he distinguished himself by his studies in History and Literature, including the French, and by winning the Chancellor's Medal with his poem *"Ely"* in 1902. Although an avid reader and of marked literary interests and talent, he did not produce anything to attract attention until 1918, when *Eminent Victorians* appeared. It is possible that the disillusionment fostered by the war was responsible for the prompt and wide circulation of the volume, for in the four portraits-- CardinalManning, Florence Nightingale, Dr.

Arnold, and General Gordon—the author demonstrated very persuasively that these English idols had feet of clay. The attempts at refutation of Strachey's characterization of Cardinal Manning in the Catholic journals have only recently subsided. With the appearance of *Queen Victoria* (1921) Strachey's fame was secured. It is generally surmised that the author originally intended to use the Queen as a target for his satirical talent; but although Victoria's weaknesses are exposed, she emerges a personable and likeable figure. Someone has called Victoria's conquest of Lytton Strachey the most remarkable phenomenon of modern biography. The brilliant essays in *Books and Characters: French and English* (1922) were interesting, chiefly to Strachey enthusiasts—of whom a considerable number had grown up—, for the subjects considered, such as Madame du Deffand, Thomas Beddoes, and Lady Hester Stanhope, were of limited appeal. Most of the biographical essays in this collection had been written long before the volume appeared. *Elizabeth and Essex* (1928) added considerably to the author's stature, for it indicated that his insight was not confined to the Victorian scene, and that he was a consistent master of a compelling style. The brief pieces in *Portraits in Miniature*, which appeared the year before his death in 1932, although concerned largely with minor figures, are all admirable examples of Strachey's ability to select the highly significant and integrate the details into a consummate whole.

Strachey has often been judged severely and justly on account of his satirical attitude toward many of the characters he portrayed. It is true that in his attempt to break away from the panegyrical tone of most of the Victorian and early twentieth-century biographies, he went often to the other extreme. The motto he introduced into *Eminent Victorians* is generally applied: *"je n'impose rien; je ne propose rien: j'expose."* Although his interest in exposing the motives of characters is plain, Strachey was more concerned with selection and unification than he was with the uses to which irony and the devices of fiction could be put. His selection of detail was invariably highly discriminating; and in the presentation of detail he employed the talent he admired so much in Racine: of making each word say everything that that one word can say. With epigram and nimbly turned phrases he did not deal; it was rather the beauties of restraint, clarity, refinement, and precision that he sought and attained.

Biography: *Eminent Victorians* (1918), *Queen Victoria* (1921), *Elizabeth and Essex* (1928), *Portraits in Miniature and Other Essays* (1931).

Essays, chiefly critical: *Landmarks in French Literature* (1912), *Books and Characters, French and English* (1922), *Characters and Commentaries* (1933).

Philip Guedalla

Differing from Lytton Strachey and from the other writers who adopted the methods of fiction and the psychoanalytical approach, Philip Guedalla (1889-1944) produced many biographical essays which are to be found in *Supers and Supermen* (1920), *A Gallery* (1924), and *Bonnet and Shawl* (1928); and several full-length lives, notable among which are *Palmerston* (1926) and *Wellington* (1931). In many respects, Guedalla was a traditionalist, for he rejected entirely the devices of the so-called "new biography" in order to view his subjects in the strong light of their historical background. "The first essential of sound portraiture," he observed in his sketch of Washington in *Fathers of the Revolution* (1926), "is background. The park, the looped curtain, the invariably decisive sea-fight behind him may tell so much about a sitter that is concealed by his impenetrable stare. Yet history, disdainful of significant detail, is lamentably apt to divorce her favorite characters from their surroundings; to present them in statuesque isolation that is all pedestal and no perspective; to leave them, insulated and gasping for air, in a sort of historical vacuum. Perhaps that is why, in her stately pages, they so rarely contrive to live. . . . Background, the full and accurate rendering of *milieu*, is the first element of historical portraiture."

Philip Guedalla was born in 1889, educated at Rugby and Balliol College, Oxford, where in 1911 he was president of the Union. He practiced law from 1913 until 1923, and during the First War he was a legal adviser in the War Office. He contested for Parliament unsuccessfully during the midtwenties, and was actively engaged in the English political and economic scene. In addition to his active participation in politics, he was a tireless student of history, especially that of nineteenth-century England and France. This interest in history is reflected in his numerous contributions to the London periodicals and his works which appeared in book form. Recognition came to him chiefly from his full-length biographies of which *Wellington* (1931), published in England under the title *The Duke*, was widely circulated on both sides of the Atlantic. He lectured in America in the early thirties, and held audiences spellbound by his compelling and often brilliant delivery. He died in London in 1944.

Guedalla did his least effective work in his short pieces in which he was frequently too given to stylistic mannerisms. Possessed of a sparkling wit of which he was well aware, he often sacrificed substance for trimly turned phrases. He justified his manner in the sketches by insisting that his essays were "after all, only studies casually detached from a prosewriter's notebook." In the essays in *Masters and Men*, *Supers and Supermen*, and *A Gallery* the author at times exasperates the reader by the deliberately casual way in which he toys with his subject. Too often the subject provides him with a framework on which he performs his stylistic calisthenics. There is at times discernment in these essays, however, and in the full-length lives there is substance as well as brilliance of style. *Palmerston* is not only a penetrating interpretation of the personality of the Prime Minister, but an illuminating record of the times, with biography and history working happily together to produce a well-integrated result. *Wellington* is equally valuable as a skillful fusion of biography and history, and there are sustained passages which show the author's talent for brilliant phrase and resonant prose.

Essays: *Supers and Supermen* (1920), *Masters and Men* (1923), *A Gallery* (1924), *Fathers of the Revolution, Published in England as Independence Day* (1926), *Bonnet and Shawl* (1928), *The Missing Muse and Other Essays* (1929).

Biography: *The Second Empire* (1922), *Palmerston* (1926), *Mary Arnold* (1929), *The Duke* (1931).

Sir Edmund Gosse

The reputation of Sir Edmund Gosse (1849-1928) has sunk greatly since his death, but during the first twenty years of the century he was an important figure in the literary world. He was the son of Philip Henry Gosse, a poor but able marine biologist, who raised his son in the severe and narrow discipline of the Plymouth Brethren. At the age of seventeen Edmund Gosse obtained, through the kindness of Charles Kingsley, a minor post in the British Museum. With independence and new friendships among men of letters Gosse broke with his father and renounced the beliefs of his youth. Making himself officially acceptable, he passed from the Museum to the Board of Trade as translator, and in 1910 became librarian of the House of Lords.

He first attracted literary notice in 1879 by his appreciative study of Ibsen, whom he was the first to introduce to English readers. Gosse's causeries on literature, polished and informative, were widely read. In 1886 he was appointed Clark Lecturer in literature at Cambridge. The lectures, published as *From Shakespeare to Pope,* drew severe strictures for inaccuracy of scholarship that damaged Gosse's reputation and for a while shook his self-confidence. Reputation and confidence were not fully recovered until the recognition by the French Academy of his masterpiece *Father and Son*. This book, published anonymously in 1907, tells in ,great detail of his youth, his spiritual struggle with his father's narrow, puritan views. It is candid without bitterness and ranks with the best autobiographical works in English. During his later years Gosse had great authority with the reading public and his judgments upon new books were widely accepted. His critical essays were a weekly feature of the *Sunday Times* from 1919 until his death.

" Gosse is a showman," his biographer says, and in a good sense that is true. He was omnivorous of literary excellence and could communicate his enthusiasms to his readers. Nor were his enthusiasms static; acquainted in his youth with Tennyson and Swinburne, he welcomed sympathetically new writers of ability whenever they appeared. Along with Arnold Bennett, whose judgments had equal weight with the reading public, he did much to establish the reputations of those young writers of the twenties who are still regarded as the best. Gosse had his faults as a scholar but as an interpreter and popularizer he served his times well.

In the European world of letters Gosse knew everyone of note, and though his unsparing sarcastic wit was widely feared he was generally known and welcome all over the continent. No British man of letters has ever carried as many foreign decorations and distinctions as he. His value as a critic apart, Gosse is an entertaining personality to include in one's reading.

Essay and criticism: *Studies in the Literature of Northern Europe* (1879), *Seventeenth Century Studies* (1883), *From Shakespeare to Pope* (1886), *A History of Eighteenth Century Literature* (1889), *Northern Studies* (1890), *Gossip in a Library* (1891), *Questions at Issue* (1893), *The Jacobean Poets* (1894), *Critical Kit-Kats* (1896), *A Short History of Modern English Literature* (1897), *English Literature, 4 v., with Richard Garnett* (1903), *French Profiles* (1905), *Portraits and Sketches* (1912), *Collected Essays*, 5 *v.* (1913), *The Future of English Poetry* (1913), *Two Pioneers of Romanticism: Joseph and Thomas Warton* (1915), *Inter Arma* (1916), *Three French Novelists* (1918), *Some Diversions of a Man of Letters* (1919), *Malherbe and the Classical Reaction* (1920), *Books on the Table* (1921), *Aspects and Impressions* (1922), *The*

Continuity of Literature (1922), *More Books on the Table* (1923), *Silhouettes* (1925), *Leaves and Fruit* (1927), *Selected Essays* (1928).

George (Edward Bateman) Saintsbury

The dean of the elder critics in 1900 before whom even Edmund Gosse walked delicately was George (Edward Bateman) Saintsbury (1845-1933) . Born in Southampton, he attended school in London and took his degree from Oxford in 1868. There followed eight years of school teaching and five more of journalism before his name became well known. From the appearance of his *Primer of French Literature* in 1881 until his death critical works and essays poured from him steadily. His best known and most ambitious are *A History of Criticism and Literary Taste in Europe* (1900-4) and *A History of English Prosody* (1906-21). In 1895 he was appointed to a chair of English at the University of Edinburgh which he held until he reached the age of retirement in 1915. At the close of the First World War Saintsbury lost a great deal of money, so that he was obliged to sell his splendid library and live cheaply in Bath. The books that he wrote from 1920 on are the pot boilers of an old and discouraged man.

Like Gosse, Saintsbury is of the school of Saint Beuve. He was a prodigious reader, as he believed every critic should be, since on no other basis can adequate generalizations and comparisons be made. Well read in most European literatures, he was, like most of the older critics, especially so in the French, which he knew nearly as well as English. He contemned narrowness of critical theory and especially any attempt to treat criticism as a pseudo-science, preferring to rest it on broad comparative judgments. He generally justifies the method in his practice, which shows him, within his limits, a sound and appreciative critic. Less of a gossip than Gosse, he had not the elasticity of mind that enabled Gosse to receive new writers sympathetically to the end of his days. Saintsbury's is always the voice of the nineteenth century with a strongly conservative tone. Politically he was a Tory and though he deprecated political criticism, the

irritating attitude expressed in his "Thoughts on Republics" (*Miscellaneous Essays*, 1893) often pervades his work.

A Primer of French Literature (1880), *Dryden* (1881), *A Short History of French Literature* (1882), *A History of Elizabethan Literature* (1887), *Essays in English Literature*, 1780-1860 (1890), *Essays on French Novelists* (1891), *Miscellaneous Essays* (1892), *Essays in English Literature*, 1780-,1860, *Second Series* (1895), *Corrected Impressions* (1895), *A History of Nineteenth Century Literature*, 1780-1895 (1896), *The Flourishing of Romance and the Rise of Allegory* (1897), *Sir Walter Scott* (1897), *A Short History of English Literature* (1898), *A History of French Literature* (1899), *Matthew Arnold* (1899), *A History of Criticism* (19001904), *The Earlier Renaissance* (1901), *Minor Poets of the Caroline Period* (1905- 1921), *The First Half of the Seventeenth Century* (1906), *A History of English Prosody* (1906- 1910), *A History of Elizabethan Literature* (1906), *The Later Nineteenth Century* (1907), *Historical Manual of English Prosody* (1910), *A History of English Prose Rhythm* (1912), *The Historical Character of the English Lyric* (1913), *The English Novel* (1913), *The Peace of the Augustans* (1916), *A History of the French Novel* (1917- 1918), *Some Recent Studies in English Prosody* (1919), *Collected Essays and Papers of George Saintsbury*, 1875-1920 (1923- 1924), *George Henry Borrow*, 1803-1881 (1924), *A Consideration of Thackeray* (1931), *Prefaces and Essays* (1933), *Shakespeare* (1934), *French Literature and Its Masters* (1946).

Charles Whibley

An uncompromising conservative, Charles Whibley (1859-1930) was, curiously, a graduate of Cambridge, the more liberal of the two great English universities. A young literary journalist in London of the eighties, he became an early contributor to the *Scots Observer* and soon the friend of its editor, W. E. Henley, the two being drawn together by their common hatred of sham as well as by their politics.

For some years Whibley continued to work closely with Henley as contributor to the National Observer and as co-editor of the *Tudor Translations* from 1892.

In 1900 he began his best known and best sustained work of literary journalism, the "Musings Without Method," which appeared in 347 issues of *Blackwood's Magazine* from their inception until shortly before his death in 1930. Over some of these years he also contributed to the London *Daily Mail* his *Letters of an Englishman,* which were issued anony mously in 1911 and 1912. It is to be regretted that T. S. Eliot never made the selection from the "Musings" which he long ago projected. Their considerable literary merit aside, these two groups of occasional writings are among the best sustained works of English journalism in the twentieth century, and, as Professor Altick has pointed out, valuable sources of reference for the social and political history of England as seen by a representative of a dying class and political party.

Whibley's more substantial work is to be found in his biographical writing. This includes sound, if old-fashioned, studies of Thackeray (1903), Pitt (1906), Swift (1917) and Lord John Manners (1925) as well as numerous biographical essays collected in such volumes as A Book of *Scoundrels* (1897), *The Pageantry of Life* (1900), and *Essays in Biography* (1913). These latter are especially good, for he was a master of the form. No one has known better how to convey the essence of a character within the limits of an essay, not bleakly but with the color of the age his subject lived in. A marked individualist, Whibley preferred to write of unusual and colorful characters, especially of the seventeenth and eighteenth centuries

A Tory of the old pattern, Whibley outlived his age and often offends the modern reader by the narrowness and vindictiveness of his political and social views. Yet to those who can overcome their resentment, he discloses himself as an able and utterly sincere writer of great ability. He is never cheap. He is urbane and scholarly, master of a richly traditional prose style, and, within the limits of his convictions, a sound judge.

A Book of Scoundrels (1897), *The Pageantry of Life* (1900), *William Makepeace Thackeray* (1903), *Literary Portraits* (1904), *William Pitt* (1906), *American Sketches* (1908), *Studies in Frankness* (1910), *The Letters of an Englishman, First Series* (1911), *Second Series* (1912), *Essays in Biography* (1913), *Jonathan Swift* (1917), *Political Portraits, First Series* (1917), *Literary Studies* (1919), *Political Portraits, Second Series* (1923), *Lord John Manners and His Friends* (1925).

John Middleton Murry

John Middleton Murry made his name as a brilliant young critic at the time of the First World War. He was born in Peckham, London, the son of a poor government clerk. His father, obsessed by insecurity, wished his son to rise in the world and to that end educated him ferociously. Murry learned to read at two, and when he entered the Board (public) School at two-and-a-half could write his multiplication table. In 1901 he was admitted on a scholarship to Christ's Hospital, the famous Blue Coat School, where Coleridge, Lamb, and Leigh Hunt had got the rudiments of their learning. Here he remained until, again on a competitive scholarship, he went on to Brasenose College, Oxford.

As the university brought him closer to the career in the Civil Service for which his father intended him, he became increasingly discontented and he left his college in 1911, returning only to take his examinations for his degree. With a college friend he had undertaken to produce a literary magazine, *Rhythm*, which vas to be "the *Yellow Book* of the modern movement." This and reviewing for the *Westminster Gazette* were his introduction to journalism. They brought him little money and for some time no recognition, but important friendships with Frank Harris, W. L. George, D. H. Lawrence, and Katherine Mansfield (q.v.) whom he later married. *Rhythm* lasted through 1912 and was succeeded by the even shorter lived *Blue Review*. Book-reviewing served him better, and soon he was reviewing for the *Daily News* and for the *Times Literary Supplement*. In 1916 he was appointed translator in the Political Intelligence Department of the War Office and at the end of three years had become Chief Censor. The war was an agony of spiritual depression and overwork but by the end of it he had made a name as journalist and critic.

In 1917 Murry had met H. W. Massingham and had been asked by him to write for the *Nation*. In 1919 he was appointed editor of the *Athenaeum*, also controlled by *Massingham*, which until it was merged with the *Nation* two years later was the most brilliant English literary weekly. In 1923 he founded the successful *Adelphi*. In the same year he suffered a heavy loss in the death of Katherine Mansfield, to whom he had been married since 1918.

Murry creative work begins virtually in 1920: before that he had published only a novel, a study of Dostoievsky, and one volume of criticism. His thirty-seven volumes since then include biography, ethics, literary criticism, and, latterly, public affairs. He has written studies of his favorite English classics, Shakespeare, Keats, and Blake, and of his friend D. H. Lawrence. His five volumes on religious subjects include the brilliant, but unorthodox, *Life of Jesus* (in the American edition *Jesus, Man of Genius*). He was the literary executor of Katherine Mansfield and collaborated in her biography. Of his critical essays the best known are *Aspects of Literature* and *Countries of the Mind* (First and Second Series).

If labels must be attached, Murry is a humanistic critic. The one valuable experience of his Oxford days was his surrender to Plato. But whereas to Wells Plato pointed the way to the realization of the world state, to Murry he disclosed the ultimate values and their relations, an eternally valid basis of judgment. He believes that "the values of literature, the standards by which it must be criticised, and the scheme according to which it must be arranged, are in the last resort moral." This does not imply any authoritarian categories like those of T. S. Eliot; it simply means that in the light of Plato aesthetic and ethic are inseparable and the critic whose duty it is to establish the one cannot ignore the other, since art "has reference to a more perfectly human morality than any other activity of man." Upon this qualitative basis the critic founds the judgments which "establish a definite hierarchy among the great artists of the past, as well as test the production of the present" and so bring order into the intellectual confusion of the modern world.

Autobiography: *Between Two Worlds* (1938).

Criticism: *The Critic in Judgment* (1913), *Fyodor Dostoevsky: A Critical Study* (1916), *The Evolution of an Intellectual* (1920), *Aspects of Literature* (1920), *Countries of the Mind* (1922), *The Problem of Style* (1922), *A Neglected Heroine of Shakespeare* (1922), *Pencillings* (1923), *Discoveries* (1924), *Keats and Shakespeare* (1925), *Studies in Keats* (1930), *D. H. Lawrence, Two Essays* (1930), *Countries of the Mind, Second Series* (1931), *Son of Woman: The Story of D. H. Lawrence* (1931), *Reminiscences of D. H. Lawrence* (1933), *The Life of Katherine Mansfield, with Ruth E. Mantz* (1933), *William Blake* (1933), *Shakespeare* (1936), *Heroes of Thought* (1938), *Katherine Mansfield and Other Literary Portraits* (1949).

Herbert Edward Read

Herbert Edward Read was born and passed his first ten years on his father's farm in Yorkshire, a place little touched by the outside world, where life was remarkably simple for modern times. Upon his father's death he was sent to boarding school, a rather bleak establishment, where until he was fifteen he had few pleasures but acquired his first taste for reading and writing. During these years his home had been broken up and his mother had moved to Leeds. On leaving the school at the end of his fifteenth year he took a post as junior clerk in a bank. Here he worked for £20 a year, educating himself in night schools and the public library until 1912, when he matriculated at the University of Leeds. He had no definite intentions beyond acquiring a sound education, majoring in Law and Economics. He did not finish his course, for in 1914 the outbreak of war found him in summer camp with the University OTC unit. A few months later he was commissioned in the Yorkshire Regiment and went to France in 1915.

After the war, in which he served with credit as adjutant of his battalion, receiving the DSO and Military Cross, Read obtained a clerkship in the Treasury, an excellent post by civil service standards, but one which left him no leisure for the literary work on which his heart was set. After a few years and at a considerable sacrifice of salary, Read exchanged it for another in the ceramics department of the Victoria and Albert Museum which allowed him greater freedom. The knowledge of the arts gained in his museum work led to a professorship of fine art at the University of Edinburgh from 1931 to 1933 and later to lectureships at Liverpool and Cambridge.

Read began as a poet, his earliest verse having been published in 1915 in an edition that was pulped after twentytwo copies had been sold. Influenced at first by Blake and Yeats, later by Donne and Browning, he worked his way toward poetic maturity through *Naked Warriors*, his war poems. His ultimate allegiance was to the Imagists, with whom he has been regularly identified.

It is as a critic, however, that Read is best known. Fundamentally a humanist with romantic leanings, he has acquired from his dual connection with literature and the plastic arts a fastidious sense of form. Among his strongest preferences, he says, "are poets like Arnold and Hopkins, novelists like Flaubert and Henry James, and painters like Poussin and Seurat, in all of whom formality is almost an obsession." His practice, however, is less strict than this statement indicates, and though his sympathies are imperfect in some directions —as are those of all critics—his range of perception and receptivity is wide. In common with most modern critics he has availed himself fully of the resources of psychology, and interprets the concrete result in terms of the conceiving mind. His judgments are expressed in a wide variety of forms from the full-length study *Wordsworth* (1930) to the brief essays of *A Coat of Many Colours*. His criticism, however, is not confined to literature. His interest in the plastic arts is as wide and the authority of his judgment as high.

For Read art and morals have a common law in the highest expression of the individual. Consequently he calls himself a philosophic anarchist. He envisions a society ordered in conformity with natural law in which every man shall have the fullest opportunity of spiritual development. It is not very different, really, from the more liberal sorts of liberalism. In his criticism his philosophy appears without doctrinal implications but simply as an integrating spirit. He is ready to welcome any work of art for what it is and to examine it as understandingly as possible, seeing all artists and arts as the variant expressions of a common impulse. A purely intellectual critic, he is never difficult or repellently highbrow. His autobiography, *The Innocent Eye*, which contains some of his best writing, offers the best approach to an understanding of his work. For the six years before the Second World War Read edited the *Burlington Magazine*.

Criticism: *Reason and Romanticism* (1926), *English Prose Style* (1928), *The Sense of Glory* (1929), *Wordsworth* (1930), *Julien Benda and the New Humanism* (1930), *The Meaning of Art* (1931), *Form In Modern Poetry* (1932), *Art Now* (1933), *In Defense of Shelley* (1935), *Art and Society* (1936), *Poetry and Anarchism* (1938), *Collected Essays in Literary Criticism* (1938), *A Coat of Many Colours* (1941), *Coleridge As Critic* (1949).

Verse: *Collected Poems* (1926), *Poems, 1914-1934* (1935), *Thirty-five Poems* (1940), *World Within a War* (1945).

Memoirs: *The Innocent Eye* (1933), *Annals of Innocence and Experience* (1940).

SOME MINOR FIGURES

Barker, George , named the most promising of the younger poets by C. Day Lewis in 1939, has only in fair measure progressed beyond the plane reached in such a fine poem as *"Munich Elegy Number* 1." His representative work is to be found in *Janus* (1935), *Poems* (1935), *Calamiterror* (1937), *Lament and Triumph* (1940), *Sacred and Secular Elegies* (1943), and *Eros in Dogma* (1944). There is no doubt that Barker has an energetic talent, as his procession of volumes indicates, but this talent has taken no particular direction or theme, nor has it progressed in manner. Severe discipline continues to be lacking: there is much which can be deleted as inept and even tasteless. Illustrative of his distinctive manner, including his lapses into mere word play, is the poem *"The Amazons."* The collection *Sacred and Secular Elegies* is probably Barker at his best.

Cecil, Lord David , literary biographer, author of *William Cowper* (1932), *Sir Walter Scott* (1933), *Early Victorian Novelists* (1934), *Jane Austen* (1935), and *The YoungMelbourne* Melbourne (1939).

Comfort, Alex, a practicing physician, educated at Highgate School and Trinity College, Cambridge, is one of the younger poets from whom more is sure to come. He has written both prose and verse: his critical perceptions are demonstrated in his brief consideration of contemporary fiction, *The Novel and Our Time* (1947); and the themes and manner of his verse appear in large part in *The Song of Lazarus* (1945). His forceful "Notes for My Son," a warning to the new generation about the deceptions of warmongers, is hardly so characteristic of his usual themes as the poems in which he is concerned with metaphysical inquiry.

Empson, William, known in America chiefly as a critic, was considered for a time the pole-star around which the younger poets of Cambridge circled. In this respect for a time he was compared with W. H. Auden. His measures are frequently those of the traditionalists, with only slight modifications and adaptations; but his themes are presented with little regard for traditionalist imagery and logical sequence. *Poems* (1935), *The Gathering Storm* (1940), and *Selected Poems* (1948) indicate his latitude of theme and manner.

Gascoyne, David identified for a time with the surrealists, although still given to the extreme use of free association rather than logical sequence, has added considerably to his stature as a poet in his later work in which his manner is aloof and stately in treating themes which seem to be essentially religious. His *Short History of Surrealism* is a notable contribution to the critical literature which concerns this curious and ephemeral movement. His early volume *Man's Life is His Meat* (1936) is plainly experimental. It is in *Poems: 1937-1942* (1943) that one finds a clearer indication of his direction and talent.

George, W. L. (1882-1926). Novelist, born in France of English parents and educated there. Remembered for his savage caricature of Lord Northcliffe in *Caliban* (1920). Author of fifteen novels besides short stories and a great deal of miscellaneous prose.

Godden, Rumer English born but has lived the greater part of her life in India, the background of three of her novels. Became generally known in 1939 with appearance of *Black Narcissus. Take Three Tenses* (1945) is an interesting technical experiment in the handling of time. Has also written *Chinese Puzzle* (1936), *The Lady and the Unicorn* (1938), *Gipsy, Gipsy* (1940), and *Breakfast With the Nikolides* (1942).

Gogarty, Oliver St. John, the original of "Buck Mulligan" in James Joyce's *Ulysses*, in addition to his work as a physician has written a sizeable amount of prose and verse in which there is a distinctive flavor. It has been reported that he never liked Joyce especially, but that he was on intimate and friendly terms with Yeats and the chief figures of the Celtic Renaissance. His memoirs *As I Was Going Down Sackeville Street* (1937) are not only illuminating of the author's life and personality, but the work makes very good reading. *Poems and Plays* (1920), *An Offering to Swans and Other Poems* (1924), *Wild Apples* (1930), *Selected Poems* (1933), *Elbow Room* (1939), and *Mad Grandeur* (1941) illustrate his themes and manner in which there is an unmistakable tone which varies between the light and the bold.

Grigson, Geoffrey, editor, anthologist, essayist, and poet, has been a considerable force among the younger generation of writers. As editor of *New Verse,* he provided poets of the advance guard with a receptacle for their offerings and exercised a moderating influence. The anthology *New Verse* (1939), and the recent collection *Poetry of the Present* (1949) indicate his preferences. His own poetry is to be found in *Several Observations: Thirty-one Poems* (1939), and the more conventional *The Isles of Scilly* (1946). His prose, often terse to the point of abruptness, is largely devoted to an attempt to illuminate and justify recent developments and movements in the arts. *The Arts Today* (1938), the introductory piece in *The Romantics* (1942), and *The Harp of Aeolus and Other Essays on Art, Literature, and Nature* (1948) show his variety of interests and critical perceptions.

Hulme, T. E. (1886-1917), although killed in action in the First World War before his theories and talent were completely developed, has been the subject of much critical attention. After leaving Cambridge, he established himself as one of the experimental poets in London. Five of his poems appeared along with Ezra Pound *Ripostes* in 1915. Herbert Read collected and edited some of Hulme's precepts concerning his art under the title *Speculations* (1924), and supplemented them in a pamphlet *Notes on Language and Style* (1929). Hulme's poetry, slight in volume, but interesting historically, scarcely warrants the critical emphasis which has been placed on it.

Lewis, Wyndham, Born in Maine of English parents but educated in England. Known chiefly as an artist and critic. Editor before the First World War of *Blast,* which he founded with Ezra Pound. Author of *Tarr,* a novel which made some stir in 1918. He had a large influence on the younger men, especially the poets, of the wartime generation. He is often confused with the journalist D. B. Wyndham Lewis.

Murray, Gilbert, classical scholar and translator, born in Australia and educated in England at Merchant Taylor's School and Oxford. Professor of Greek at Glasgow University, 1889-1908; Regnis Professor of Greek at Oxford, 1908-36; Charles Eliot Norton Professor of Poetry at Harvard, 1926. He is known for his translations of the Greek dramatists, especially for his renderings of Euripides in Swinburnian measures. Highly readable, these are not always looked on with favor by his fellow classicists. *Euripides and His Age* (1913), *The Classical Tradition in Poetry* (1927), *Aristophanes, A Survey* (1933), and *Aeschylus: The Creator of Tragedy* (1940).

Quiller-Couch, Sir Arthur (1863-1948), King Edward VII Professor of English Literature at Cambridge since 1912. For many years he wrote stories and novels of his native Cornwall under the pen name "Q." He is better known for his later lectures and critical essays, among which are *Studies in Literature* (1918, 1922, 1929), *The Art of Reading* (1920), and *Charles Dickens and Other Victorians* (1925).

Scarfe, Francis, educated at Durham University and the Sorbonne, and a member of the tutorial staff at Cambridge University for a time, has written discerningly about his contemporaries in *Auden and After: The Liberation of Poetry* (1942). His verse in *Inscapes* (1940), a title which suggests at once Gerard Manley Hopkins, is more interesting to the experimentalist than to one who is seeking a significant theme presented in a readily comprehensible way.

Thirkell, (Mrs.) Angela, was born Angela Mackail, daughter of J. W. Mackail, classicist and professor of poetry at Oxford. Like her brother Denis Mackail, she is a popular novelist. Though she first published in 1930 she was not well known to American readers until 1939. Her novels of genteel country life closely imitate those of Anthony Trollope but though amusing have none of his solid quality.

Waddell, Helen J, medieval scholar born in Japan of Irish parents and educated in Belfast. She taught and lectured for many years at Oxford and at Bedford College, London, and has received a great many academic distinctions. Her principal book is *The Wandering Scholars* (1927) but her translations from medieval Latin and her novel *Peter Abelard* (1933) are nearly as well known. Williams, Emlyn, Welsh actor-dramatist, author of *Night Must Fall* (1935), *The Corn is Green* (1938) and other less-well-known plays, some of them as yet unpublished. Williamson, Henry, miscellaneous writer of considerable ability, known for his studies of nature, especially *Tarka the Otter* (1927) and *Salar the Salmon* (1935). These are not juvenile books, as their titles might suggest.

Chapter 8

The Drama

INTRODUCTION

For the London theatergoer of the later nineties who asked more than entertainment the table was not bountifully spread. There was Shakespeare in the expert hands of Henry Irving and Ellen Terry, but little modern fare. The conviction of Oscar Wilde in 1895 had driven his plays temporarily from the stage and no heir to his brilliant, epigrammatic wit had appeared. George Bernard Shaw, now known for half a dozen plays, was also Irish and brilliant but with an uncomfortable difference. His wit was the lambent surface of a fierce puritanism that probed and questioned everywhere and raised disquieting thoughts. Beneath it he was too much like the serious foreigner Ibsen, with whose praises he belabored the public in the *Saturday Review*. London had put up a stout resistance to Ibsen. Ever since his discovery by Edmund Gosse in 1879, intelligent critics and managers had been trying to persuade the English public to accept him, but though the season of 1890-91 had seen five of his plays, audiences remained shy and the theatrical world had learned that he did not pay.

As an alternative to Shaw and Ibsen there were smoothly constructed and less disturbing social problem plays of Henry

Arthur Jones and Arthur Wing Pinero. Jones, already a veteran who had been writing for twenty years, caused a sensation and something of a scandal in 1896 with *Michael and His Lost Angel,* a play dealing with clerical adultery. It closed after eleven nights but established for his plays a reputation greater than they deserved. For some years afterward he enjoyed great popularity. Pinero scored his greatest success with *The Second Mrs. Tanqueray* in 1893 and *The Notorious Mrs. Ebbsmith* in 1895, but *Trelawney of the "Wells"* (1898) and *The Gay Lord Quex* (1899) sustained his reputation, and in 1909 *Mid-Channel* was the most controversial play of the year. Both of these men were exceedingly deft technicians, whose plays owed more to skill of construction than to intellectual content. Their handling of social problems was far more timid than Shaw's and the old-fashioned conventionality of their work caused it to be quickly outmoded. Yet by putting the problem play in terms that were acceptable to English audiences they did more perhaps than Shaw's ruthless attack to prepare the public taste for a more serious drama, and they deserve credit for an important part in the effort to raise the English theater out of the low estate into which it had fallen in the nineteenth century.

In this effort the dramatist had the support of the Stage Society, which produced plays that could not get a hearing in the commercial theater, and of a group of brilliant journalists. Aware of how the continental drama was advancing in the hands of Ibsen, Strindberg, Maeterlinck, and Sudermann, the leading dramatic critics, Shaw, A. B. Walkley, William Archer, and soon Max Beerbohm, deplored the flaccidity of the London theater and labored hard to raise the standard of appreciation. There was no lack of theatrical talent: Johnston Forbes-Robertson, John Hare, Herbert Beerbohm Tree, Cyril Maude, Lilly Langtry, Janet Achurch, and Mrs. Pat Campbell were as fine a group of actors as the English stage has had at any time. All things were propitious for the revival of the drama which had already begun.

The first vigor of the new movement appeared in Dublin where W. B. Yeats, Douglas Hyde, Lady Gregory, and George Moore founded the Irish National Theater Society. Though denounced by young James Joyce in an early pamphlet, *The Day of the Rabblement* (1901), as a prostitution of art to political ends, the movement was artistically sincere and became practically effective with the opening of the Abbey Theater in 1904 under the management of Miss Annie Elizabeth Horniman to produce the plays of native authors. The dramatic strength of the Abbey Theater was supplied by the genius of John M. Synge, a discovery of Yeats's, who from its opening until his early death in 1909, wrote for it the finest plays that Ireland has yet produced. They sometimes offended the touchy patriotism of Dublin audiences, and *The Playboy of the Western World* (1907) caused rioting in theaters on both sides of the Atlantic by its alleged misrepresentation of the Irish character. Lady Gregory contributed short comedies of peasant life in the amusing "Kiltartan" dialect, some of them translations from the Gaelic writings of Douglas Hyde. Yeats's plays were too poetic in their conception to be effective on the stage and George Moore took no active part in the venture. In 1908 the Abbey produced *The Clancy Name,* a tragedy by a young playwright, Lennox Robinson. Two years later he became stage manager, taking the players to the United States in 1912. Later still from Belfast came St. John Ervine, whose John Ferguson was produced at the Abbey in 1914 and who succeeded Robinson as manager in the following year.

In 1908 Miss Horniman left Dublin to manage the Manchester Repertory Theater. Inspired by the success of the Abbey, this movement developed some able dramatists in the Midlands of whom the best were Stanley Houghton, Harold Brighouse, and Alan Monkhouse, all vigorous realists. Masefield *Tragedy of Nan* (1909) was the theater's first sensation, and Houghton *Hindle Wakes* its greatest success. Repertory theaters were also founded in Glasgow, Birmingham and Liverpool, but these were less important.

Meanwhile in London Harley Granville-Barker and J. E. Vedrenne, encouraged by J. T. Grein's experiment with the Independent Theater, took over the management of the Royal Court Theater to produce plays of real merit, and were so successful that in 1907 they moved to the larger Savoy. The genius of Gordon Craig, Ellen Terry's son, was employed to furnish a new simple decor that broke away completely from the detailed realism that was then the established fashion in stage settings. Granville-Barker was himself a dramatist, having made his debut in the Stage Society's production of *The Marrying of Ann Leet* in 1901. By the time he retired from management in 1914 he had made a substantial reputation as a playwright with *The Voysey Inheritance* (1905), *Waste* (1907), and *The Madras House* (1910).

James Barrie, after the lavender and old lace of *Quality Street* (1901), had showed in *The Admirable Crichton* (1903) that he was capable of pointed social satire, and the next year had as great success with the best beloved children's play in the language, Peter Pan. At the Court Theatre in 1906 John Galsworthy began a successful dramatic career with *The Silver Box*. The problem plays of his first period were felt to be "challenging," like those of Pinero, and were for some time overestimated. So were the showy but ephemeral social plays of Alfred Sutro. Somerset Maugham was doing steady journeyman work, his successes *The Circle* and *The Letter* still far in the future after the war. These four writers, with Shaw, gave London its most serious plays, with a preponderance of social criticism, until the First War.

For the first few years of the century Stephen Phillips had a great name as a poetic dramatist. Paolo and Francesca was generally acclaimed by the critics in 1900, as were his three following plays, *Herod* (1901), *Ulysses* (1902), and *The Sin of David* (1904), after which, as their rhetoric and theatricality become more apparent, even praise for the genuine if slight talent in his work ceased. In 1910 he was eclipsed by Masefield, whose *Tragedy of Pompey* the Great promised more than his really narrative genius could sustain in the drama. Gilbert Murray's translations of the Greek dramatists, while attacked by scholars as betrayals of their originals, were, under Granville-Barker's management, dramatically effective. The exotic fantasies of Lord Dunsany, though their charm of "strange beauties and strange dooms" has not lasted, appealed strongly to the taste of the prewar public.

The war put an end to the demand for serious plays, life having quite enough problems for everyone. Galsworthy, engaged in war work, wrote only one trifle; Barrie furnished the sentimental with *The Well Remembered Voice*, *Barbara's Wedding*, and *The Old Lady Shows Her Medals*. Shaw, equal to any war, produced *O'Flaherty V. C.*, *The Inca of Perusalem*, and *Augustus Does His Bit*. But for the most part the theater offered reviews and light diversion. *Chu Chin Chow*, a lavish oriental spectacle, ran to packed houses for over three years.

Shaw, Galsworthy, and Barrie were still the leading dramatists in the twenties, Galsworthy doing his best work with *Loyalties*, *The Skin Game*, and *Old English*. Frederick Lonsdale, who had been writing without great distinction since 1908, scored a success with *Aren't We All?* in 1923. His suavely sophisticated social dramas, in the tradition of Pinero with a postwar difference, held the stage until in the late thirties they began to seem outmoded. A similar belated success came to John Drinkwater, whose chronicle plays enjoyed a decade of popularity after the success of Abraham Lincoln in 1918.

The first of the new playwrights to appear was A. A. Milne, an established humorist of the staff of Punch who had begun his dramatic writing while in the army. His whimsical comedies with an exquisite sense of the ridiculous in situation and dialogue were just what audiences of the twenties wanted to help them forget the war. In 1924 the younger generation knocked unmistakably at the door with the appearance of *The Rat Trap*, the first play by Noel Coward. As his amazing versatility unfolded he showed perfect competence, and often more, in sophisticated comedy (Private

Lives, Design for Living), drama (The Vortex), historical spectacle (*Cavalcade*), and fast-paced revue (*This Year of Grace, Words and Music*). His hard cleverness and nostalgic sentiment are intensely characteristic of his generation and he has become its most efficient spokesman in the theater. J. B. Priestley has appealed to a less sophisticated middle-class audience. He did not turn to the theater until 1932, when he was a well-established novelist, but the popular success of his plays has been as great as that of his books. A sturdy socialism and interesting experiments with time hardly relieve the mediocrity of his work, through most of which there runs a distinct reminiscence of Barrie. *An Inspector Calls* (1947) is an effective parable of social responsibility and probably his strongest play since *Dangerous Corner* (1932). John Van Druten was lost to the English theater through his emigration to the United States in 1926.

Meanwhile in 1923, at the end of Lennox Robinson's second period of management, the Abbey Theater had produced The Shadow of a Gunman, by Sean O'Casey. It was soon clear that he was the best Irish dramatist since Synge, but like Synge he offended national susceptibilities and *The Plough and The Stars* (1926) provoked the same sort of rioting that had greeted *The Playboy*. He has been better appreciated in England and the United States than in his own country.

As the thirties drew on there was a marked decline of new dramatic authorship. Here and there an isolated success was scored such as R. C. Sherriff's war play *Journey's End* in 1929 or Walter Greenwood's socialist document *Love on the Dole* in 1933, but they led to nothing. Lawrence Housman, who for thirty years had been writing unpopular, and often censored, religious plays, scored a remarkable success in 1934 with *Victoria Regina*. The Welsh actor Emlyn Williams appeared as author in 1930 and has written a number of steadily better plays of which *The Corn Is Green* (1938) is the best so far. Keith Winter showed considerable promise in *The Shining Hour* (1934) but has not sustained it in his later work.

W. H. Auden and Christopher Isherwood have collaborated in three plays of very modern technique: The *Dog Beneath the Skin* (1935), *Ascent of F* 6 (1937), and *On the Frontier* (1938). These, however, are more suitable for reading than for production. An interesting revival of the religious drama was instituted at the Canterbury Festival with plays presented in the Cathedral Chapter house. For this T. S. Eliot wrote *Murder in the Cathedral,* the martyrdom of St. Thomas à Becket, in 1935, and Dorothy Sayres *The Zeal of Thy House* in 1937 and *The Devil to Pay,* a version of the Faust story, in 1939.

The rehabilitation of the English drama since 1890 has been accomplished against serious obstacles. The low estate into which the nineteenth-century drama fell was due in part to the great vogue of the novel and in part to the wholesale pirating of foreign plays by London managers, both of which drove the best literary talent into the field of fiction. The English playwright has also had to support the incubus of the censor who, with his power to refuse a license for a play upon his unsupported judgment, has been a virtual dictator of the theater. The poor fare offered as a consequence to the Victorian theatergoer depressed and vitiated the public taste to such a degree that the education of the modern public to the appreciation of serious plays has been slow and often discouraging.

The period from 1890 to 1920 with the work of Wilde, Shaw, Barrie, Galsworthy and Synge, not to mention the lesser writers, was the most brilliant that the English theater had seen since the Restoration. In those thirty years the intellectual level was astonishingly raised. A public whose aver age taste was fairly represented by *Charlie's Aunt* had been brought to accept and support a drama of serious social criticism, to recognize wit above the level of farce, and to associate again the once wholly divorced worlds of the stage and of reality.

Since 1920 there has been a noticeable decline from the abundant excellence of the prewar period. In spite of many interesting technical experiments and many individually good plays there is a comparative thinness of dramatic achievement. So far only three men have produced substantial bodies of dramatic work and if one makes such a comparison as Milne with Barrie, Priestley with Galsworthy, and Coward with Wilde, it is only in the last instance that the younger man's work will bear it. Only time will allow this period to be correctly evaluated but from the uncertain standpoint of the present a peak appears to have been passed.

Among the British playwrights who were influenced by Ibsen whose dramas of social import were produced in London during the nineties, none was more popular than Sir *Arthur Wing Pinero* (1855- 1934). Between 1887 and 1928 he wrote more than thirty plays, some of which such as *The Second Mrs. Tanqueray* (1894), *The Notorious Mrs. Ebbsmith* (1895), *Trelawny of the "Wells"* (1898), and *MidChannel* (1909) had very long runs and have been frequently revived. As late as 1924 Ethel Barrymore gave one of her finest performances in *The Second Mrs. Tanqueray* as Paula, a role which had given Mrs. Patrick Campbell much of her fame. Although all of Pinero's social themes are no longer considered profound, and his management of them is now regarded as sketchy and superficial, his plays, especially the tragedies, are generally moving and theatrically effective.

Arthur Wing Pinero

Arthur Wing Pinero was born in London in 1855, the son of a well-to-do solicitor of Portuguese-Jewish ancestry. His education did not extend to the university, for soon after completing his classical studies at Birkbeck Institute he became interested in the theater, and at the age of twenty-four made his first appearance as an actor in Edinburgh. A few years later he was with Sir Henry Irving's company, with which he remained from 1876 to 1879 and in which he no doubt received much valuable training for his chosen profession of playwright. It was while he was associated with Irving's group that he wrote his first plays, but it was not until 1880 that he forsook his work as an actor to devote his time to writing for the stage. During the eighties and early nineties his plays were produced at frequent intervals, but it was with *The Second Mrs. Tanqueray* (1894) that he became famous. In 1909 he was knighted in recognition of his services to the English stage. His plays written after the First World War show ingeniousness but a perceptible falling off in dramatic effectiveness. He died in 1934.

Pinero's plays divide themselves into the dramas of social import such as *The Second Mrs. Tanqueray* and *Mid-Channel*, and the Comedy of Manners plays such as *The Weaker Sex* and *The Gay Lord Quex*. In the dramas of social import, problems are raised and in some measure answered. For example, Aubrey, in *The Second Mrs. Tanqueray*, risks marrying Paula, a woman with a past. The catastrophe becomes apparent when it is disclosed that Ellean, Aubrey's daughter by a previous marriage, has fallen in love with one of her stepmother's former lovers. Paula, who has tried in her way to be a good wife to Aubrey, sees no way out of the difficulty and commits suicide. Pinero's method of solving the problem seems real enough, but there is nothing of striking inevitability about the tragedy. In *Mid-Channel*, a more universal problem is presented, that of a childless couple who find upon reaching middle age little by way of common bond and no ideal or illusion toward which to strive. Pinero manipulates the characters and situation with great skill, with the result that the climax seems not only entirely plausible, but inevitable. Although even now it is not generally recognized, it was with light social comedy that Pinero did some of his finest work. Possessed of a talent for ingenious situation and witty lines, he wrote more than a score of comedies which in spite of their dated mannerisms are genuinely entertaining. In all of his work his resourcefulness as a technician is outstanding.

Mayfair (1885), *Lady Bountiful* (1890), *The Hobby-Horse* (1892), *Sweet Lavender* (1893), *The Second Mrs. Tanqueray* (1894), *The Weaker Sex* (1894), *The Notorious Mrs. Ebbsmith* (1895), *Trelawny of the "Wells"* (1898), *The Gay Lord Quex* (1899), *Iris* (1901), *The House in*

Order (1905), *The Thunderbolt* (1909), *Mid-Channel* (1909), *The Big Drum* (1915), *The Enchanted Cot- tage* (1921), *A Private Room* (1926), *Child Man* (1928).

Sir James Matthew Barrie

Sir James Matthew Barrie (1860- 1937) was born at Kirriemuir, Forfarshire, Scotland, the ninth of ten children of David Barrie, a poor handloom weaver. The death of an elder brother made him very early the favorite child of his mother Margaret Ogilvie (so called in the family by her maiden name, according to Scots custom) and his whole childhood and youth were shaped by his close and tender association with her.

Barrie had his schooling at Glasgow Academy, where his brother was classical master, and later at Dumfries Academy, still under the eye of his brother, now Inspector of Schools for that district. He showed some aptitude for writing and more for amateur theatricals of all kinds, and took a normal schoolboy interest in sports. In his last years at school he decided upon a literary career, disappointing his mother's hopes of seeing him a minister, and in 1878 entered the University of Edinburgh in order to study English literature under Professor David Masson. He was now a very short. thin youth of eighteen, shy among strangers because of his physical insignificance, a good but not remarkable student. Like most literary undergraduates he conceived numbers of literary projects, but beyond his academic essays he wrote nothing at the University except some dramatic criticisms for the Evening Courant. He took his degree in 1882 without having made any mark in college life.

Barrie, now with his family's whole-hearted support, began his literary career as "leader" (editorial) writer for the *Nottingham Journal*, which he joined in January, 1883. For a weekly salary of £3 he produced twelve columns of matter, including, in addition to daily editorials, a weekly article and a column of notes. At the end of a year of this servitude he left the paper—whether he resigned or was discharged is not clear—and thereafter remained a free lance. He returned home for a while, and then, in 1885, encouraged by the sale of his articles, went to London. For the next four years he lived in the Bloomsbury district, working desperately hard, increasing his acquaintance among editors, and gradually establishing a reputation.

The work that first brought Barrie popular recognition began with an article entitled *An Auld Licht Community*, published in 1884. The "Auld Lichts" formed a very strict sect of Presbyterians to which Margaret Ogilvie had belonged before her marriage. It was from her reminiscences, for he never himself entered an "Auld Licht" church, that Barrie drew his material, filling it out with character and local color from his own knowledge of Kirriemuir. The success of the first sketch brought editorial requests for more, and in 1888 these were collected in a volume as *Auld Licht Idylls.* With the critical and popular appreciation of these, Barrie ceased to be an obscure journalist. He had found a rich vein in the atmosphere of his native place and he went on to exploit it fully in *When a Man's Single* (1888), *A Window in Thrums* (1889), and *The Little Minister* (1891). *Sentimental Tommy* (1895) and *Tommy and Grizel* (1900) brought him to the height of his power and of his reputation as a novelist. His success inspired a number of imitators the so-called "kailyard school," exploiting the humor and pathos of humble Scottish life and the picturesqueness of the "lallans" speech, on the whole the most important group of new regional writers before 1900.

Meanwhile Barrie had been working away from fiction toward the theater. His first successful play, *Walker, London* (1892), dramatizing material drawn from *When a Man's Single*, ran for 511 performances. The heroine was played by Mary Ansell, who two years later became Barrie's wife. This play was followed by *The Professor's Love Story* (1895) and a dramatization of *The Little Minister* for Charles Frohman in 1897. All of these plays Barrie had regarded as experiments or potboilers, but from 1900 with Frohman as his producer and Maude Adams as his leading lady he seriously undertook the works that at once brought him enormous popularity. *Quality Street*, a delicate romantic comedy, appeared in New York in 1901 and a year later in London, where it was very soon followed by *The Admirable Crichton*, on the whole the best he ever did. The Christmas holidays of 1904 saw the historic first performance of *Peter Pan*, that all but immortal fantasy for children, that for more than a generation has been revived annually. To many now middle aged, Maude Adams as Peter Pan is an ineffaceable part of their childhood. His next important play, What *Every Woman Knows*, a comedy of Scottish character recalling his early stories, appeared in 1908 and brings to a close the first period of his dramatic work.

In 1909 Barrie's wife left him for Gilbert Cannan, the novelist, and was soon afterward divorced. The failure of his marriage was a severe blow to Barrie and for a while paralyzed his creative effort. For the next few years he produced chiefly one-act plays, of which the best known is *The Twelve-Pound Look*. In 1913, when the title meant little to him, he was made a baronet.

The war years 1914-18 saw him writing again with his former energy. In addition to three one-act plays, *The New Word, A Well Remembered Voice, and Barbara's Wedding*, he produced two of full length, *A Kiss For Cinderella* and *The Old Lady Shows Her Medals*. Apart from these "war plays," in 1917 was *Dear Brutus*, a serious comedy on the theme that "If there were second chances in this world, few of us would take them." For one scene drawn straight from Barrie's own childless unhappiness, this is his most powerful work. In 1920 appeared the only partially successful *Mary Rose* and two years later *Shall We Join the Ladies?*, a one-act thriller.

In the same year, 1922, Barrie was granted the Order of Merit, an honor then held only by Meredith and Hardy, and was elected Rector of St. Andrews University. He was now a wealthy man, living opposite Shaw in the Adelphi Terrace, and his career was all but over. He wrote one more prose story, *Farewell, Miss Julie Logan*, for the Christmas Eve supplement to the *Times* in 1931, and an unsuccessful biblical drama, *The Boy David*, in 1936. He died the following year.

Besides all these, and some minor pieces not mentioned, Barrie wrote *Margaret Ogilvie* (1896), an affectionate study of his mother, and his pleasant but unreliable autobiography, *The Greenwood Hat*. His exact relation to "Daisy Ashford's" hilarious *The Young Visitors*, of which he appeared as sponsor, remains a mystery.

With genuine pathos and humor, with a gift for telling a story dramatically and with an unfailing mastery of "good theater," Barrie was handicapped as a dramatist by weaknesses which have been attributed to his spiritual dependence on his mother. Certainly Margaret Ogilvie is responsible for the frequency in his plays of efficient, motherly women who dominate their men, and possibly for the escapism that he shares with D. H. Lawrence and Shaw, who were also much under maternal influence. But Barrie's sentimentalism, his greatest defect, is all his own. Before 1918 it was accepted and even applauded because it was exactly on the emotional level of the theater-going middle class, but in retrospect it seems so glaringly false as to vitiate a large part of his work. *The Admirable Crichton* contains good social satire, *What Every Woman Knows* humor of character, and *Dear Brutus* the genuinely pathetic figures of Dearth and his dream-daughter—enough to sustain them for some time to come. But it is doubtful whether even the wistful magic of Peter Pan still has its old appeal to children, and for the rest Barrie's inventions seem already to belong to a faded past.

Fiction: *Better Dead* (1887), *Auld Licht Idylls* (1888), *When a Man's Single* (1888), *A Window in Thrums* (1889), *The Little Minister* (1891), *A Holiday in Bed* (1892), *An Auld Licht Manse and Other Sketches* (1893), *A Powerful Drug* (1893), *A Tillyloss Scandal* (1893), *Two of Them* (1893), *A Professor's Love Story* (1895), *Sentimental Tommy* (1896), *Tommy and Grizel* (1900), *The Little White Bird* (1902), *Peter Pan in Kensington*

Gardens (1906), *Peter and Wendy* (1911), *Farewell, Miss Julie Logan* (1932).

Plays: *The Little Minister* (1898), *The Wedding Guest* (1900), *Walker London* (1907), *Quality Street* (1913), *The Admirable Crichton* (1914), *Half Hours* (1914), *"Der Tag"* (1914), *What Every Woman Knows* (1918), *Echoes of the War* (1918), *Alice Sit-by-the-fire* (1919), *A Kiss for Cinderella* (1920), *Dear Brutus* (1922), *Mary Rose* (1924), *Shall We Join the Ladies* (1928), *Peter Pan* (1928), *The Boy David* (1938).

Memoirs: *The Greenwood Hat* (1937).

George Bernard Shaw

George Bernard Shaw (1856-1950) at his death was much more than the Grand Old Man of English letters; like Queen Victoria he had become an institution. Two generations always had G.B.S. there to delight, frighten, stimulate, or exasperate them. He was a brilliant young arrlviste of *Yellow Book* days; he debated with Belloc and Chesterton in their Edwardian prime; he commented on the First World War with authority, on the second as a sage. It was hard to believe that he had temporal origins.

He was born in Dublin, the third child and only son of George Carr Shaw, a retired civil servant turned corn factor, an unsuccessful and sometimes intemperate man, who bequeathed his son little but his saving wit. The family was kept solvent largely through the efforts of Mrs. Shaw, the daughter of a Wicklow squire, a woman of great strength and independence and an accomplished musician. Up to the age of fourteen Shaw was given a haphazard education at the Wesleyan Connexional School and other institutions, but was idle and learned little. Music he got from his mother; literature from his wide and largely undirected reading.

At fifteen Shaw was put to work in a Dublin land agent's office, where he did so well that when, a year later, the cashier's position fell vacant, he was chosen to fill it. For four years he competently performed duties that were supposed to require maturity and experience. This was the first evidence of the business ability he showed throughout his life.

In 1876, at the age of twenty, Shaw left Dublin to join his mother in London, where she was teaching music. For nine years he tried to make a place for himself in literature and journalism without the least success. His statement: "I did not throw myself into the struggle for life: I threw my mother into it" is an exaggeration of course, but certainly she was his principal support in these years. Between 1879 and 1883 he wrote five novels, Immaturity, *The Irrational Knot, Love Among the Artists, Cashel Byron's Profession,* and *An Unsocial Socialist,* all of which except the first were published before 1890. Immaturity did not appear until 1930.

Journalism became his means of livelihood in 1885 when through William Archer he obtained a place on the reviewing staff of the *Pall Mall Gazette* and later as dramatic critic of *The World.* From 1888 to 1890 he contributed articles on music to *The Star* and from 1890 to 1894 to The World. His public reputation as a critic was made by his dramatic criticisms in the *Saturday Review* (1895- 1898). It was confirmed by his two books *The Quintessence of Ibsenism* (1891) and *The Perfect Wagnerite* (1898). Out of his unsuccessful attempt to collaborate with William Archer in 1885 came also his first play, Widowers' Houses, performed and published in 1892. This was followed during the next four years by some of his best work, The Philanderer, Mrs. Warren's Profession, Arms and the Man, Candida, The Man of Destiny, and You Never Can Tell. All of these were published in 1898 in two volumes as Plays: Pleasant and Unpleasant.

Thus by 1898 Shaw had established a reputation as novelist, critic, and dramatist but he had severely overworked himself to do so. His health broke down completely. During a long convalescence, he married Miss Charlotte Françis Payne-Townsend, a woman capable at once of caring for him, of appreciating his art, and of sharing his work in the Fabian

Society. In these happier circumstances Shaw began the second, and most creative, period of his work.

This began with The Devil's Disciple, Caesar and Cleopatra, and Captain Brassbound's Conversion, published in 1901 as *Three Plays for Puritans*. Man and Superman followed in 1901, John Bull's Other Island and Major Barbara in 1905, and *The Doctor's Dilemma* in 1906. In these years he was gradually securing a theatrical as well as a reading public. At first his plays antagonized critics and audiences unused to intellectual satire and social propaganda, and performances of Mrs. Warren's Profession were forbidden on both sides of the Atlantic, but between 1905 and 1910 he won acceptance in the theatres of London and New York. Down to *Heartbreak House* in 1917 Shaw produced at least one remarkable play a year. It was then that the mythical figure of G. B. S., half genius, half bogey-man was formed in the public mind.

Shaw was now past fifty and recognized even by his severer critics as the foremost English playwright. He had managed his affairs well and was materially as well as artistically a successful man. His plays appeared less frequently and declined in quality. Back to Methuselah (1921) is really a sequence of five plays beginning in Genesis and ending in the forty-second century A.D. in a static, passionless world in which man, through knowledge, has almost escaped from the web of life. Saint Joan (1923) is an attempt to capture some of the sublimity of tragedy entirely beyond the scope of Shaw's purely comic genius, and insofar is a failure. The play becomes a treatise on toleration that obscures the human significance of the heroine. The Apple Cart (1929) is amusing but a trifle, and padded. His later plays have added nothing to his reputation.

If Shaw was for a long time resented and often misunder stood, it was largely his own doing. A witty Irish provincial without the cachet of an English public school—an outsider, in short—trying to break into the London literary world, he realized that to succeed he must advertise himself by eccentricity. His virgin red beard, his Jaeger clothing, his alpinstock, and such paraphernalia were all part of a calculated campaign to impress the public. So was much of his intellectual arrogance.

"For ten years past," he wrote in the *Saturday Review* in 1898, "with an unprecedented pertinacity and obstination, I have been dinning into the public head that I am an extraordinary witty, brilliant and clever man. That is now part of the public opinion of England . . ."

In all his long life he was never able to resist the Irishman's impulse to muddle and befool the Saxon, and the public was not greatly to blame if often it was not able to separate the superlative buffoon from the artist. But the artist beneath the baffling, irritating antics of the buffoon was of such consistent principle and purpose from the start that what was written of him forty-odd years ago may stand today without the alteration of a word.

Saved by his mother's energy and intelligence from the consequences of his father's fecklessness and kept under her influence until he was past forty, Shaw developed an abhorrence of wasteful, stupid, and sensual ways. He was ascetic, sexually prudish, a teetotaler, a nonsmoker, a vegetarian. Though he was never confirmed in any religion and came to recognize God only as a Life Force, his outlook has always been uncompromisingly puritan. In his eyes the contemporary world had fallen into a quagmire of false idealisms that made it incapable of managing its own affairs or even of seeing them realistically. Socialism seemed to him the only rational way for modern man and he became one of the earliest members of the Fabian Society. Throughout his career he was a revolutionist, a consistent propagandist for his own highly individual interpretation of Fabian principles.

Shaw's first two plays were direct attacks upon specific social evils; thereafter he gradually developed the idea of a realistically ordered society emancipated from the stupidity of idealism. But here he encountered the problem of all social planners, that of adequate direction. Who is to bring about the regeneration? The Webbs looked practically to a carefully selected and trained civil service; Wells revived the Platonic ideal of a dedicated aristocracy. Shaw was not a democrat; he never believed in the power of the mass of men to raise or guide themselves. He exalted the born leader, subtly intelligent, clear-sighted, self-confident, strong of will and completely free of prejudice. He has dressed this character in every sort of costume and shown him in every variety of situation; he is that "master of reality" through whose eyes Shaw looks at humanity, "the slaves of reality." Here as Chesterton pointed out (*Heretics*, 1905) is the fatal defect in Shaw's thought. The leader who is to free us from ideals is himself an ideal and an inhuman one that can furnish no solution to purely human problems. The most effective part of Shaw's work is iconoclastic; he swept up a lot of rubbish and knocked down a lot of idols, and it is good fun, but his Superman can build no new world. In Back to Methuselah the empty life of the Ancients, drained of all humanity and passion, is a virtual admission of defeat.

Like the morality plays, of which they continue the tradition, like the poetry of Browning, like the novels of Wells and Huxley—like all literature having the discussion of ideas for its purpose—the plays of Shaw tend toward dialogue and ultimately monologue. Action becomes merely accessory, to be imposed upon the dialogue by clever device or its absence covered by local color and the wit of the lines. To this the conventional playgoer finds it hard to adapt himself; he wants to "cut the cackle and come to the 'osses," but with Shaw the cackle is the 'osses and he has not the humorist's resources for involving it in significant action. For a humorist, however he may ridicule humanity, fundamentally accepts it and finds significance in whatever men do: to Shaw the humanity of human nature is too often an offense, and his moral situation becomes a monotonous opposition between Intelligence, represented by his brilliant spokesman, and stupidity variously manifested in most of the other characters. It is the greatest evidence of Shaw's power that with this serious limitation he has achieved so many characters that transcend their puppet origins and are memorable as created persons.

Like Dryden, Shaw has found the play form too narrow for the full expression of his thought and has overflowed into copious prefaces and appendices. They are the principal continuation of his critical work through his dramatic period and survey, not always accurately, a wide field of politics, sociology, and criticism. Other by-products of the time include such various books as *Socialism and Superior Brains* (1910), *Common Sense About the War* (1914), *The Intelligent Woman's Guide to Socialism and Capitalism* (1928), *Adventures of a Black Girl in Search of God* (1932), and *William Morris as I Knew Him* (1936). His musical criticisms and other fugitive writings have been collected, and a collected edition of his works appeared 1931-1934.

Shaw's later life was, except for public outcry at his provocative utterances, uneventful. He always maintained his eccentric pose, largely as a barrier to keep the public at a distance. He avoided the honors usually given to literary men, accepting only the Nobel Prize for literature in 1925. He generally resisted the popularization of his works. Arms and the Man was adapted as a musical comedy in 1911 as The Chocolate Soldier, but it was not until 1938 that he permitted any of his plays to be filmed. Since then Pygmalion, Major Barbara malion, Major Barbara, and Caesar and Cleopatra have all had marked success on the screen.

Shaw deliberately made himself hard to sum up partly by allowing his mind at times to follow tracks only tangent to his main line of thought, partly, like an Irishman, by saying a lot of things that he only half meant. It may take some time to distill the quintessence of Shavianism but it is pretty clear that he was the best English dramatist since the Restoration.

Novels: *Cashel Byron's Profession* (1886), *An Unsocial Socialist* (1887), *Love Among the Artists* (Chicago, 1900), *The Irrational Knot* (1905), *Immaturity* (1930).

Plays: *Widowers' Houses* (1893), *Plays Pleasant and Unpleasant* (1898), *Three Plays For Puritans* (1901), *Man and Superman* (1903). *John Bull's Other Island, and Major Barbara; also How He Lied to Her Husband* (1907), *Press Cuttings* (1909), *The Doctor's Dilemma, Getting Married, and The Showing Up of Blanco Posnet* (1909), *Misalliance, The Dark Lady of the Sonnets, and Fanny's First Play* (1914), *Androcles and the Lion, Overruled, Pygmalion* (1916), *Heartbreak House, Great Catherine, and Playlets of the War* (1919), *Back to Methusalah* (1991), *St. Joan* (1924), *Translations and Tomfooleries* (1926), *The Apple Cart* (1930). *The Complete Plays of Bernard Shaw* (1931), *Too True to Be Good, Village Wooing, and On The Rocks* (1934), *The Simpleton, The Six, and The Millionairess* (1936), *Cymbeline Refinished* (1937), *Geneva* (1938), *In Good King Charles's Golden Days* (1939).

Miscellaneous: *The Quintessence of Ibsenism* (1891), *The Perfect Wagnerite* (1898), *The Author's Apology From Mrs. Warren's Profession* (1905), *Dramatic Opinions and Essays* (1906), *The Sanity of Art* (1909), *The Dying Tongue of Great Elizabeth* (1920), *The Intelligent Woman's Guide to Socialism and Capitalism* (1928), *The Adventures of a Black Girl in Her Search For God* (1932), *Major Critical Essays* (1932), *Pen Portraits and Reviews* (1932), *Our Theatres in the Nineties* (1932), *Music in London, 1890-94* (1932), *Prefaces* (1934). *London Music, 1888-89* (1937), *Sixteen Self Sketches* (1949).

Letters: *Letters from George Bernard Shaw to Miss Alma Murray* (1927), *Ellen Terry and Bernard Shaw: A Correspondence* (1931), *Some Unpublished Letters of George Bernard Shaw* (1939).

Index

C

D

E

F

G

H

I

J

K

L

M

N

O

P

Q

R

S

T

U

V

W

Y